A SAFE PLACE

A MARRIAGE ENRICHMENT RESOURCE MANUAL

BARRY AND PAULA DAVIS

Paula and Barry have been able to make a life-changing impact not only in my marriage but those of hundreds of others in Sri Lanka. It has been a true blessing to work alongside this couple and to see this book being developed with all the experience they have gathered through their amazing work in a variety of cultures over many years.

Robert Silva, Head of Counselling, Connect for Life, Sri Lanka; Board Member, Asia Christian Counseling Association

The marriage training addressed common issues couples have in many areas of our country. Husbands realised that their wives and children wanted more of them than their function and practicalities. Wives recognised their value was much more than being in servitude to the family and learned to speak from the heart and risk sharing their deepest needs and feelings. Some of the pastors recognised that they had been concentrating on their church family to the detriment of their wives and children. We particularly benefited from being able to begin to share and talk about our dreams for each other and the future.

Priscilla and Baddraka Ruhunage, Marriage Facilitators, Sri Lanka

This couple's approach and methodology of Marriage Ministry changed, challenged, touched and unclogged the "communications veins" of many a couple that attended their training. Barry and Paula's shared vulnerability caused couples to look into their own lives and, despite our "do not rock the boat culture", the training prompted sincerity and openness between spouses. As a result, many wounds were healed and couples embarked on a new road to a healthier marriage.

Vivian Kityo, Director of Wakisa Ministries, Kampala, Uganda

Ministering with Paula and Barry over a number of years in various parts of Uganda was foundational to our enduring friendship. I was amazed by their honest and candid dialogue as a communication tool for couples who were simply existing in their marriages. They did this using their own relationship as an example, becoming very vulnerable and transparent. I was particularly encouraged by the way they handled culturally sensitive questions. Their approach to marriage enrichment and support has greatly influenced my counselling with married couples and also those desiring to get married. They touched the lives of many couples, especially the pastors and their wives.

Theo Niringiye, Counselling and Training Director, Relate Communications, Kampala, Uganda

What made Paula and Barry unique for us was that they did not just offer tools and techniques; they invited us into their story, which they are willing to live out loud. Together we began to explore the primal feelings and longings that were the power source in our lives. We learned what it means to really connect and not just talk. We learned to compassionately "wallow" in each other's pain, fears, ambitions, dreams etc. without losing sight of our personal healing. Any couple can relate to their wealth of good and bad personal relationship experiences. They access these experiences when sharing with others in a way that is up-building, healing and gives hope. We discovered the compatibility of our very different personalities and characters and how they complement each other and the potential synergies we can enjoy moving forward.

David and Lisa Minor, serving as missionaries in East Africa

Barry and Paula's conversations during the marriage sessions are so real and genuine, and address many of the core challenges of marriage and how to overcome them. Each of the couples in our Bangalore workshops still hold dear the learnings and the experiences. Marriages are being transformed as a result. We benefited immensely through the marriage workshops and also during the training they conducted on how to minister to other couples. The program for trainers equips couples to effectively have input into other families by offering tools that are simple and adaptable across cultures.

Philips Dayanidhi and Reupah Dayanidhi PhD, Counselling Psychologist, Primecare Multispeciality Clinic, Bangalore, India

Through their unique experiential style and brilliant dialogues, we were able to mine layers of who we are as individuals, and as a couple. The demonstration of various tools and skills facilitated the weaving of them into our own narrative and we were able to create our unique, rich and intimate story. They modelled transparency, spontaneity, vulnerability and did not shy from pain through their own journey. Brave, daring, not sugar-coated either but indeed very contagious and effective.

Drs. Sam and Sanaa Labib, General Practitioners, Sydney, Australia

Over the last five years we have had the immense privilege of receiving tools and support from the marriage enrichment ministry. This has been a gift to us and has given our marriage a scaffolding that ensures we continue to grow stronger as a couple. Together we have faced challenges that had we not been equipped, may have damaged our relationship. We are forever thankful for the huge gift this has been to us.

Mike and Fiona Smith, Sydney, Australia

CONTENTS

PART B: A SAFE PLACE

PART C: MANAGING GROUPS AND EVENTS

LIST OF WORKSHEETS AND EXERCISES

FOREWORD

What a privilege to be invited to write a foreword to such a useful book! Paula and Barry have not only gathered a wealth of material, they have distilled and refined it, made it more available and, in the process, added their own unique perspective. This is not only a 'how to' book but also a 'why' and 'when' book. Appropriately, they have sought to honour those who went before, recognising that they are standing on others' shoulders.

We had the privilege of contributing to Paula and Barry's training as marriage enrichment leaders. We saw and listened to their robust encounters with each other, their obvious respect and love for each other and their respect for other couples in the training group. We probably did not realise at the time just how much leadership potential they had. Since then we have developed great love and respect for them.

Since training, Barry and Paula have gone on to lead many marriage enrichment events, across different cultures and among survivors of wars and natural disasters in some emerging nations. Such events place great stress on marriages. But, as David and Vera Mace (pioneers of marriage enrichment) recognised, strong, healthy marriage relationships can be a real resource for others in such situations. Barry and Paula have led retreats and run leader training programs in a number of such environments, thereby contributing healing and empowerment not only within individual marriages, but also within their wider communities. In fact, it is probably fair to say that this ministry has become a passion, as well as a concrete expression of their Christian faith.

A major part of the methodology of Mace-style marriage enrichment is the willingness of the leaders to use their own relationship, including its strengths and vulnerabilities, as a resource for the participating couples. This has proved to be a powerful teaching tool but it can be tough on the leader couples! Of course, it can also be very enriching for them. In the book Paula and Barry model this process well, and it is a joy to see them doing it and also reaping the rewards of increased intimacy.

We cannot help but think that David and Vera Mace, who trained us, would like this book.

Gerlinde and Ian Spencer

April 2020

PREFACE

Marriage enrichment (ME) is about intentional marriages. Marriage is a gift to treasure but often the pressures and burdens of daily life leave this relationship impoverished. The goal of ME is to create a safe place where married couples can take time out to nurture and strengthen their relationship and to grow towards increased intimacy.

Thank you for setting aside the time and energy to learn about conducting safe and effective ME events. The underlying desire to be a leader couple of an ME event is usually motivated by loving concern for the well-being of other couples in your community. However, the immediate outcome is the continuing growth of our own relationship, which is, after all, the basis for anything we may wish to offer others. If we hope for commitment by other couples to their marriages, we must first be committed to ours. If we desire other couples to communicate well and solve their problems creatively, it needs to begin with us.

Our aim in facilitating this resource manual is to share the tools, techniques and experiences we have discovered that foster a safe place for marriage growth. The role of the leader couple in reaching for a level of vulnerability that shares both strengths and weaknesses cannot be over-emphasised. Leader couples can offer direction and hope to other couples and the possibility of true intimacy when vulnerability meets vulnerability. A skilled leader couple will seemingly lead the process with relaxed informality and ease.

Therefore, this resource manual is intended to highlight the possibilities as well as shape the sensitivity and skills necessary for authentic leadership of couples as they seek to grow in their marriages. We believe that amid the difficulties and struggles of life, genuine delight, freedom and love is possible for married couples who take the time to grow towards it. It is our hope that this resource manual will be a landmark for you as a couple and that, whatever the benefits for other couples, you will find it a real stimulus to your own growth and that this will flow out to others in a vital and effective way. We desire to support you in appropriate ways. Therefore, the resource manual is accompanied by a series of live training videos available for purchase through our website, http//www.connectingmatters.com.au.

It is important to declare that our Christian faith informs every aspect of our lives and will sometimes be reflected in the pages of this manual. However, from our cross-cultural experience we have learned that the principles, truths and concepts we explore in relationships have universal application, whether in a faith-based community, a culturally specific group or otherwise.

Moreover, it is good to be reminded that we all start from zero. Therefore, we ask that you approach this resource manual with a beginner's mind: that is, an open mind and heart seeking wisdom. Individual and couple spirituality can only be discovered if it there is a genuine spiritual search for the Divine Mystery. And we ask that you come as a participant from beginning to end and not as an observer. Marriage, like life itself, is not a spectator sport.

The aim of this resource manual is to assist leader couples to design and deliver engaging ME events. Overall, the task of the leader couple is to create a safe place for participants to share their stories in a group setting shared with other couples. Safety is created through community building activities, leader couple modelling and designing ME sessions that are engaging and provide a transformational place where couples can learn, grow and change.

The manual has four parts, organised as follows:

- Part A introduces the role of Marriage Enrichment in marital growth and the principles of a Marriage Enrichment event. These include a commitment to effective communication, creative use of conflict, personal growth and flexibility. Part A also explains the elements of Marriage Enrichment events, couple leadership and cultural issues.
- Part B is about creating a safe place for participants to risk vulnerability and marital growth. Creating a safe place involves community-building, modelling and designing engaging Marriage Enrichment sessions.
- Part C explores issues that may arise in Marriage Enrichment, including practical elements of Marriage Enrichment; such as planning, the importance of good closure and evaluating effectiveness. Participatory elements include handling difficult situations and giving feedback.
- Part D includes additional resources and worksheets that can be photocopied and used in Marriage Enrichment sessions. It contains practical information on common topics for workshops and referenced material supporting the concepts detailed in other sections.

Personal vignettes containing our story and experiences of Marriage Enrichment are peppered throughout the resource manual.

In order to get the best out of this resource manual, it is important to remember that "the only person who can bring about change is the person who is willing to be changed" (author unknown). If you decide to become a Marriage Enrichment Leader Couple, at times you may have to take risks that may feel like you are swimming in deep water. Often this is the place of personal and marital growth. We hope that our resource manual supports you in this growing venture.

Barry and Paula Davis

Sydney, Australia

September 2020

ACKNOWLEDGEMENTS

"Those of us who have working, satisfying marriages should stand up and say so and be willing to share some of how it can be done."[1] These are the words of David and Vera Mace, founders and leaders of the Association for Couples in Marriage Enrichment (A.C.M.E.) from 1973 to 1980. David Mace shared his hope for mainstream Marriage Enrichment events in his book, *Close Companions*:

> Our hope was that it might be quite natural (with no direct religious, political or professional connections of any kind) and might, therefore, become a coordinating agency for other organizations that were developing programs in this new field; that it might undertake the task of setting standards for leadership; that it might encourage the development of local chapters which could promote in their communities the cause of better marriage.[2]

David and Vera pioneered the technique of a leader couple dialogue using their own relationship as a teaching tool. They coined the term "couple dialogue" for this process, establishing its current meaning in Marriage Enrichment circles. More information can be found on the Better Marriages USA website at https://www.bettermarriages.org. David and Vera's books, *Close Companions* (1982), and; *How to Have a Happy Marriage: A Step-by-Step Guide to an Enriched Relationship* (1980) are no longer in print at the time of this writing. However, it is a privilege to share and build on their material.

We are also indebted to Ian and Gerlinde Spencer, who worked as therapists and supervisors for the Family Life Movement of Australia (now Interrelate). In the 1980s, we attended a Marriage Enrichment weekend at Family Life, Strathfield, Sydney, facilitated by Ian and Gerlinde. Immediately we were impressed by their skill, vulnerability, dedication and courage to move into risky areas. Their facilitation of professional events, encouragement and friendship over the years has been a source of inspiration, both personally and in our marriage.

This resource manual utilises unpublished material originally found in resource material for Couples for Marriage Enrichment Australia (CMEA) (2006) now called Better Marriages. Diligent effort has been made to locate authors and copyright ownership of material quoted in this manual. Where we cannot identify the original source (because notes and clippings have been given to us), we would appreciate hearing from those who can, so that corrections can be made and proper credit given.

Notes

1 D. R. Mace (1982). *Close Companions*. Continuum.

2 Ibid., p. 246.

PART A

FOUNDATIONS OF MARRIAGE ENRICHMENT

CHAPTER 1

INTRODUCTION TO MARRIAGE ENRICHMENT

Overview

This chapter explores the concept of marital growth and provides some ideas to initiate couple growth during a marriage enrichment event. The chapter is organised under the following headings:

⇒ The Benefits of ME

⇒ The Concept of Marital Growth

⇒ Initiating and Increasing Awareness of Marital Growth

⇒ Foundational Principles of ME

The Benefits of Marriage Enrichment

Marriage Enrichment (ME) offers couples a safe space to develop relational skills and a growing intimacy within their marriages. Marriage is what David Schnarch, author of the book *Passionate Marriage*, calls a "Human Growth Machine".[1] Susan Johnson, the founder of Emotionally Focused Therapy, believes that the quality of our love relationships hugely influences our physical, mental and emotional health and that positive love connections promote resilience against the suffering life throws at us.[2] The old adage rings true; "Suffering is a given; suffering alone is intolerable".[3] Rather than being "the icing on the cake of life", love is actually "a basic primary need like oxygen and water".[4]

> "The persistent human cry is hold me tight."
> (Donald Joy)

Johnson's research revealed that, five years into a marriage, it is not how the couple manage conflict that predicts relationship breakdown, but rather lack of emotional responsiveness. It seems we are continually asking each other (mostly non-verbally): Can I count on you? Do I and my feelings matter to you? Will you be there for me when I need you or do I have to do it alone? If the answer is "no", our spouse receives the message: Your distress signals do not matter, and I do not care that there is no emotional engagement or connection between us.

> It's the nature of emotional engagement that defines the quality of a relationship.

John Bowlby, the founder of attachment theory, noted that separation distress in children resulted in three stages: protest, despair and detachment.[5] Later research confirmed that this is also true of adults – when I reach for you and you are not there, I start to get angry. Bowlby called this the "anger of hope". There is nothing worse than no response, so I will do everything to get you to respond to me. This can become a destructive dance that is returned to again and again. It goes like this: I encounter a stressful situation. I give out distress signals. You are emotionally unresponsive to my signals or, worse, you blame me for the problem ("If you changed, things would be much better for us.

> "Secretly we long to perpetuate that one astounding moment in the Garden of Eden. We long to stand in awe of one another, just as Adam and Eve must have done when they first locked gazes. We long for our whole body to tingle with the thrill of knowing that this one fascinating being, this being of a different gender, has been created especially for us and given to us unreservedly for our help, comfort and joy. Men and women ache for the heart with which to see one another (and therefore themselves) as the astounding miracles they are..." (M. Mason, *The Mystery of Marriage*, p. 20)

If you weren't so … this wouldn't happen."). It rarely helps, but we repeat the same dance, hoping for a different outcome. But since I still cannot get a response, I go into the pain of despair, believing that the connection I deeply long for will never happen (there is enormous evidence that marital distress sets us up for depression). Then, if my distress signals are still ignored and connection does not happen, I move to detachment, which signifies grieving, letting go or moving away. This stage is very difficult to come back from.

> An alternative term for Marriage Enrichment is Intimacy Training.

From another perspective, John Gottman, a relationship researcher who has studied thousands of couples, says: "If you don't have a goal, objective, or specific outcome in mind, or if you don't know what your and your partner's needs are and how best to fulfill them, how can you know whether or not you're being successful in your partnership?"[6] Perhaps this lack of success is because many couples fail to notice the difference between closeness and intimacy. Closeness tends to be comfortable, while intimacy involves a risky vulnerability. Thus, an alternative term for ME is "intimacy training". To illustrate, a review of marital intimacy-enhancing interventions among married individuals claims: "The depth of intimacy that people understand in their communications depends on their ability to handle correct, effective, and clear communications with the expression of feelings, needs, and desires."[7]

Hence, the ME process has particular application where couples desire something better from their relationship and are prepared to risk gaining increased vulnerability, insight, understanding and change.

Pause for Reflection

What does the word "intimacy" mean to you?

What does the word "vulnerability" mean to you?

Additionally, ME events involve self-disclosure. Self-disclosure accompanied by an empathic response is also known to increase couple intimacy, because "when people trust each other and share their thoughts, feelings, and internal reality, it helps them strengthen the intimate communication in couples".[8] Thus, ME involves intimacy training.

> There is a difference between closeness and intimacy. Closeness tends to be comfortable, while intimacy involves a risky vulnerability.

Moreover, other studies confirm the benefit of ME. Masoumi et al. claim that "[e]nrichment skills are the skills that help satisfy the strongest desires of families… and are used in almost all cultures" and that "enrichment training is a preventive and non-invasive program and can prevent deterioration into marital conflict".[9] This meta-study of whether marriage and relationship education are effective focused on relationship quality and communication skills and the researchers found both were effective for white, middle-class couples.

> ME has been found to increase marital happiness.

ME has also been found to increase marital happiness. A study by Isanejad et al. found that relationship enhancement education is effective across cultures in increasing marital happiness.[10] Findings from a study by Hickmon, Protinsky and Singh demonstrated that ME groups produced a statistically significant increase in marital enrichment.[11] A further study by Kardan-Souraki found that communication skills training leads to the reduction of problems and "the enhancement of agreement, affection, truthfulness, and fulfillment of commitments and generally the level of intimacy between spouses".[12] Thus, relationship enhancement significantly increases marital happiness.

The Concept of Marital Growth

Many couples participating in a ME event for the first time are surprised by the concept of marital growth. Currently, the prevailing emphasis of counselling

> There are three participants in the marriage: the self, the spouse and the relationship.

is on individual and personal growth without a commensurate emphasis on growth as a couple. The importance of marital growth (couple growth) cannot be stressed enough. It is not unusual for a leader couple to introduce this component of ME only to find the response from some couples is, "We don't really need to grow" or "We don't really understand what you mean." It is helpful to convey that there are three participants in the marriage: the self, the spouse and the relationship. Therefore, one of the important aspects of ME is to open the window for couples to this new dimension of couple growth.

At the end of an ME event, couples are given the opportunity to draw up a growth plan (worksheets for marital growth are included at the end of this chapter). If they have not understood what is meant by growth, this plan will not be done well or with understanding. Moreover, struggling with a growth plan will frequently reveal deeper issues in the relationship, requiring clinical intervention. ME is not designed to be marriage counselling. It is recognised that this requires a different set of clinical skills. Couples needing this kind of deeper assistance are encouraged to consider carefully whether participating in an ME event would be helpful, because at times the conversations and sharing will heighten the sense of what is lacking in their relationship.

ME events are oriented towards couples who feel positive about their marriages and want to see them grow and strengthen. The purpose of ME is to:

- increase each spouse's awareness of self and spouse, with an emphasis on the positive aspects, strengths and growth potential of the individuals and the relationship;
- develop and encourage the use of effective communication, problem solving and conflict resolution skills;
- identify directions for relationship growth;
- learn skills and discover ways in which positive growth can take place; and
- increase mutual intimacy and empathy.

Initiating and Increasing Awareness of Couple Growth

Many people come to ME with considerable ambivalence. Spouses often attend only because their partner wanted to come and could not attend without them. Participants may also have unrealistic hopes and fears of what the experience might produce. Frequently, the anxiety is increased by the discovery that the activities are experiential and they cannot comfortably maintain silence or play a simple observer role.

> The initiation of marital growth is akin to the spark that lights a bush fire.

The initiation of marital growth is akin to the spark that lights a bush fire. It has been observed many times that once couples gain perspective on the marital growth concept, they are off and running. They realise almost instantaneously a wide range of issues in their relationship where there is yet more to accomplish and nurture. They are able to analyse these opportunities and are particularly responsive to concepts of developing their marital potential.

It is a matter of starting from scratch. Leader couples can work on the fairly safe assumption that this idea of marital growth will be a new one for everybody. In the leader couple's sharing of dialogue and marriage journey, stories of growth experiences will emerge and will help flesh out what is meant by the term. In other words, couples can be led into an

> Make a point of collecting activities and exercises that have a growth dimension to them.

awareness of marital growth by what they learn from our experiences as leader couples. Then it will not be too long before they are able to begin to consider what growth might mean for them.

There are a number of exercises that are ideal to further stimulate the growth process. Their purpose is to help couples identify areas where there is room for increased understanding, energy and application. The *Three Good Things* exercise below and the *Our Marriage Potential Inventory* at the end of this chapter are ideal for this purpose. Remember to introduce these and other similar exercises so that couples know the purpose behind undertaking them. Make a point of collecting activities and exercises that have a growth dimension to them.

A couple on a retreat or participating in some other ME-related event is already committed to the view that their marriage is worthwhile and worthy of intentionality. As a result, they are well placed to focus on marital growth once it has been understood. It is a good idea, particularly through couple dialogue, to encourage couples to share their insights on marital growth as a retreat proceeds.

While the concept of marital growth is crucial, the purpose of ME is to increase couples' awareness of the strengths and growth areas of their relationship. The tasks to raise this awareness are:

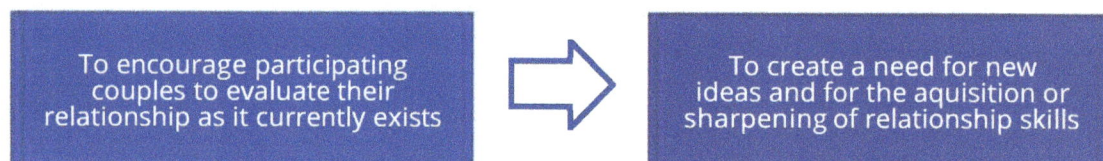

To encourage participating couples to evaluate their relationship as it currently exists	⇨	To create a need for new ideas and for the aquisition or sharpening of relationship skills

A commonly used exercise, *Three Good Things,* can be used to accomplish this.[13]

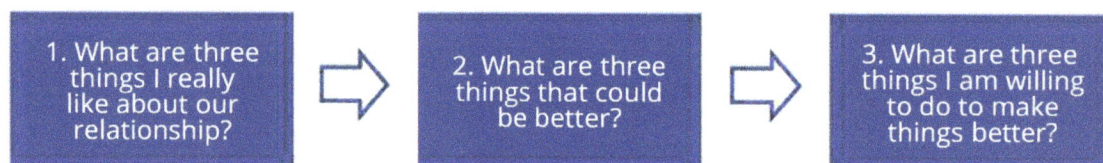

1. What are three things I really like about our relationship?	⇨	2. What are three things that could be better?	⇨	3. What are three things I am willing to do to make things better?

> The purpose of marriage enrichment is to increase couples' awareness of the strengths and growth areas of their relationship.

This *Three Good Things* exercise sums up the essence of awareness building. As the emphasis in ME is on the positive, couples are asked to first identify the areas in which they are functioning well. However, an assumption of ME is that all marriages have unfulfilled potential. Consequently, helping couples identify where they need to grow in their relationship creates a need for learning and sets the stage for the process of growth. In order to create receptivity to new learning, it is important to allow couples to discover for themselves where growth is desirable. In initiating this step, the simple exercise noted above may be useful.

Awareness building is actually a continuing activity throughout longer ME events. As the group moves from one issue to another, awareness enters into the process. Couples become aware of where they are in relation to each issue that comes before the group. The simple

Three Good Things exercise can be adapted to a variety of issues, such as communication, conflict resolution, time management, leisure activities, sexuality etc. For example, if the group is dealing with sexuality, the *Three Good Things* exercise can be altered as follows.

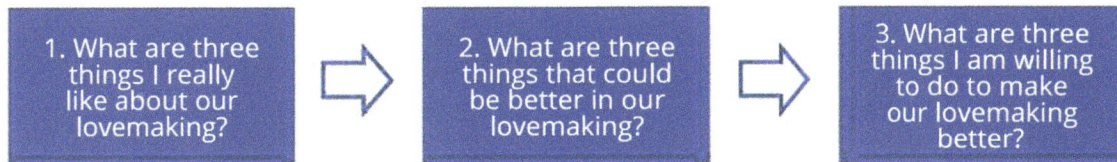

1. What are three things I really like about our lovemaking?	⇨	2. What are three things that could be better in our lovemaking?	⇨	3. What are three things I am willing to do to make our lovemaking better?

There are also many other scales, dialogue questions and inventories that can be used to help couples assess the strengths and growth areas in their relationship.

The above adaptation could be used effectively in a 90-minute ME workshop on sexuality or in the sexuality session of a weekend retreat. The leader couple might model the exercise with open dialogue before asking the other couples to engage with the

> The leader couple's willingness to be vulnerable helps create an environment in which participant couples can risk being vulnerable with each other.

topic. The leader couple's openness in discussing their sexuality and their willingness to be vulnerable will help create an environment in which participant couples can take risks in discussing sexuality, either with the group or with their spouses.

Open couple dialogue may also be used as a tool for developing awareness. Once an issue is introduced, a couple can be asked to dialogue about their experience of that particular issue. When one couple has dialogued, another couple may then be willing to talk together, perhaps followed by another. It is unlikely that all the couples will enter into the open dialogue. Whether they do or not, the process of identification leads to increased awareness of how couples handle issues.[14]

Foundational Principles of Marriage Enrichment

David and Vera Mace, the founders of ME, identified four foundational principles of the ME process. These are:

1. A commitment to effective communication

2. A commitment to creative conflict

3. A commitment to personal growth

4. A commitment to flexibility

These principles will be addressed in the following chapters.

Our Story

I (Barry) am crying. Not gasping sobs, but a steady trickle of tears. I am watching television and the actor, an older man, is holding his first grandchild. I am caught in the anticipation of my first grandchild in a few short months. My emotions are a tumbling mixture of happiness, excitement and anticipation but also anxiety and reflective redemption. My tears are for the smell and feel of a baby that will be mine again. I did not realise how much longing had been held within me until the image of the old man and the newborn drew me to the place of tears. I am comfortable with my tears and the inward places they take me. I smile and reflect on my travels from an event many years ago.

Paula and I take our name tags and sit in the circle of couples joining us in the first ME event we attend. Our marriage is struggling and so are we. Help is needed desperately. This step is foreign to me as, in my family of origin, we do not declare our neediness. Rather, we endeavour to resolve problems within the structure. I feel awkward, but if you ask me what I am feeling at this time I cannot answer. In fact, that is exactly what the facilitators do. "Please state a feeling you are experiencing now; we will start on the left and move around the circle."

I am stunned. I am in my thirties and have no idea of what I am feeling. This is not a practice I am used to. I have feelings, but I do not articulate them, nor am I able to readily connect with them. Anger is familiar, but growing up it was forbidden to be displayed or conveyed. My wife is also stunned by this request, because her feelings overwhelm her and cannot be isolated in the burden of an avalanche of pain and shame. She is aching for my meaningful involvement. We need help.

I am drawn to the husband facilitator. I watch him fluently navigate and name his feelings in a masculine way. I have not had this modelled well. My parched heart awakens and I consent to the desire to be able to do as he is doing. I am to be a grandfather of a little girl and the tears trickle, now in a "manly way".

Chapter Summary

- There is an innate desire in each of us for closeness and connection. Married couples long for the other to be there for them when they are distressed.
- ME has been found to increase marital satisfaction and happiness.
- Initiating marital growth occurs as the leader couple model risky vulnerability in their relationship.
- Through well-timed activities and exercises, ME increases couples' awareness of their strengths and the growth areas of their relationship.
- The four foundational principles of ME are:
    1. a commitment to effective communication;
    2. a commitment to creative use of conflict;
    3. a commitment to personal growth; and
    4. a commitment to flexibility.

Worksheets on Marital Growth

Our Marriage Potential Inventory

Good relationships do not just happen, they require intentionality; that is, specific effort by couples to reach their full marital potential. In the areas below, rate how well you believe your relationship is faring, with 1 being low and 10 high. Add up and discover the potential for growth in your relationship, which is the difference between your score and 100! (Low scores may mean hard marking or high expectations.)

I/I am

___ Pleased with the way we talk to each other

___ Think we handle conflict constructively

___ Content with the way we spend our time

___ Satisfied with our sex life

___ Happy about the level of appreciation and affection

___ Comfortable with the way we manage our money

___ Believe our parenting is healthy

___ View us as a pretty good team

___ Satisfied with our commitment to marital growth

___ Appreciate your attitude toward my family

___ Total   Date: _____

Reflecting On Our Differences...

Do alone.

1. I consider my strengths to be

2. I consider my weaknesses to be

3. I consider my spouse's strengths to be

4. I consider my spouse's weaknesses to be

5. The situation that would be most threatening to my spouse is

6. If I were to use my uniqueness as a male/female to support my spouse, it would look like

7. The following is likely to be stressful for me in the near future

8. I need you to support me in

Share sensitively with your spouse.

Notes to Chapter 1

1. Cited by J. Gottman (2020). *The Marriage Minute.* The Gottman Institute. Retrieved from https://www.gottman.com/blog/seriously-whats-point-marriage-growth/
2. S.M. Johnson (2008). *Hold Me Tight: Seven Conversations for a Lifetime of Love.* Little Brown Spark.
3. Ibid., p. 25.
4. Ibid., p. 27.
5. J. Bowlby (1969). *Attachment. Vol 1: Attachment and Loss.* Basic Books.
6. Gottman, *The Marriage Minute.*
7. M. Kardan-Souraki, Z. Hamzehgardeshi, I. Asadpour, R. A. Mohammadpour & S. Khani (2015). A review of marital intimacy-enhancing interventions among married individuals. *Global Journal of Health Science,* 8(8): 89. DOI:10.5539/gjhs.v8n8p74.
8. Ibid.
9. S.Z. Masoumi, S. Khani, F. Kazemi, F. Kalhori, R. Ebrahimi & G. Roshanaei (2017). Effect of marital relationship enrichment program on marital satisfaction, marital intimacy, and sexual satisfaction of infertile couples. *International Journal of Fertility & Sterility,* 11(3):197-204, p.204. DOI: 10.22074/ijfs.2017.4885.
10. O. Isanejad, S.A. Ahmadi, F. Bahrami, I. Baghban-Cichani, O. Etemadi & Z. Farajzadegan (2011). Study of effectiveness of relationship enhancement on marital happiness and optimism in Iranian couples. *Australian Journal of Basic and Applied Sciences,* 5:200-206.
11. W.A. Hickmon, H.O. Protinsky & K. Singh (1997). Increasing marital intimacy: Lessons from marital enrichment. *Contemporary Family Therapy,* 19(4):581-589. DOI.org/10.1023/A:1026191223476.
12. Kardan-Souraki et al., Effect of marital relationship enrichment program on marital satisfaction, marital intimacy, and sexual satisfaction of infertile couples, p.89.
13. The Three Good Things exercise is adapted from R.A. Emmons & M.E. McCullough (2003). Counting blessings versus burdens: An experimental investigation of gratitude and subjective well-being in daily life. *Journal of Personality and Social Psychology,* 84(2):377–389. DOI: 10.1037/0022-3514.84.2.377, and from M.E. Seligman, T.A. Steen, N. Park & C. Peterson (2005). Positive psychology progress: Empirical validation of interventions. *American Psychologist,* 60(5):410–421. https://doi.org/10.1037/0003-066X.60.5.410.
14. P. Dyer & G. Dyer (1989). *Marriage Enrichment, Process, Methods and Techniques.* Association for Couples in Marriage Enrichment.

CHAPTER 2

FOUNDATIONAL PRINCIPLE: A COMMITMENT TO EFFECTIVE COMMUNICATION

Overview

This chapter explores a foundational principles of marriage enrichment - a commitment to effective communication. The chapter is organised under the following headings:

⇒ What is Effective Communication?

⇒ What Does Effective Communication Involve?

What is Effective Communication?

Effective marital communication is incredibly risky, because it is an opportunity to offer the core of ourselves to another. "But if I tell you who I am, you may not like who I am, and that is all that I have".[1]

> "But if I tell you who I am, you may not like who I am, and that is all that I have"
> (John Powell, *Why Am I Afraid to Tell You Who I Am?*)

Effective communication is also an important component of marital adjustment. Moreover, educating couples about communication skills has positive effects on their relationship.[2] Thus, addressing effective communication is a crucial part of a ME event.

Communication is essentially the two-way process of exchanging information. It is the means by which two people attempt to bridge their separateness. Effective communication leads to understanding. It

> "To reveal myself openly and honestly takes the rawest kind of courage."
> (John Powell, *Why Am I Afraid to Tell You Who I Am?*)

provides tools by which we can know and be known by another person. Marital spouses can tolerate disagreement much better when there is understanding between them. Effective communication prevents spouses from feeling isolated from each other, increases their ability to be affirming, aids creative conflict resolution and encourages intimacy.

A good place to begin a session on effective communication is the house metaphor. The house with doors that can be locked or opened with a key is a good metaphor for a couple's communication. As a leader couple, draw the outline of a house plan on a whiteboard. Then

tell the following story. A marriage can be likened to a large house with many rooms that a couple inherits on their wedding day. Their hope is to use and enjoy these rooms, as we do the rooms in a comfortable home, so that they will serve the many activities that make up their shared life. But in many marriages, doors are found to be locked – they represent areas in the relationship which the couple are unable to explore together. Attempts to open these doors lead to failure and frustration. So, the couple resign themselves to living together in only a few rooms that can be opened easily, leaving the rest of the house, with all its promising possibilities, unexplored and unused.

The leader couple can ask couples for some examples of locked doors. Typical responses are:

- finances and spending
- religious faith
- raising children
- in-laws
- specifics of death
- specifics of sexual intercourse
- deep feelings of joy, fear, pain or anger.

There is a *key* that the couple can use together, and that key is *effective marital communication.*

> "The most important thing in communication is hearing what isn't said."
> (Peter Drucker)

The leader couple can ask couples: "Do you think couples ever get to the point where they can no longer communicate?" When couples say they can no longer communicate with each other, they actually have good communication. At times what is not said speaks louder than what is spoken. It is what we *do not* say to each other that is so important that we are afraid to say it. It is so important that our spouse does not want to hear it. Communication is not a virtue unless we can say what needs to be said. It is being able to say it, not because a spouse wants to hear it, but because our relationship might end one day if we don't, and we will never convince ourselves that we loved our spouse. Thus, communication is the process of sharing ourselves, verbally and non-verbally, in such a way that the other person can both know and understand what we are sharing. Communication is to a relationship as blood is to life.

What Does Effective Communication Involve?

> "Communication is the oxygen of relationships." (Anonymous)

Guidelines for effective communication are essential. The multi-faceted process of creating intimacy consists of interrelated components which can be learned as skills.[3] We suggest you make copies of the section on *Communication Guidelines* below. Hand out copies to participants and ask them to quickly read them. After a few minutes, ask for questions. Discuss questions briefly and call attention to any you believe need emphasis. Be careful not to let this become an intellectual discussion. You might say something like, "Rather than just talking about these, let's work on some specifics to see how they might apply to actual communication in our marriage".

Communication guidelines

- It is impossible not to communicate. Everything said or done transmits information.
- Communication takes two forms. Verbal or spoken communication occurs when messages are translated into words. Nonverbal or unspoken communication relies on behaviour and behaviour conveys a message.
- In human interaction, there is no one truth, only points of view.
- Positive messages can and need to be both spoken and unspoken. Negative messages need to be spoken to avoid misunderstanding and to allow for discussion.
- All communication occurs at two levels. The first level consists of the simple content of the message; for example, "I don't want to go." The second level makes a statement about the spousal relationship. The point of view one uses in terms of tone of voice, timing, and other unspoken factors conveys certain intentions toward the spouse.

- Totally open communication – for example, conveying every thought one has – is disruptive to relationships. All communication should be monitored. In caring relationships, positive messages outnumber negative messages at least five to one.

> "Anybody who has been in love knows love is easy, loving is not. Being a good partner is difficult and for most doesn't come naturally. If you want a relationship to last it takes a lot of work."
> (Theodore Waters)

- Negative feelings cannot be ignored. In time, the negative feelings will have an impact on the relationship.

Active listening

Active listening is *not* passive. Listening requires some amount of interaction between spouses. The idea brings to mind a "give and take" – a reciprocal arrangement in which both spouses are responsible for the success of the exchange. A shift often occurs when the spouse feels valued and understood, allowing elements of selfhood to appear. Consider the benefits of active listening. It:

> "To really listen is to be open to change... We may be physically present with another person while out minds and hearts are far away. We may have internalized the cultural lie that our value is wrapped up in how busy we are. The more we do, the more we are in motion, the more significant we are."
> (Adam McHugh, *The Listening Life*)

- shows the sender you are interested;
- proves you have heard and understood;
- checks on the accuracy of your understanding;
- gives the sender a chance to ventilate;
- communicates acceptance of the sender;
- allows the sender to define his/her own problem;
- forces the sender to move from the artificial and superficial to the underlying problem;
- helps the sender to deal with feelings, not just facts;
- stimulates insights;
- encourages openness and honesty; and
- promotes intimacy and friendship.

What makes a good listener?

Note: The leader couple may want to create a handout from the principles below on What Makes a Good Listener.

Good listeners see conversations as divine encounters. They show respect for each person they talk to, even those with differing opinions. In contrast, certain behaviours are sure signals that a person is *not* listening. Here are some common complaints about poor listeners:

> "There is no such thing as a worthless conversation, provided you know what to listen for. And questions are the breath of life for a conversation." (James Nathan Miller)

- He doesn't give me a chance to talk.
- Whenever I try to say something, he interrupts.
- She never looks at me when I talk.
- He constantly fidgets with a pencil, a paper, fingernails, etc. How can he do that and listen too?
- She asks questions as if she doubts everything I say.
- Whenever I offer a suggestion she throws cold water on it.
- He is always trying to get ahead of my story and guess my point, sometimes finishing my sentences for me.
- He begins arguing with me before I have a chance to finish making my point.
- Everything I say reminds him of an experience he had or heard of recently.
- She acts like she can't wait for me to stop talking so she can interject something.
- Whenever I have a good idea, she takes credit by saying something like, "Oh yes, I've been thinking about that, too."

- He overdoes being attentive with too many nods, mm-hm's or uh-huh's.
- She makes jokes when I'm trying to be serious.
- She keeps looking at her mobile phone while I'm talking.

Common attributes of a good listener include the following.

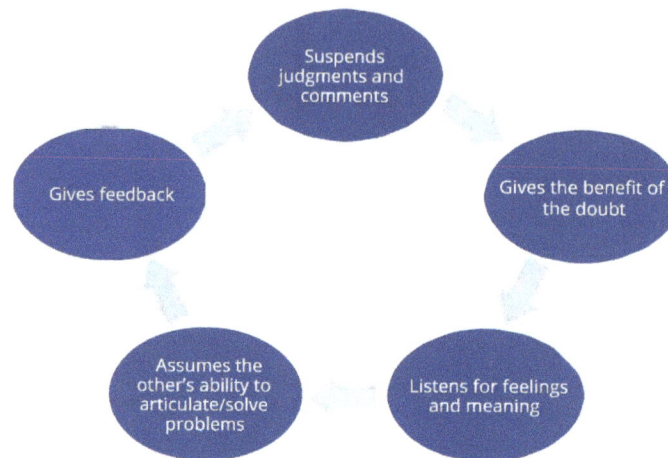

- Good listeners suspend their own judgements and comments in order to give the other person's ideas priority. When they ask questions, it is to draw the speaker out; for example, "Tell me more about that".
- Good listeners give the speaker the benefit of the doubt. Rather than jumping in to disagree, the good listener first seeks to understand as much as possible about where the speaker is coming from.
- Good listeners listen for feelings and meanings beneath the words and reflect them back to convey understanding.

> "Most of us feel that others will not tolerate such emotional honesty in communication. We would rather defend our dishonesty on the grounds that it might hurt others and having rationalised our phoniness into nobility, we settle for superficial relationships."
> (John Powell, *Why Am I Afraid to Tell You Who I Am?*)

- Good listeners assume their spouse is able to articulate and solve their own problems, rather than needing to "fix" them or give unrequested answers.
- Good listeners give feedback that lets the speaker know they have been understood. One way of doing this is paraphrasing: "Let me see if I have this right, George. You said that......... Is this correct?"

Additionally, good listeners turn towards their spouse when he/she is in need. Encourage couples to pay attention to "turning towards" behaviours.

DO

- Listen to the tone of voice
- Repeat what you hear in terms of feeling and meaning
- Repeat until sender is satisfied with your level of understanding
- Watch body language, posture, etc.
- Prime the pump (encourage exploration)
- Watch your spouse's face
- Listen with your third ear (offer total presence)
- Share roles of helper and helpee

DON'T

- Criticise
- Be defensive
- Ignore feelings
- Judge
- Rush
- Make comments
- Discount or minimise
- Interrupt
- Withdraw

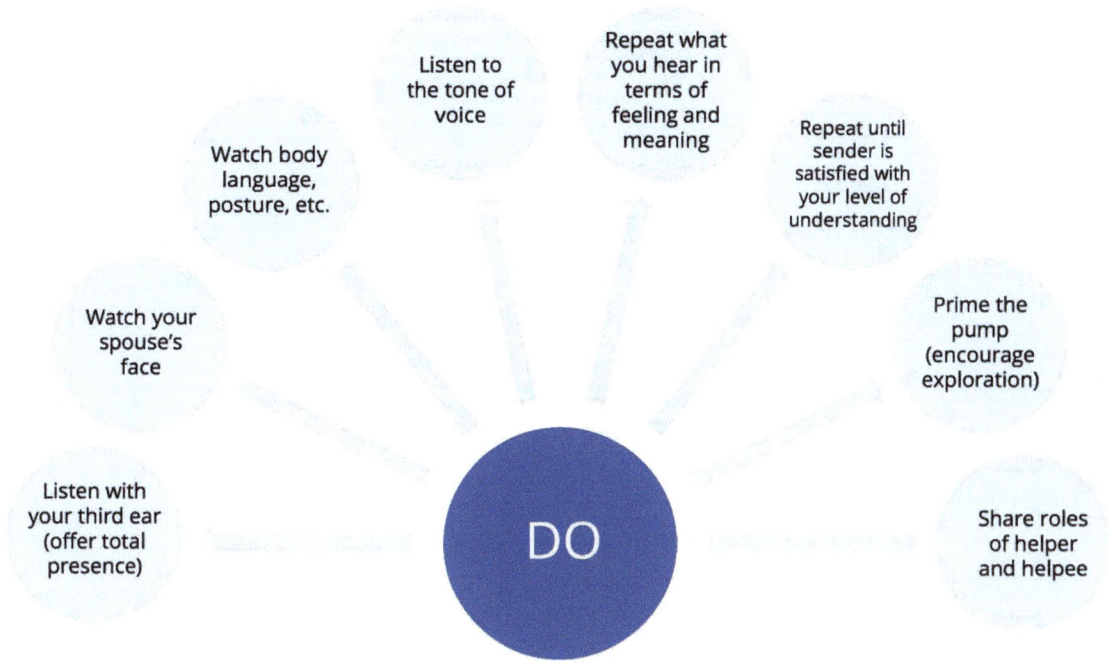

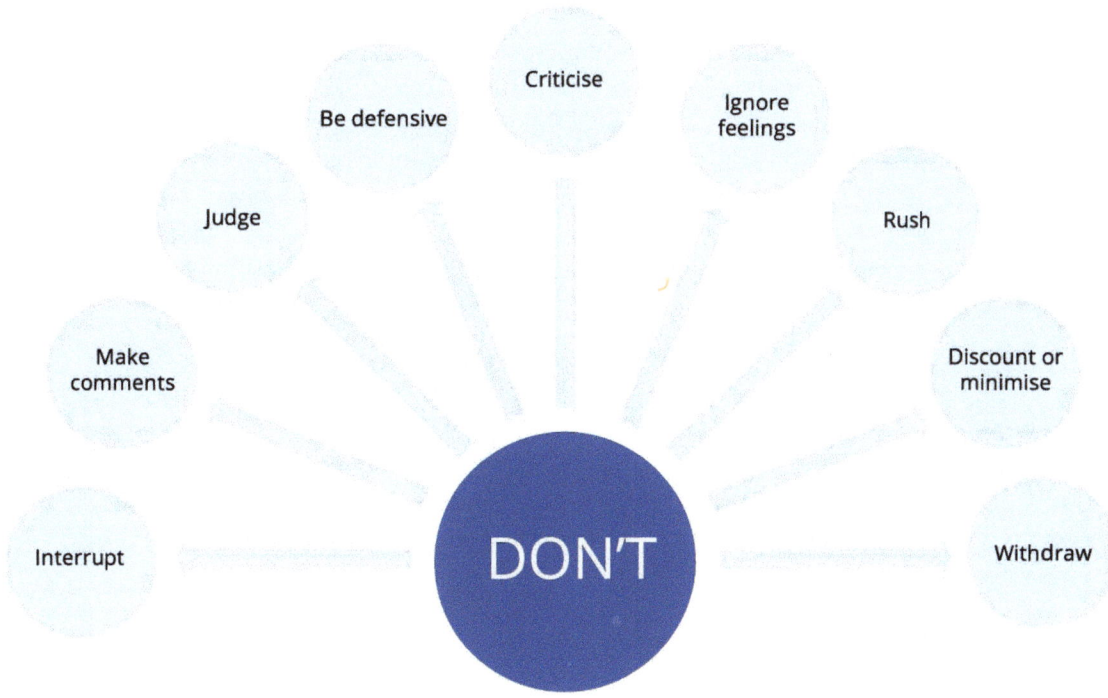

(Adapted from T. Gordon (2000). *Parent Effectiveness Training*)

To summarise, active listening involves the following:

Turn off your own self-talk

Listen for key words related to your spouse's thoughts, feelings and wishes

Ask yourself "What is my spouse really trying to say?"

Active Listening

Our Story

Active listening appears to be caught, not taught. A Sri Lankan husband described our couple dialogue: "What you [the leader couple] shared was very clear, especially to help us to listen. That was the main key. Not only the words, but underneath the words – the feelings, the emotions. Our weakest part is listening. Teaching us to listen and to respect each other's feelings; just to give a safe place for sharing – that was a great thing." Another husband reflected on his usual way of interacting with his wife. "We always talk on the run, but today I had to look into her eyes and I could not escape the feelings I saw in her eyes."

Our leader couple dialogue modelled vulnerability that facilitated vulnerability for other couples. Vulnerability creates a safe place that not only gives couples a voice, but enables them to experience active listening. This appears to override cultural constraints of emotional discipline and containment and results in increased engagement, communication skills and participation, especially among those who would normally remain silent. Leader couple dialogue creates a stimulating learning environment that facilitates significant self-disclosure for other couples.

Paraphrasing

To paraphrase is to say what the other has said in your own words. To paraphrase is to repeat your spouse's words or what you understand your spouse to have said to check if you have heard correctly.

- Use paraphrasing for specific information; for example, "So, you will meet me at 9:30 in the car?"
- Use paraphrasing for understanding more complex messages; for example, "So, let me see if I've got this right…"
- Carefully interrupt your spouse for clarification if he/she says more that you can paraphrase; for example, "Wait a second, let me be sure I understand what you have said."
- Use a tentative or questioning tone; for example, "OK, so are you saying…?"; "Do you think…"; "It sounds to me like you are feeling…"; "What I understand is…".
- Use the same key words that your spouse uses so that she/he feels heard.
- Paraphrase both the positive and the negative parts of your spouse's message; for example, "On the one hand you seem to be saying that you want connection, but on the other hand, you tend to push it away. Is this right?"

Note: A good way to teach the skills of paraphrasing is to demonstrate them in a personal dialogue.

Message received equals message sent!

When trying to convey an important message to your spouse, have you ever had the feeling you were like two ships passing in the night? You were both there, but not connecting at all. One of the major needs

> The message sent must equal the message received. Paraphrasing is a skill that is designed to do just that.

in communication is to be sure that *message sent equals message received*. Communication is such a complicated process that there is actually a strong chance that the message you want to send will not be the message your spouse receives. For spouses to achieve essential understanding, the *message sent must equal the message received*.

Our Story

Paula's doctoral research participants were required to keep "reflective diaries" to provide feedback as to how helpful the Trauma Recovery Program was in dealing with the psychological impact of their war experience. Paula is sharing some of these diary notes (with permission) as we enjoy a cup of tea, the first of the day. As I (Barry) watch the steam drift off my tea, I waft between the memories and the moment.

Communication has always fascinated me. The part that really intrigues is what is heard. I know what I want to convey, but what does my listener hear? The reflection diaries are giving us valuable insight into this transaction, but one in particular draws me from my state of reverie, as there is a deeper level of honesty. Her disclosure is personal and attracts me. I listen. She describes a time where we share our experiences from an exercise called The Tree of Life. Left-brain rational defences are bypassed and the participants are in touch with their pain. The sharing is raw and honest and at a depth that had not been previously explored. The young woman writes that she is pleased to be in a place of tears. Nevertheless, she declares, "I am not strong enough to cry. I begin and my body shakes and I find it difficult to breathe and I pull back." I sit with my cup of tea and a tear is released. My mind tumbles through the assumptions of how she holds on to that precipice of tears. Paula continues reading but I am stuck in the moment.

One of the communications and teaching tools that entices me to change is Jesus's use of paradox. I can spend hours in the suspended state between two seemingly opposing concepts that eventually give birth to one transforming principle. I imagine Him with a grain of wheat in hand explaining that unless it dies it cannot produce a crop and that if we want life, the way to obtain it is to refrain from holding onto it.

Throughout my younger years in school and community, I lived with two brothers and my father, a Second World War veteran, whom I never saw cry. The message I perceived was "Men don't cry... tears are a sign of weakness." This message has changed in more recent times but a lingering doubt still rests in my inner psyche, because tears come easily to me and sometimes their presence is embarrassing. The young lady was unable to completely convey why she could not cry, but she was afraid of what might happen if she allowed herself the release. "I am not strong enough to cry." My beliefs about tears changed in that moment.

Later that morning Paula and I begin to communicate in one of those conversations that unlock a locked door in our relationship. A gnawing thought is in my mind since we tried to understand the propensity that we have to pay out on each other when under pressure. I begin to realise that there is a pattern in my response after the workshops, and sometimes during them. I say to Paula: "I found it difficult to stay connected when I felt pushed away." In fact, I thought she was disconnected and self-protectively withdrawing, but what about my pattern?

Our communication continued, with Paula sharing her learning from a book titled *Trauma*, by Professor Gordon Turnbull (2011). She explained how she exhibits trauma responses using examples of Turnbull's interactions with loved ones after he had been helping trauma victims. It was good to have a better understanding of what was happening, but I was struggling with the ostensible escape from responsibility, because in my view I was the major recipient of her "trauma responses". She then asked me what I meant by disconnection, because she felt that even though she was writing and processing things, she was doing it in my presence and felt connected to me. "Maybe you're the one that disconnects." Insight is not a daily occurrence in my life, and when it happens it is an internally explosive moment.

This touches memories from earlier, darker days in our marriage, when I would fill my life with work and busyness in order to not feel the loneliness and emptiness in my life. I can persevere with this mode of operation and be helpful, practical and caring, but even though I am functioning, I am retreating deep within. Hearing the trauma stories triggered a need to have someone to connect with, to assure me there is still a place of belonging that is safe for me. But Paula cannot be there for me because she is struggling with her own responses. This constitutes a very painful conundrum. It appears that neither of us can offer a safe place to the other in the moment.

Slowly, I realise that the trauma stories we have heard and the visual evidence has me in a quandary of existential questions that all seem to start with "Why?" I am comforted that what is happening for both of us is, in some way, parallel to what our traumatised friends are experiencing. Paula and I have been given an invitation to explore and then communicate our struggles and trauma responses, to create a safe place in the pond of brokenness. I am reminded how the prophet Jeremiah saw God as the source of his pain ("you break my teeth" – Lamentations 3:16) but also the solution ("your mercies are new every morning" – Lamentations 3:22–24). I, too, see this same paradox in my relationship with Paula. My experience of both her and God invites me to go to that place of paradox and ambiguity as a willing learner and patiently wait for the touch of God. This is a precious moment. Maybe I am strong enough to cry!

Chapter Summary

- Effective communication is a foundational principle in marital adjustment. It is the means by which two people attempt to bridge their separateness. Communication provides the tools by which we can know and be known by another person and decreases the sense of aloneness and isolation.

- The metaphor of a house with rooms with locked doors can represent a couple's communication system. The key to opening the doors is communication.

- Communication guidelines involve understanding the patterns that occur between couples. The skills of active and good listening, paraphrasing, and recognising that the message sent must equal the message received are all crucial in the communication process.

Worksheets on Communication

Reflections On Our Communication

Do alone.

To me communication means:

_____

_____

_____

_____

Three things about our patterns of communication that please me the most are?

1. _____

2. _____

3. _____

Three things about our patterns of communication that I would like to be different are?

1. _____

2. _____

3. _____

How Well Do We Communicate?

Do alone.

Circle the response which best fits how you presently communicate about the areas listed.

1 = Not at all
2 = Poor
3 = OK
4 = Good
5 = Excellent

Values and beliefs	1 2 3 4 5
Aims and goals	1 2 3 4 5
Financial decisions	1 2 3 4 5
Decision making	1 2 3 4 5
In-laws	1 2 3 4 5
Friends	1 2 3 4 5
Time spent together	1 2 3 4 5
Decisions about leisure time /activities	1 2 3 4 5
Household tasks	1 2 3 4 5
Work-related matters	1 2 3 4 5
Raising children	1 2 3 4 5
Handling disagreements/conflict	1 2 3 4 5
Showing affection	1 2 3 4 5
Sexual satisfaction	1 2 3 4 5
Personal habits	1 2 3 4 5

In what areas do we communicate well?

What areas need improvement?

What is one area we can choose to work on?

Share sensitively with your spouse.

Levels Of Communication

Do alone. Circle the response that is closest to how you feel. Then put yourself in the place of your spouse and indicate how you think they would respond. Then share sensitively with your spouse.

1. Strongly disagree
2. Disagree
3. Uncertain
4. Agree
5. Strongly agree

ME   MY SPOUSE

1 2 3 4 5	I am satisfied with my ability to communicate	1 2 3 4 5
1 2 3 4 5	I feel I really listen to my spouse	1 2 3 4 5
1 2 3 4 5	I trust my spouse	1 2 3 4 5
1 2 3 4 5	I am careful with areas that are sensitive for my spouse	1 2 3 4 5
1 2 3 4 5	I can't seem to find the right words to express what I want to	1 2 3 4 5
1 2 3 4 5	I share my concerns and problems with my spouse	1 2 3 4 5
1 2 3 4 5	I share how I really feel with my spouse	1 2 3 4 5
1 2 3 4 5	My spouse is aware of my needs and desires	1 2 3 4 5
1 2 3 4 5	I'm afraid to expose my inner self to my spouse	1 2 3 4 5
1 2 3 4 5	I'm not convinced anything will change if I try to talk	1 2 3 4 5
1 2 3 4 5	I'm afraid I'll be squashed if I talk	1 2 3 4 5
1 2 3 4 5	I handle conflict in a constructive way	1 2 3 4 5
1 2 3 4 5	My spouse is my best friend	1 2 3 4 5
1 2 3 4 5	I am affectionate with my spouse	1 2 3 4 5
1 2 3 4 5	I am open with my spouse	1 2 3 4 5
1 2 3 4 5	I think our relationship is intimate	1 2 3 4 5

What are your feelings about completing this?

Locked Doors

It is often more difficult to talk to a spouse on some topics than others. Which of the areas below represent locked doors for you and your spouse?

___ Your finances and spending

___ Handling the kids

___ Your spiritual walk

___ The specifics of intercourse

___ Your deep feelings (joy, fear, pain, anger)

___ Your needs and desires

___ Your past

___ Other (specify)..............................

___ Other (specify) ....

What needs to happen to unlock the door?

My Listening Habits

Tick the responses that apply to you most of the time.

Barriers I use to protect myself from listening to my spouse:
____ Read the paper
____ Absorb myself in screen time and social media
____ Iron or clean
____ Keep busy or watch television so my spouse will be asleep when I go to bed
____ Bury myself in my work
____ Bury myself in the children and their concerns
____ Bury myself in ministry or helping others
____ Blame my upbringing: "That's just the way I am."
____ Other

My personal listening habits:
____ I change the subject
____ I joke my spouse out of feeling miserable
____ I talk too much
____ I switch the topic to me
____ I don't answer
____ I stick to safe topics
____ I interrupt
____ I finish my spouse's sentences
____ I spiritualise
____ I can't wait till my spouse finishes so I can give my opinion (solution)
____ I evaluate what my spouse says in terms of its acceptability
____ I listen through my own filters

Barriers to sharing myself:
____ I was brought up to hold things inside
____ I have an image that to share feelings is a sign of weakness
____ I am scared I will be ignored or dismissed
____ I don't want to hurt or offend my spouse
____ I am scared of appearing dumb or stupid
____ I am scared of being ridiculed or shamed
____ I am scared of intensity of emotions
____ I fear being out of control
____ I am concerned that my spouse will tell other people
____ I am scared that our relationship will change
____ I am afraid my opinions will be wrong
____ I am too angry to talk
____ I am not convinced it will help if I share myself
____ I can't seem to find the right words to say to express what I feel

My Responses To My Spouse's Communication

Do alone. Circle responses which best describe you. Then share with your spouse.

Never   Mostly

1 2 3 4 5   I respond defensively

1 2 3 4 5   I give quick apologies

1 2 3 4 5   I tend to attack my spouse

1 2 3 4 5   I usually correct my spouse's feelings

1 2 3 4 5   I like to give advice/solutions

1 2 3 4 5   I pressure my spouse to change

1 2 3 4 5   I criticise a lot

1 2 3 4 5   I communicate acceptance of my spouse if they do what I like them to

1 2 3 4 5   I tend to be judgemental

1 2 3 4 5   I listen through my own filters and expect my spouse to be like me

1 2 3 4 5   I usually give no response

1 2 3 4 5   I ask too many questions in order to stay on a rational level

1 2 3 4 5   I tend to dismiss my spouse's feelings

1 2 3 4 5   I tend to 'preach' to my spouse

1 2 3 4 5   I tend to lecture my spouse

1 2 3 4 5   I want my spouse to do something to help themselves

1 2 3 4 5   I usually do nothing and hope the problem goes away

1 2 3 4 5   I am a peace-at-any-price person

1 2 3 4 5   I tend to agree with my spouse to keep peace

1 2 3 4 5   I usually blame my spouse

1 2 3 4 5   I use name-calling and threats

1 2 3 4 5   I often shame my spouse into changing

1 2 3 4 5   I joke my spouse out of it

1 2 3 4 5   I reassure my spouse a lot that everything will be OK

1 2 3 4 5   I am a "rescuer" - I feel responsible to fix my spouse

My feelings about this are?

CHARACTERISTICS THAT HELP ME STAY SAFE

Tick those that are true for you, then tick those you think are true for your spouse.

ME   MY SPOUSE

___ I put myself down a lot   ___
___ I get depressed a lot   ___
___ I'm shy and insecure   ___
___ Im fairly compliant and tend to feel taken advantage of   ___
___ I find it difficult to say "No", get overcommitted, and then resent it   ___
___ I hate conflict. I want peace at any price   ___
___ I find criticism from my spouse extremely difficult to bear   ___
___ I tend to be a person who retreats and withdraws   ___
___ I am mostly a stingy person   ___
___ I often think other people don't like me   ___
___ I tend to manipulate my spouse to get him/her to do what I want   ___
___ I have a strong personality and strong opinions   ___
___ I think I'm a boring person   ___
___ I get angry easily and find it difficult to control myself   ___
___ I tend to be impulsive and irresponsible   ___
___ I like to take the easy path in our relationship. It requires too much   ___
     effort to listen and be involved
___ I am a fearful person   ___
___ I am anxious and worry a lot of the time   ___
___ I lack tact and my spouse would call me insensitive   ___
___ I like to be in control of myself and my emotions. I don't let them show   ___
___ I have a strong need to be liked and accepted so I try to please others   ___
___ I feel responsible to "help" or "fix" people's problems, including my spouse's   ___
___ I seldom take time to examine my inner world and my motives   ___
___ I am a dependent person, wanting others to rescue and come through for me   ___
___ I get hurt easily and am very sensitive   ___
___ I am quite individualistic and tend to be somewhat rebellious   ___
___ I tend to be a threat to people   ___
___ I appear to be very competent and together   ___
___ I like to feel needed   ___

What would you like to change about yourself?

How would like to see your spouse change?

Sensitively compare lists with your spouse.

I Will Find It Hard To Share My Feelings If...

Do alone. Circle which of the following applies to you.

- I HAVE BEEN TAUGHT TO IGNORE MY FEELINGS.
    I'll be uncomfortable with mine and yours.

- I HAVE HAD BAD EXPERIENCES WITH `EMOTIONAL' PEOPLE.
    I want to avoid a repeat.

- I DON'T KNOW WHAT TO DO TO HELP YOU.
    I feel helpless (and don't like it).

- I AM AFRAID OF MY OWN EMOTIONS.
    I may explode or go crazy and out of control.

- I HAVE BEEN LAUGHED AT WHEN I SHOWED MY FEELINGS.
    I will never let you see me again.

- MY OWN FEELINGS WERE CONSTANTLY IGNORED.
    I numb myself for protection.

Share the ones that apply to you with your spouse.

Self-Disclosure

1. Write down at least three things about what makes it difficult for you to share heart-to-heart (allowing yourself to be known, or self-disclose etc.) to your spouse? (Examples: "I am afraid if I share something really important to me that it will be minimised.")

2. What would need to happen for you to feel safer to share your heart with your spouse? (Example: "I need to take the risk even if I get a response I might not like.")

3. Write it in a sentence. (Example: "I need you to stop finishing my sentences for me!")

4. Share it with your spouse.

5. Tell them what that is like for you. (Example: Did you feel scared, excited, loving etc.)

Notes to Chapter 2

1. J. Powell (1969). *Why Am I Afraid to Tell You Who I Am?* Fount Paperbacks.
2. M. Sharifian, S. Najafi & F. Shaghaghi (2011). An investigation of couple communication program (CCP) on the life's quality and intimacy of unsatisfied women. *Social and Behavioral Sciences, 30*:1991-1994. DOI:10.1016/j.sbspro.2011.10.387
3. D.A. Bagarozzi (2001). *Enhancing Intimacy in Marriage: A Clinician's Guide.* Routledge.

CHAPTER 3

FOUNDATIONAL PRINCIPLE: A COMMITMENT TO CREATIVE USE OF CONFLICT

Overview

This chapter explores a foundational principle of ME – a commitment to creative use of conflict. The chapter is organised under the following headings:

⇒ What Is Effective Conflict Resolution?

⇒ How Do Learned Responses Influence Anger and Conflict?

⇒ What Are Some Options for Resolution?

What Is Effective Conflict Resolution?

Anger and conflict can be either destructive or constructive. Anger is an emotion most of us regard as negative, destructive, unpleasant and sometimes frightening. Many of us have been taught that anger is "sinful" unless it is "righteous anger", expressed on behalf of another person or an important cause. However, constructive anger and conflict show that two people care enough about each other, and their relationship, to work at all the issues, even the painful ones in their lives.

Understanding anger and conflict

Resolving conflict will require an understanding of anger and conflict in the marital relationship. The following reflections may help.

- *The reality of difference.* Conflict in marriage is inevitable and normal, because we are different from each other. Learning to understand and deal with our differences is a step towards conflict resolution. The end result is a sound and satisfying marriage in which differences are valued.

    > Learning to understand and deal with our differences is a step towards conflict resolution.

- *Accepting anger and dealing with anger.* Anger is a signal that all is not well. We cannot deal well with anger while it's hot – it takes time to defuse the bomb of anger. Venting anger can be difficult to handle, because it can produce hurt, retaliation, distance and lack of safety. Uncontrolled anger may be a learned method of getting our own way. Suppressing anger can also be difficult to handle, because it can lead to hostile withdrawal, passive-aggression and distance. Both these behaviours, venting and suppression, can become destructive patterns that destroy the capacity for tenderness. Replacing these patterns with love and patience requires action by both spouses. Destructive patterns *can* be changed over time.
- *Defusing Anger.* Anger must be defused before an issue can be addressed productively. Defusing anger has physical implications – we need time to deal with our bodily arousal, increased heartbeat, adrenalin flow, sensations of threat or danger and the confusion that many of us experience.
- *Anger is part of the relationship.* It needs to be worked on together. Anger alerts us to the growing edges of our relationship and can provide the opportunity to increase intimacy through a greater understanding and consideration of each other.
- *Anger is an automatic physical response.* Anger is bodily response triggered by threat or pain. When we feel threatened or hurt, physically or emotionally, our body responds by getting us ready to fight the attacker or run from danger; for example, fear in a

Anger is an indicator of the growing edge of our relationship.

mother whose child is lost may often trigger anger, rather than joy, when they are reunited. In traumatic circumstances, we might also freeze and be powerless to act. In survival mode, our heart rate and breathing increase as adrenalin is pumped through our body, our muscles tense, our stomach and gut contract and we are primed for survival.

How Do Learned Responses Influence Anger and Conflict?

In certain families, and in collective societies, there are strong restraints on the open expression of anger. Most people tend to possess a personal dislike and distrust of anger. Yet, the fact is that in the face of threat or danger, we have little conscious control over our bodily reactions. In a relationship, we tend to have different anger responses that are generally learned from our families in childhood; for example, one spouse may come from a family where anger:

- is expressed indirectly such that the person who is angry feels justified in blaming, accusing or belittling their spouse's behaviour, rather than acknowledging their own anger and seeking to understand its cause;
- is displaced onto the spouse, the office junior, the dog or the kids. Displaced or indirect anger can play havoc with our digestive system and can result in raised blood pressure;
- is vented to excess. This results in anger feeding on itself, signalling to the angry person's body that the danger is continuing or increasing. When anger becomes rage, it is hard to rein in;
- blazes out suddenly or ends in tears. Sometimes this kind of anger can turn into rage and frighten everybody in its path;
- is turned against the self, rather than openly facing it in the presence of a loving spouse; or
- is suppressed in an emotional mechanism that automatically suppresses the strength of our physical reactions. This does not allow for awareness of anger. Expressing natural responses to threat or pain (such as rejection or abuse) is to be aware of strong emotions like hurt, fear, powerlessness or inadequacy. If suppressed, these feelings may later find expression in depression or resentment and cause withdrawal and continuing discomfort.

We may discover that anger can be the servant of love and assist us in our growth as human beings.

These learned responses can be very unpleasant and are usually unproductive. So, what can be done to express anger in such a way that it heals the relationship? How can anger serve us and be a useful force in helping us build a better home, society and world? Perhaps it occurs when we recognise that anger:

- is a warning signal that all is not well;
- is energy waiting to be harnessed;
- can give us the courage to act when we are afraid;
- is an indicator of the growing edge of our relationship; and,
- can be constructive.

Anger can also be a power for good; for example, anger can be constructive if:

- we allow ourselves to feel our anger;
- we take the time to understand what is happening and channel how we react;
- those of us who are quick off the mark learn to respond more slowly;
- those people who are slow to recognise anger give it more room/acknowledgement;
- we learn that sometimes we get the signals mixed, that there is no threat or hurt intended;
- we learn ways of discharging the excess physical energy;
- we learn to tune into our body so we know what is happening there;

- we learn how to take ourselves and others less seriously;
- we are willing to express anger cleanly, without accusation and without backing down on the strength of our feeling;
- we realise that anger is a signal to tell us that something needs to change and can mobilise us into action; and
- we care enough about ourselves and our relationships and our world.

Then, we may discover that anger can be the servant of love and assist us in our growth as human beings.

What Are Some Options for Resolution?

Research shows that increasing marital adjustment between couples in conflict can be achieved by the acquisition of new skills.[1] The skills of conflict

> Remember, if one spouse wins, we both lose.

resolution can draw couples closer to each other, as they jointly search for win–win solutions.[2] There can be a powerful shift from being adversaries to being co-operative spouses so that each person benefits. In their book *Everyone Can Win*, Cornelius et al. claim that conflict resolution skills enable us to bypass personal differences and to open up to possibilities (the Conflict Resolution Network provides valuable resources at http://www.crnhq.org).

Creative use of anger includes increasing awareness of it, as anger is a warning signal that all is not well. Some strategies are to let your spouse know you are

> Avoid using 100% phrases such as "you always" or "you never".

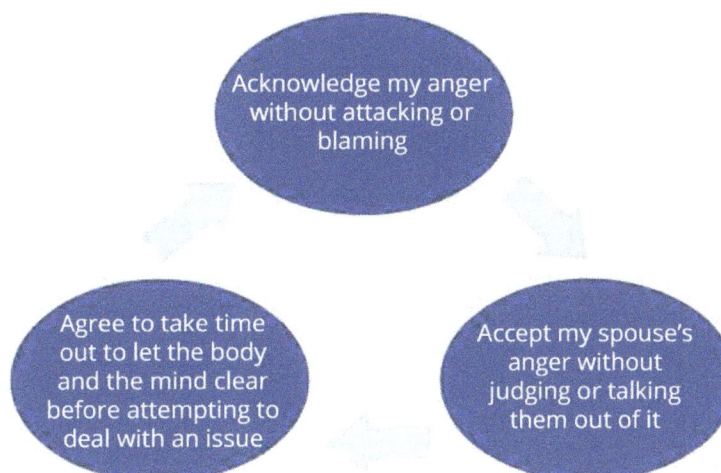

angry, without blame or accusation. Take *Time Out* to calm down if you need it. Ask your spouse if they are able to listen and set a time if needed. Address the cause of the anger between you, either alone or with your spouse's permission and support. Alternatively, take turns to listen to and try to understand each other. The following guidelines are useful when anger needs defusing so that conflict can be dealt with in a constructive way.

Acknowledge my anger without attacking or blaming

Accept my spouse's anger without judging or talking them out of it

Agree to take time out to let the body and the mind clear before attempting to deal with an issue

In addition, the following guidelines are useful in learning to deal with conflict constructively. Reflect on those you generally use.

- Pick your time to raise contentious issues.
- Postpone dealing with the issue to a definite time.
- Agree to discuss. Use reflective listening where needed.
- Stay with one subject at a time.
- Tackle the problem, not the person.
- Try hard to stick to the facts.
- Be honest about your feelings and show them.
- Avoid using 100% phrases such as "you always" or "you never".
- Explore what can be changed and what cannot.
- Listen without interruption.
- Check that you have understood correctly and whether you have the same understanding of meanings.
- Check the accuracy of both verbal and non-verbal messages when you sense a misunderstanding.
- Be patient with your spouse when they have difficulty understanding what you are saying.

The anger volcano

On ME evaluations, the volcano is often mentioned as being the most powerful and valuable take-away from any ME event. A volcano is an opening in the earth's crust that allows molten rock, gases and debris to escape to the surface. Whilst molten lava spews out the top, the real power and energy emerges from deep within the earth. Our couple relationship can be likened to a volcano. Sometimes one spouse longs for more closeness and connection and reduces stressful situations by moving towards their spouse to talk it through. The other spouse tends to reduce stressful situations by distance, withdrawal and silence. Both feel their needs are not met by the other when this dance of pursue/distance occurs at the top of the volcano. This is what we can observe, the lava, but the power is generated from deep within.

When a pursuer moves towards their spouse and there is distance, they sense a disconnection in the relationship and they panic. They want to talk about it and work it out, but their spouse's withdrawal propels them into blaming and criticising in order to deal with the pain of disconnection. In their protest they attempt to bash down their spouse's locked door.

On the other hand, the withdrawer typically believes that if they show up, their spouse will criticise and blame them and then leave the relationship. Ironically, they are trying to protect the relationship. As their spouse is incredibly important to them, they do not want to lose them. Therefore, they shut down or lock the proverbial door so that nothing comes in or out. Of course, this leaves their spouse feeling alone and abandoned.

As couples, we often unconsciously create a destructive dance at the top of the volcano. The pursuer/withdrawer dance creates conflict and disconnection. We are "hard-wired" for connection and the key issue in marital conflict is the security of the emotional bond.[3] The strength of the emotional bond is based on how we answer the following questions.[4]

- How responsive are you when I am distressed? Can I count on you? Can I rely on you to respond to me emotionally?
- How accessible are you? Will you be there for me when I need you? Can I reach you?
- How engaged are you? Overall, do I know you will value me and stay close?

When the pursue/withdraw dance is in full swing, it tends to tap into our own painful unresolved issues and neither is able to offer anything to the other. Instead, our interactions become rigid and our relationship becomes locked up and unsafe with no possibility of being there for each other.

How do we learn to dance to a different tune? Distinguishing between primary and secondary emotions is a good place to begin. Secondary emotions communicate a powerful message to our spouse and dictate their reactive response; these emotions occur "above the line" of the volcano. Primary, below-the-line emotions connect us to our inner worlds. The distancer often experiences a sense of helplessness and failure underlying their withdrawal. For the pursuer, there is often a sense of loss beneath their anger, criticism and complaint – they feel alone, abandoned and desperate.

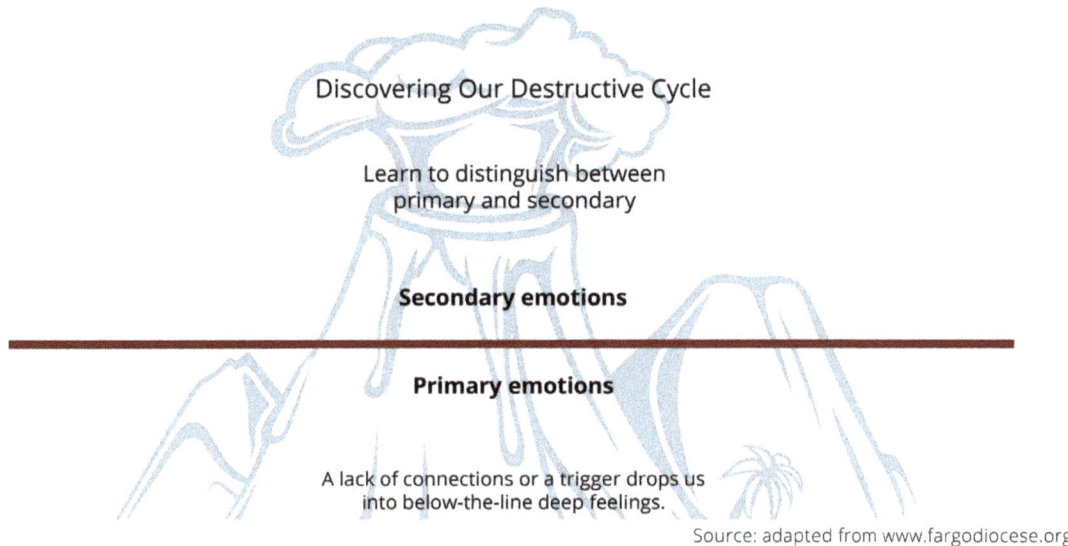

Discovering Our Destructive Cycle

Learn to distinguish between primary and secondary

Secondary emotions

Primary emotions

A lack of connections or a trigger drops us into below-the-line deep feelings.

Source: adapted from www.fargodiocese.org

Secondary, above-the-line emotions or reactions to our spouse's responses are a way to cope by avoiding primary, below-the-line emotions. Identifying primary, below-the-line emotion can change the destructive dance to a more constructive

> "We are 'hard-wired' for connection and the key issue in marital conflict is the security of the emotional bond."
> (Susan Johnson, *Hold Me Tight: Seven Conversations for a Lifetime of Love*)

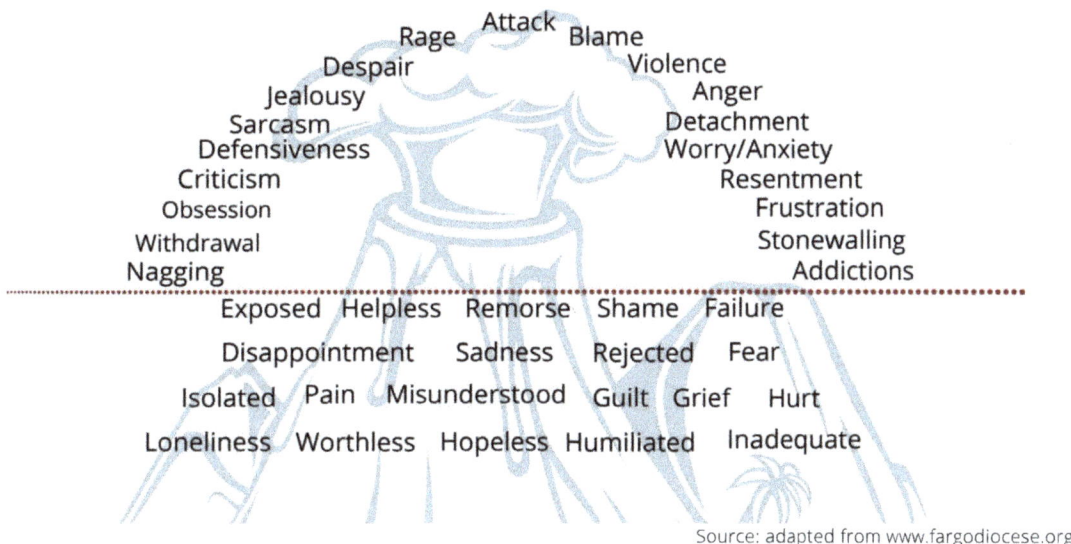

one; for example, fear (below the line) is often expressed as anger (above the line). When the primary emotions underlying our dance steps are experienced and acknowledged, new healing emotional conversations can occur.[5] Successful, connected couples are those who are good at repair.[6]

Rage Attack Blame
Despair Violence
Jealousy Anger
Sarcasm Detachment
Defensiveness Worry/Anxiety
Criticism Resentment
Obsession Frustration
Withdrawal Stonewalling
Nagging Addictions

Exposed Helpless Remorse Shame Failure

Disappointment Sadness Rejected Fear

Isolated Pain Misunderstood Guilt Grief Hurt

Loneliness Worthless Hopeless Humiliated Inadequate

Source: adapted from www.fargodiocese.org

We have found that it is helpful to give couples an exercise. Ask them to draw a volcano to represent their relationship. Suggest they think of a recent conflict in order to narrow their focus. Firstly, request they identify their destructive dance of secondary emotions at the top of the volcano and name their dance. Secondly, ask couples to identify the primary emotions beneath the line. An example of a handout is shown below.

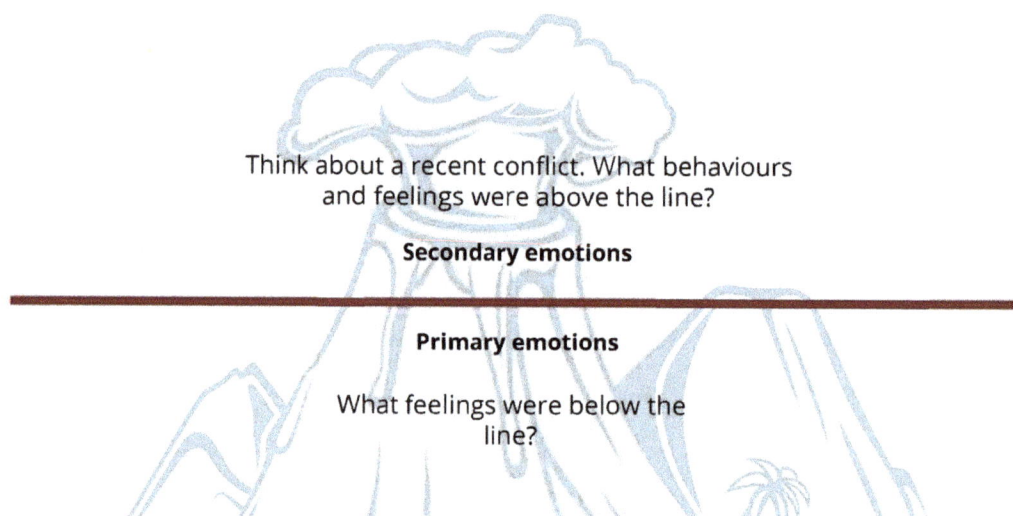

Think about a recent conflict. What behaviours
and feelings were above the line?

Secondary emotions

Primary emotions

What feelings were below the
line?

It is always beneficial for the leader couple to dialogue about their destructive dance at the top of the volcano. This enables them to draw a volcano on a whiteboard and ask the couples to guess what behaviours and emotions are above and below the line, not only encouraging vulnerability but also demonstrating the skill. The leader couple can ask for a volunteer to dialogue about their own volcano and draw it on the whiteboard, allowing for cross-identification.

Processing beneath the line

We have observed that processing anger and conflict, both in our own relationship and those of others, involves ultimately coming to a place of giving ourselves permission to feel the primary, painful feelings and grieve our losses. If we refuse or deny our primary feelings and their pain, the wound festers and we will be triggered again and again. Our relationship will be fraught with continual cycles of conflict. When conflict in our relationship is constant, we live with unmet needs and it is easy to descend into shame (a primary feeling).

Shame triggers tend to be different for men and women. According to Brené Brown, "While women are faced with a web of many layered, competing, and conflicting expectations, there seems to be one major expectation for men – do NOT appear weak".[7] Women tend to feel shame when they perceive they fall short of the standards they impose on themselves. They seek core validation. If it is not forthcoming, women tend to blame themselves and move away from their vulnerability; for example, women often long to be a good wife, mother, daughter, sibling, friend and so on. When these relationships fail they feel they are without a voice, abandoned and unseen. Instead of sharing these painful primary feelings, women often respond by being controlling, demanding, desolate or needy.

On the other hand, men often long to feel that they are courageous, that their words, decisions and life matter and have impact. They experience shame when they sense they have failed or lack the strength to give on behalf of others; for example, they respond to an early message of "You are not good enough" by blaming others, using aggressive words, shutting down or moving into passivity. In some men it is expressed as violence. James Gilligan remarks, "I have yet to see a serious act of violence that was not provoked by the experience of feeling shamed and humiliated, disrespected and ridiculed, and that did not represent the attempt to prevent or undo this 'loss of face'".[8] Men often oscillate between being a victim and being an offender.

> "Successful, connected couples are those who are good at repair."
> (John Gottman, *The Seven Principles for Making Marriage Work*)

In order to deal with conflict in our relationship we return to the volcano to determine the primary emotions below our repetitive destructive cycle that spews from the top. Conversations then centre on sharing our primary feelings. We have learned that we cannot sit through the painful feelings if we are in reactive mode. We have also learned that through sharing our primary feelings, they lose their power and we begin to heal.

Eventually, we come to the place of forgiving those who hurt us. They, too, are hurt, because hurt people hurt others. Forgiveness enables us to let go of blaming ourselves or others or feeling responsible for the hurt. Forgiveness allows us to cease accusing ourselves or our spouse for how we feel.

The parroting skill

The "parroting" skill – also called the *Imago Dialogue Process*[9] – enables us to deal with anger and conflict in a way that reduces reactivity to each other. On ME evaluations, the parroting skill is also mentioned as being a powerful and valuable take-away from ME events. Parrots love to imitate and repeat words or phrases. Parroting as a couple involves repeating (as closely as possible) what we hear our spouse saying. Parroting is a type of structured communication technique that can be used to communicate with each other when we are frustrated, do not feel understood or just want to feel closer. This dialogue technique[10] is a way to talk about conflict in our relationship in a way that lets each feel heard.

To practise the technique, first ask your spouse, "Is now a good time to talk?" If they say "Yes", ask them to join you in a comfortable place where you can sit facing each other (knee to knee) and dialogue together. Through taking turns, you will each have time to share your thoughts and feelings on a topic that you agree to talk about. Start with something easy and not too frustrating. Remember, this may feel ridiculous and unnatural at first. However, if you practise this technique, later on it will become a beneficial tool to help you both to feel heard and seen by each other when you want to discuss something difficult or conflictual in your relationship.

> "Do not despise your inner world... A creature without any needs would never have reasons for fear, or grief, or hope, or anger. But for that very reason we are often ashamed of our emotions, and of the relations of need and dependency bound up with them... So people flee from their inner world of feeling, and from articulate mastery of their own emotional experiences... What is the remedy of these ills? A kind of self-love that does not shrink from the needy and incomplete parts of the self, but accepts those with interest and curiosity, and tries to develop a language with which to talk about needsand feelings
> (Martha Nussbaum, *Frontiers of Justice*)

Second, choose who will be the sender and who will be the receiver. The sender begins with a short discourse about the topic. The receiver then parrots what they hear, checking if it is correct. They follow this by asking, "Is there more?", continuing to parrot until the sender says, "That's enough for now." The receiver then validates the sender's feelings and empathises. They then switch roles with the receiver and respond by sharing their perspective on the issue.

This is a good format to practise as you continue to move into more difficult conversations. Remember, parroting means simply repeating what you hear your spouse saying; for example, if your spouse says, "I appreciate you listening to me without interrupting", you simply reply by parroting, "You appreciate that I am listening without interrupting. Is there more?" It is helpful to check with your spouse to see if what you understood is what he/she meant; for example, "Is that correct?", or "Did I get all of it?", or "Am I in the ball park?", or "Am I hearing you correctly?" The confirmation may be spoken or non-spoken; "Yes, that's it!", or an affirmative nod or touch. If the understanding is not what the sender meant, then the sender clarifies the message and the process begins again. Parroting or mirroring makes your spouse feel seen and heard and gives a space for the dialogue to continue without reactive, strong emotions. It also allows you some time to listen and hear what your spouse has to say without having to think of a reply or jump into any interpretation. Review the accompanying simple sender and receiver worksheets that give specific directions for you to follow.

The Imago Dialogue
The Sender

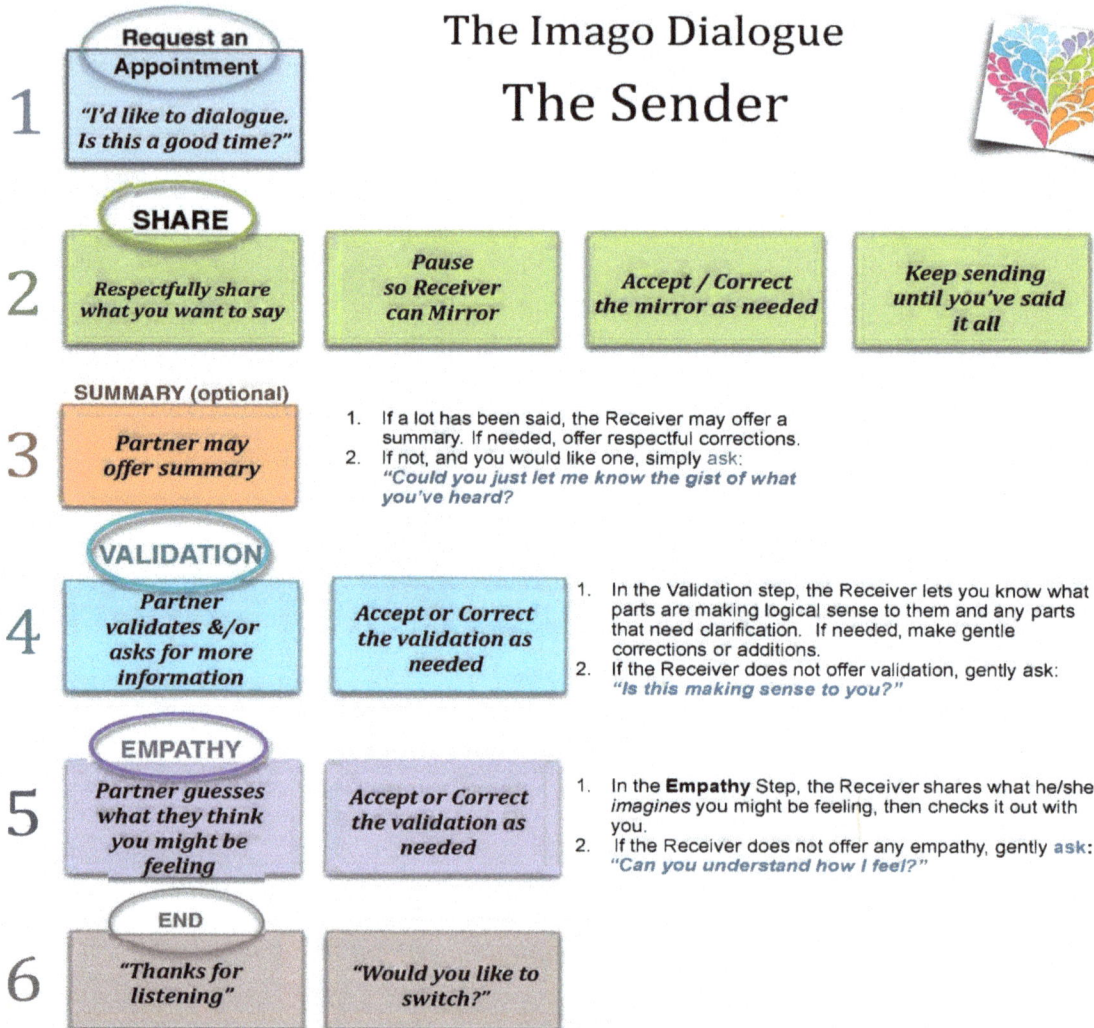

1 **Request an Appointment**
"I'd like to dialogue. Is this a good time?"

2 **SHARE**

Respectfully share what you want to say	Pause so Receiver can Mirror	Accept / Correct the mirror as needed	Keep sending until you've said it all

3 **SUMMARY (optional)**

Partner may offer summary

1. If a lot has been said, the Receiver may offer a summary. If needed, offer respectful corrections.
2. If not, and you would like one, simply ask: "Could you just let me know the gist of what you've heard?

4 **VALIDATION**

Partner validates &/or asks for more information

Accept or Correct the validation as needed

1. In the Validation step, the Receiver lets you know what parts are making logical sense to them and any parts that need clarification. If needed, make gentle corrections or additions.
2. If the Receiver does not offer validation, gently ask: "Is this making sense to you?"

5 **EMPATHY**

Partner guesses what they think you might be feeling

Accept or Correct the validation as needed

1. In the **Empathy** Step, the Receiver shares what he/she imagines you might be feeling, then checks it out with you.
2. If the Receiver does not offer any empathy, gently ask: "Can you understand how I feel?"

6 **END**

"Thanks for listening"

"Would you like to switch?"

NEGATIVE FEELING PROMPTERS

frustrated	sad	rejected	overwhelmed	betrayed
irritated	anxious	abandoned	unheard	cheated
angry	helpless	lonely	discounted	guilty
hurt	hopeless	alone	invisible	embarrassed
criticized	insecure	controlled	unloved	humiliated
attacked	scared	pressured	confused	ashamed
depressed	neglected	trapped	manipulated	enraged

(Source: Used with permission. Barbara J. Reichlin, Imagoworks at http://imagoworks.com/the-imago-dialogue/sender-flowchart/)

The Couples Dialogue
The Receiver Flowchart

• Reflect back everything your partner says • Ask partner to pause &/or repeat as needed

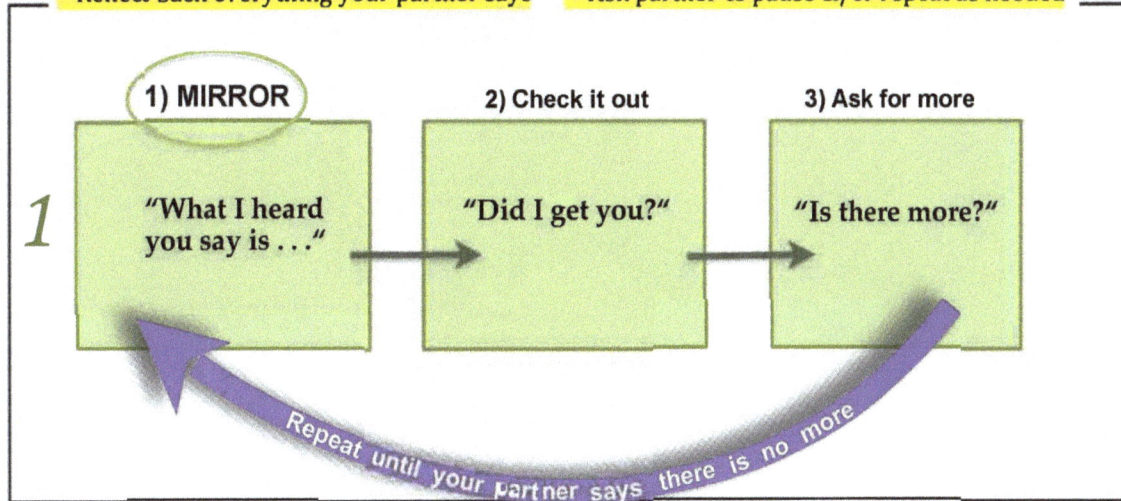

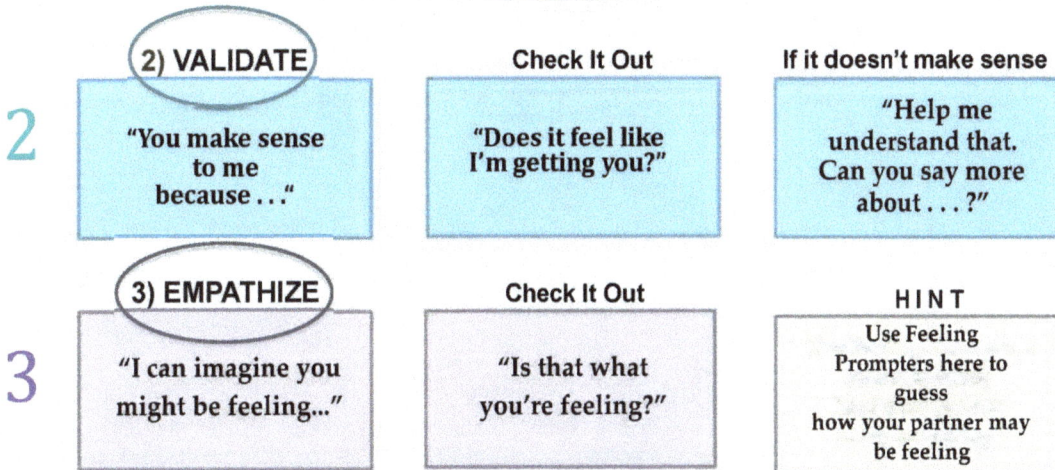

1

1) MIRROR	2) Check it out	3) Ask for more
"What I heard you say is . . ."	"Did I get you?"	"Is there more?"

Repeat until your partner says there is no more

2

2) VALIDATE	Check It Out	If it doesn't make sense
"You make sense to me because . . ."	"Does it feel like I'm getting you?"	"Help me understand that. Can you say more about . . . ?"

3

3) EMPATHIZE	Check It Out	HINT
"I can imagine you might be feeling..."	"Is that what you're feeling?"	Use Feeling Prompters here to guess how your partner may be feeling

NEGATIVE FEELING PROMPTERS

frustrated	sad	rejected	overwhelmed	betrayed
irritated	anxious	abandoned	unheard	cheated
angry	helpless	lonely	discounted	guilty
hurt	hopeless	alone	invisible	embarrassed
criticized	insecure	controlled	unloved	humiliated
attacked	scared	pressured	confused	ashamed
depressed	neglected	trapped	manipulated	enraged

Barbara J Reichlin, MA, LMFT, LPC • 713.660.9988 • breichlin@swbell.net • imagoworks.com

(Source: Used with permission. Barbara J. Reichlin, http://imagoworks.com/the-imago-dialogue/receiver-flowchart)

Restoration following conflict

As mentioned earlier, successful couples are good repairers of conflict. The following steps can be useful to both parties, but are chiefly designed to assist the offender's reflections on the conflict.

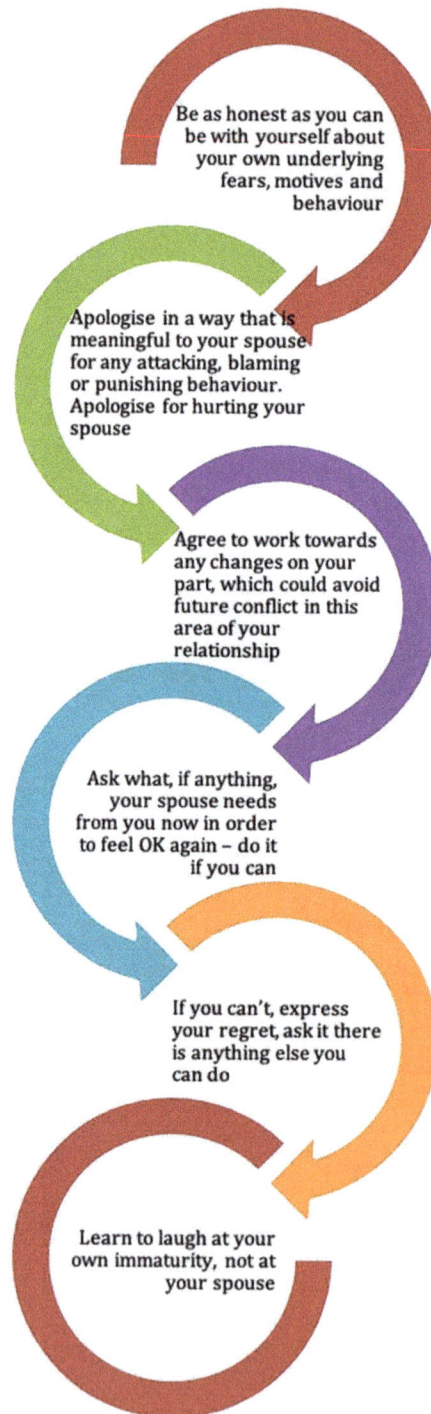

Be as honest as you can be with yourself about your own underlying fears, motives and behaviour

Apologise in a way that is meaningful to your spouse for any attacking, blaming or punishing behaviour. Apologise for hurting your spouse

Agree to work towards any changes on your part, which could avoid future conflict in this area of your relationship

Ask what, if anything, your spouse needs from you now in order to feel OK again – do it if you can

If you can't, express your regret, ask it there is anything else you can do

Learn to laugh at your own immaturity, not at your spouse

(Source: Used with permission. Gerlinde & Ian Spencer 2001)

Our Story

The beauty of Mullaitivu, Sri Lanka, belies its history. Each day the road we travel to our training venue passes an achingly beautiful lagoon. The fleeting, breathtaking colours of sunrise and sunset ward off the darkness. Many drowned in the lagoon in the final battle. The decades-long war has ended but the devastation is fresh. Suffering is not easy on the eyes. It is surreal. The landscape is scarred and desolate. A few brave families are resettling amid the ruins and I (Paula) am moved by the sweet resilience of these precious people.

This is the backstory to what happens next. It is the commencement of the first trauma recovery program in the war-torn area. The participants are profoundly broken in body and spirit, the pain etched on their vacant faces. Some are physically blinded by bombs and land mines, others are paralysed, all have lost loved ones; some bear outward scars, all bear inward scars. Our hearts break for them, raw and visceral.

We invite participants to begin drawing on a large sheet of paper a tree as a metaphor of themselves. The roots represent the past, including family history and influences. Unexpectedly, one lady gives me a gift but I do not recognise it yet. I sit. Her tree has no words or symbols. Her head is slumped into her slender, coffee-coloured hands. I strain to hear half-whispered replies, as I ask her about her drawing. She cannot draw her roots because they are so broken. Suddenly, I am untethered, as her plight touches deep, unhealed wounds in me.

I ground myself to complete the workshop. I am hurting and hurt people hurt others. That is exactly what happens, as I grapple with the volcano that has erupted inside me. There is no time to process and rest. I yearn to go somewhere quiet, to hide and lick my wounds, but I feel disabled and alone. Exhaustion claims me as I try to contain the depth of suffering that is lodged deep within.

However, this is not the worst of it. We return to our guest house, passing the beautiful lagoon with its dark secrets. I ache for the refuge of our room, where I hope to surrender to my accumulating grief. I long for Barry to want to know what is happening in me, to inquire how I am. I fall on the bed and begin to cry and this is where the real trouble begins. Barry enters our room and contemptuously states, "This is a collective society. You should be out there with the team, not shut away in your room." Hot anger flares. The breaking is complete. I am ripped open.

In the aftermath of Mullaitivu, I thought I would never come back from the brink. It takes nine months to comprehend that this heartbroken Sri Lankan woman has offered me a priceless gift wrapped in pain. With the support of a kind lady skilled in therapy my heart begins healing. Previously inaccessible primal trauma can blow me apart in a blink – or should I say propel me to come together? The broken Sri Lankan woman invites me to risk hope, to be willing to release my pain and come alive.

My heart has discovered afresh that, "I am not what has happened to me. I am what I choose to become." My mess becomes my message. I long for Barry to know this about me. Intriguingly, I realise as I approach the source of my sadness that I have been unable to cry over the pain of my own past traumas. I know the piercing agony of despair. I have been there. I know the excruciating struggle to climb out of the pit, to reach for life and risk hope. I know what it is to feel shattered inside, like the essence of me has died and is too broken to ever be stitched. I comprehend, too, that the pit has steep, slick sides and that climbing out is a slippery business. My tears finally unblock and I cry for their pain, my pain, and for the universal desire to be seen and known by another, deeply.

One year later we are participants in a marriage enrichment weekend. During a break-out time we revisit Mullaitivu, like a dog returning to a bone. I ask Barry, "What would you like to have done?" Instantly, a dawning realisation shakes him to the core. He says, "I wanted to flop on the bed and cry." Contempt for his needs has followed him since childhood. How does one recognise and move into the needs of a spouse if they are unaware of their own?

We begin to share our deep feelings below the line of the volcano and it changes us and our relationship. We no longer react to each other from our wounding, but reach across the space to find understanding and connection. We forgive and find that "Forgiveness is the fragrance the violet sheds on the heel that has crushed it" (Mark Twain).

Chapter Summary

- Conflict in marriage is inevitable and normal. Anger and conflict can be either destructive or constructive. Constructive conflict shows that two people care enough about each other and their relationship, to work at all the issues, even the painful ones, in their lives.
- Conflict resolution skills enable us to bypass personal differences and to open up to possibilities.
- Accepting anger and dealing with anger, defusing anger, viewing it as the growing edge in a relationship and an automatic physical response are all important parts of conflict resolution.
- Cultural and societal restraints can include learned anger responses to either vent or suppress.
- Options for anger and conflict resolution include acknowledging anger without attacking or blaming, accepting a spouse's anger without judging or talking them out of it, and agreeing to take time out to let the body settle and the mind clear before attempting to deal with the issue.
- The metaphor of a volcano can be used to illustrate pursue-withdraw patterns and distinguish between primary and secondary emotions.
- The parroting skill (The Imago Dialogue process) is a tool to learn to listen to a spouse's issue and reduce emotionality.
- The offender's reflections on the conflict and learning skills to deal with them can lead to restoration.

Worksheets on Anger and Conflict

How Are We Currently Handling Anger And Conflict?

Do alone first, then together. Recall a recent or current conflict.

Not well   Very well

```
|--+--+--+--+--+--+--+--+--+--|
0  1  2  3  4  5  6  7  8  9  10
```

Where do I place myself? (Put a cross)

Where do I place us? (Put a tick)

Reactions to Anger and Conflict

IGNORE OR MINIMISE YOUR ANGER

    (Do something to subdue it but do nothing to process it; for example, chop wood, thump a pillow, etc.)

DENY YOUR ANGER

    (Depression, manipulation, blackmail, etc.)

KEEP IT DOWN IN THE PIT OF YOUR STOMACH

    (Withdraw, sulk, place distance between you, cut-off, etc.)

DUMP IT ON YOUR SPOUSE

    (Throw things, yell and scream, put-downs, sarcasm, name-calling, violence)

REFUSE TO LET IT GO

    (Bitterness, malice, power struggles, intimidation, etc.)

GET EVEN, GET REVENGE, PUNISH

    (Do it in public, withhold, threaten to leave/divorce; etc.; this can be spoken or unspoken)

BLAME YOUR SPOUSE

    (Refuse to see your part in it)

DON'T LEARN FROM YOUR ANGER

    (Don't use it to build your relationship, or express what is important to you and learn what is important to your spouse)

DIVORCE

    (I never have to resolve it and learn from it)

How Do I Express Anger?

Do alone. Circle the one that best fits and then tick how often you use it; for example, sometimes or mostly.

	Sometimes	Mostly
I must win (control)	——	——
I surrender (give in for peace sake).	——	——
I stay cool / uncommitted.	——	——
I withdraw / go silent / walk away.	——	——
I sulk / brood / cry.	——	——
I am afraid of you / unsure of you.	——	——
I blame / shame / put you down.	——	——
I throw things / stomp around.	——	——
I ridicule / interrupt / feel superior.	——	——
I yell / explode / become physical.	——	——
I am unpredictable / violent.	——	——
I call you names / intimidate / threaten.	——	——
I generalise / analyse / rationalise / intellectualise.	——	——
I criticise / use sarcasm / swear	——	——
I exaggerate / overreact.	——	——
I drink / ignore you / eat.	——	——
I give advice / preach / lecture.	——	——
I save it up and use it for future ammunition.	——	——
I use other people to prove my point.	——	——
I undermine you / try to trap you.	——	——
I play the martyr / I say nothing is wrong.	——	——
I try to confuse you.	——	——
I become resentful / bitter / feel sorry for myself.	——	——
I am straightforward / consistent.	——	——
I am willing to share.	——	——
I give honest feedback / open.	——	——
I am open to feedback from you.	——	——
I try to move toward you.	——	——
Other:	——	——

Now, go back and underline the one you think fits your spouse and place a cross (x) next to the appropriate sometimes or mostly box.

Share sensitively with your spouse.

Unfair Fighting

Do alone. Circle the responses that apply to you.

___ I raise the issue when my spouse is overloaded, overworked or overwhelmed.

___ I am critical of my spouse in front of friends or the kids.

___ I drop difficult things out as I am walking out the door.

___ I use my anger to distance and/or block communication.

___ I suppress my anger, withdraw or use the silent treatment.

___ I express my anger so that it causes uncontrolled damage.

___ I repress my anger, refuse to admit or accept it or ignore it.

___ I insist on my own way and/or maintain power struggles.

Share sensitively with your spouse.

Fair Fighting Rules

BEWARE OF THE TIMING

Fatigue, pressure, etc.

KEEP FIGHTING PRIVATE

Choose a time when kids not around. However modelling of some constructive conflict is a gift to children.

KNOW WHAT YOU ARE FIGHTING ABOUT

STICK TO THE POINT

BE DIRECT

How you feel / what you require

ATTACK THE PROBLEM NOT THE PERSON

Don't attack
Blame
Talk each other down
Hit below the belt
Wear the belt too high
Bring up the past and use as ammunition
Use physical violence

OWN YOUR FEELINGS

Start sentences with "I feel" not, "You make me feel"

DON'T READ YOUR SPOUSE'S MIND

DON'T EXPECT YOUR SPOUSE TO READ YOUR MIND

LISTEN BENEATH THE WORDS

People fight when they feel they are not being heard

DON'T TRY TO CHANGE YOUR SPOUSE

However, it is okay to invite change beginning with, "What I would like is..."

How Do We Handle Anger?

Complete alone. Recall a recent situation when you both felt angry (or still do!)

	ME	MY SPOUSE
When I am angry, I am… (Choose six words from the Feeling Word List, describing how you feel when you are angry.)		
Afterwards I feel… (Choose three words from the Feeling Word List, describing how you feel when your anger subsides.)		
Then I… (withdraw, get even, take the blame, sulk, etc.)		
In the future, I would like to handle anger differently by…		

Together, share your ideas, discuss gently and lovingly, as anger can be a touchy subject.

Feeling Word List

PLEASANT FEELINGS

affectionate
alive
amused
beautiful
brave
caring
cherished
comfortable
confident
contented
calm
carefree
delighted
close
comforted
competent
cooperative
ecstatic
energetic
enthusiastic
excited
forgiving
fulfilled
generous
grateful
happy
hopeful
humourous
joyful
light
lovable
loving
passionate
peaceful
playful
pleased
relaxed
safe
satisfied
soft
special
strong
supported
tender
thankful

thrilled
victorious
warm

ANGRY FEELINGS

aggressive
angry
belligerent
bitter
contemptuous
defiant
disgusted
enraged
exasperated
frustrated
furious
hateful
hostile
impatient
irritated
outraged
powerful
resentful
stubborn
touchy
violated
unforgiving

uptight

FEAR FEELINGS

afraid
alarmed
anxious
beaten
breathless
cautious
confused
defeated
edgy
evasive
fearful
inadequate
insecure
locked in

panicky
paralysed
powerless
tense
terrified
threatened
timid
uptight

SAD FEELINGS

bewildered
burdened
choked up
depressed
despairing
desperate
devastated
disappointed
discouraged
grief-stricken
helpless
hopeless
hurt
lonely
miserable
overwhelmed
rejected
sad
tearful
tired
weary
weepy

OTHER FEELINGS

apologetic
appealing
ashamed
ashamed
awkward
bored
cold
compassionate
courageous
defensive
dependent

deprived
determined
dishonest
distant
dominant
dull
embarrassed
empathetic
envious
estranged
firm
foolish
humiliated
frisky
guilty
horrified
humble
in control
independent
jealous
miserable
mixed up
neglected
open
proud
relieved
respectful
self-pitying
sexy
shy
sick
sinful
sorry
stretched
submissive
surprised
sympathetic
taut
tired
tolerant
understanding
unloved
untrustworthy
useless
vulnerable
wrong

Notes to Chapter 3

1. B.M. Yalcin & T.S. Karahan (2007). Effects of a couple communication program on marital adjustment. *Journal of the American Board of Family Medicine*, 20: 36-44. DOI:10.3122/jabfm.2007.01.060053.
2. H. Cornelius, S. Faire & E. Cornelius (2006). *Everyone Can Win: Responding to Conflict Constructively* (2nd ed.). Simon & Schuster.
3. S.M. Johnson (2008). *Hold Me Tight: Seven Conversations for a Lifetime of Love.* Little Brown Spark.
4. Ibid.
5. Ibid.
6. M. Gottman (2000). *The Seven Principles for Making Marriage Work: A Practical Guide from the Country's Foremost Relationship Expert.* Harmony.
7. B. Brown (2004). *Women and Shame: Reaching Out, Speaking Truths and Building Connection.* 3C Press.
8. J. Gilligan (2016). *Violence: The Enduring Problem* (3rd ed.). SAGE Publications, p. 110.
9. H. Hendrix (2007). *Getting the Love You Want: A Guide for Couples* (20th anniversary ed.). Henry Holt & Co.
10. This technique is adapted from T. Nelson (2015). Communication using imago. Retrieved from http://www.yourtango.com/experts/tammy-nelson/communication-using-imago, and from A. Williams (2012). What is imago? Retrieved from http://www.imago.com.au/#WII06.

CHAPTER 4

FOUNDATIONAL PRINCIPLE: A COMMITMENT TO PERSONAL GROWTH

Overview

This chapter explores a foundational principle of ME – a commitment to personal growth. The chapter is organised under the following headings:

⇒ Becoming Real

⇒ Passages of a Marriage

⇒ Bringing Personal Growth to ME

Becoming Real

Marriage is an invitation to personal and spiritual growth. Like a garden, it needs lots of tending and attention to produce a bountiful crop. A commitment to effective communication and creative use of conflict are necessary, but behavioural change can be merely surface change. Only when these skills emanate from a heart's desire for authenticity, vulnerability and intimacy are lasting change and deep connection possible. Marriages encounter various passages that require negotiation. Successful negotiation compels us to do our personal work, involving a search for the true self. Unhealed heart and soul wounds hold us back from healthy relating, because they determine the way we respond to our spouse's words and how we treat them. We learn that holding our spouse responsible for our pain only produces more pain. We alone are responsible for how we respond to our wounds.

A powerful part of healing in marriage is the ability to offer each other "a corrective emotional experience". When this radiates from personal presence it fulfils our longings to know and be known and for genuine intimacy. When this gift is brought to other couples in an ME event, we can be a conduit to move them towards their own personal and marital growth.

> "We all leave childhood with wounds. In time we may transform our liabilities into gifts. The faults that pockmark the psyche may become the source of a man's or woman's beauty. The injuries we have suffered invite us to assume the most human of all vocations- to heal ourselves and others." (Sam Keen)

Healed wounds can become a source of great inspiration and wisdom to other couples.

A commitment to personal growth is based in a search for authenticity. The story of *The Velveteen Rabbit* makes a startling point about realness:

> Weeks passed, and the little Rabbit grew very old and shabby, but the Boy loved him just as much. He loved him so hard that he loved all his whiskers off, and the pink lining to his ears turned grey, and his brown spots faded. He even began to lose his shape, and he scarcely looked like a rabbit any more, except to the Boy. To him he was always beautiful, and that was all that the little Rabbit cared about. He didn't mind how he looked to other people, because the nursery magic had made him Real, and when you are Real shabbiness doesn't matter.[1]

When the Boy sees the Velveteen Rabbit as beautiful and accepts even the ugly parts, it enables the Rabbit to see himself in the same light and bask in the Boy's unconditional acceptance. In marriage, the challenge is to be able to love like this.

We want to become real but most of us tend to love from the false self. The notion of "True Self" and "False Self" was introduced into psychoanalysis by Donald Winnicott in 1960. Richard Rohr later wrote about it from a spiritual perspective.[2] The true self is claimed to be a sense of self based on our authentic experience and accompanied by a feeling of aliveness, sometimes termed "the real me". In contrast, our false self contains a defensive cover-up – the persona we present to the world to stifle our truth. When we live from our false self it leaves us feeling empty and dead on the inside.

"When we think of people giving up on their marriage, divorce usually comes to mind. But many people who give up on their marriage (or themselves or their partner) don't leave; they stay in the comfort cycle— until their marriage presents the inevitable dilemma: venture into the growth cycle or face divorce, loss of integrity, or living death."
(David Schnarch, *Passionate Marriage: Keeping Love and Intimacy Alive in Committed Relationships*)

Winnicott's original theory emerged from observations of neglected infants. Instead of assigning blame to the parents, the infants blamed themselves for their neglect, thereby creating a false version of self in the hope of persuading caregivers to offer the love and attention they craved. This false self contains the internalised mental paradigms of caregivers, especially the mother, that are also applied when societal pressures and demands require the child to be a certain way in order to gain acceptance. The internal pressures and demands to meet these external standards are set up early in life. False self is essentially a survival strategy about who we think we are and who we need to be to survive in this world with the crumbs of belongingness.

"[Spiritual bypassing is a] tendency to use spiritual ideas and practices to sidestep personal, emotional 'unfinished business,' to shore up a shaky sense of self, or to belittle basic needs, feelings, and developmental tasks."
(John Welwood, *Toward a Psychology of Awakening*).

Many religious couples also engage in spiritually bypassing personal growth. "Spiritual bypassing" is a concept defined by John Welwood, a psychotherapist and author in the field of transpersonal psychology, as a "tendency to use spiritual ideas and practices to sidestep personal, emotional 'unfinished business,' to shore up a shaky sense of self, or to belittle basic needs, feelings, and developmental tasks".[3] Perhaps these couples completely miss the goal of spiritual practices that are designed to support transformation and transcendence. Ingrid Clayton claims that:

> Although the defense [spiritual bypassing] looks a lot prettier than other defenses, it serves the same purpose. Spiritual bypass shields us from the truth, it disconnects us from our feelings, and helps us avoid the big picture. It is more about checking out than checking in—and the difference is so subtle that we usually don't even know we are doing it... usually because we cannot tolerate what we are feeling, or think that we shouldn't be experiencing what we are feeling.[4]

If we want to love well, we need to abandon our defences and replace them with a commitment to personal growth. According to David Schnarch, "A solid sense of self develops from confronting yourself, challenging yourself to do what's right, and earning your own self-respect".[5] As couples, when one or both of us live from our false selves, we may end up feeling disconnected, alone and lonely.

Passages of a Marriage

Every marriage goes through predictable stages or passages.[6] The false self tends to exhibit itself early in a marriage – in the first flush of love we believe we will live happily ever after. Sometimes called the honeymoon stage, we tell ourselves this is it! Lots of eye and body contact and often high sexual activity characterise this passage, even though some habits begin to irritate. Usually, there is not much knowledge of self, often resulting in fusion rather than intimacy, where we relate to our spouse out of neediness. Internally we say, "I need you to tell me who I am. My sense of self is how you reflect it. If you change, I will have no sense of identity".[7] Even though this is evident in abusive relationships, it is a common scenario (albeit to a lesser extent) in most marriages. In a sense, the marriage is in trouble because we are too important to each other. A common misconception is that to have more contact with you, I have to give up myself, and this creates great anxiety; for example, if there are difficulties in the relationship and my spouse responds to me in an accepting way, the relationship is experienced as loving and validating (but this depends on my spouse's response).[8] On the other hand, if my spouse does not respond in an accepting way, my sense of self is threatened. Marriage is learning who you are in the face of someone who is more than willing to tell you![9]

The second passage of marriage occurs when we begin trying to change our spouse into our image. It is characterised by lots of game-playing and power struggles, where our spouse's faults are now easy to see. Communication declines, but we deny anything is wrong and mentally blame the other. Interest in sex tends to decline. Criticism, anger and negative thoughts and feelings characterise this stage, but we are unable to share them, resulting in a loss of confidence. The relationship degenerates into suspicion, tension, hostility and resentment, and is often accompanied by either frequent fighting or stony silence. Energy levels deplete and feelings of failure and despair dominate our relationship. A sense of isolation and alienation from each other causes our relationship to deteriorate over time and we become stuck, evidenced by sexual difficulties, power struggles, financial struggles and malicious fighting or punishing. Mentally, we prepare for separation or divorce.

> "Your marriage... [s]hould have within it a secret and protected place, open to you alone. Imagine it to be a walled garden, entered by a door to which only you have the key. Within this garden you will cease to be a mother, father, employee, homemaker or any other role which you fulfill in daily life. Here you are yourselves, two people who love each other. Here you can concentrate on one another's needs. So take my hand and let us go back to our garden. The time we spend together is not wasted but invested. Invested in our future and the nurture of our love." (Anonymous)

Marriage is designed to end aloneness, not increase it. These difficulties can motivate us to look at our unresolved issues but we tend to refuse to go there – we want our spouse to validate us instead. When it is more important to get the response we want than to be known, we reach our final scream.

If we choose not to divorce at this point, we enter into the third passage of a marriage – acceptance of the reality of our situation. This leads to four choices. Reflect on the choice you are making.

Settle for less, drift, give up, or withdraw. Depleted energy can lead us to turn ourselves over to our spouse and define ourselves by what they want. We try to accommodate and appease them, especially sexually, but this can lead us to do things we do not like or want to do. Alternatively, we do just enough, but withdraw internally and withhold the very thing we know our spouse wants. Then we can still maintain some sense of self. We keep ourselves together by appeasing our spouse but not giving in to them.

The second passage of a marriage becomes our normal. We continue to play the victim, get even and hold onto resentment, sometimes resulting in a breakdown. Alternatively, we control, dominate or take over our spouse. We make sure we get a response, but it is never the one we really want.

Begin a new relationship. A hasty, rebound choice can be a poor match, resulting in more conflict and suffering.

Choose to stop playing destructive games and come out of hiding. A shift comes when one spouse ceases to allow the other to play with their reality. This choice allows us to focus on personal growth that makes room for change. We intentionally allow ourselves to be pushed back into our own unresolved issues. The tension in our relationship may increase, but we will be more able to tolerate it, as the problem shifts from "between us" to "inside me". This choice often pushes us into the spiritual area to obtain the motivation and faith to endure. At this point, we are ready to enter into the fourth passage of a marriage.

The fourth passage of a marriage is an invitation to personal growth characterised by risk-taking and hope. Intentionality and owning responsibility for the part we play in our relationship difficulties characterise this passage, as do personal honesty and an openness to knowing ourselves and our spouse. We slowly begin to understand our own and our spouse's needs. Forgiving ourselves and our spouse and letting go of the past can lead to a resolve to build new life with renewed commitment. New communication skills are acquired and we learn how to regulate our emotions instead of demanding our spouse do so. Friendship deepens as we discover each other's uniqueness.

The fifth passage of a marriage involves life-building and intimacy. We recognise that our spouse is not an object to satisfy us but a gift from God to cherish and end our aloneness. We discover that what we want for ourselves and what we want for our spouse is of equal priority. Now we strive to be there for another as opposed to demanding that our partner be there for us. We are no longer dependent on each other to tell us who we are, because we have discarded the false self and embraced realness.

This stage is characterised by unconditional intimacy, renewed energy and enthusiasm and self-confidence. We begin achieving shared goals. It is like a second honeymoon where satisfaction and freedom bring renewed joy. We are free to be close (not smothered by closeness) and free to be apart (not devastated by separateness). Interdependence emanates from mutual independence.

Bringing Personal Growth to ME

When we bring our personal growth to ME events, we find that the longing for realness and intimacy is caught rather than taught. If we are successfully negotiating the passages of a marriage and possess the foundational feature of a commitment to personal growth, we become a source of hope to other couples. Our vulnerable dialogues in front of the group become an inspirational model for couples who have not yet begun the journey of personal growth and those who are struggling through the various passages of their marriages.

Pause for Reflection

Reflections on Our Relationship...

1. What old family-of-origin wounds hold me back from genuine intimacy? (For example, alcoholic father, child abuse, controlling mother, enmeshment, old girlfriend/boyfriend relationships etc.)
2. What old wounds in my marriage steer me away from genuine intimacy? (For example, you weren't there when I was in distress... or when I really needed you...)
3. What assumptions have I made about how my spouse sees me? (For example, I assume my husband is no longer interested because I am now less attractive, I assume she is no longer interested in me sexually because she no longer wants me, etc.)

4. What fears and resentments do I hold that my spouse won't reciprocate my efforts to connect? (For example, Do I resent the time he spends at work? Do I resent her holiday preference? Am I afraid to talk to him/her about this because I will probably get a negative reaction?)

5. What am I willing to give with integrity in order to gain connection? (For example, am I willing to go to a football game with him? Fishing? Am I willing to attend an opera with her? Shopping? How much time am I willing to spend talking through our continuing issues? How far am I willing to go?)

6. How am I willing to change? (For example, how will I move towards my fears of deep intimacy? Am I willing to address past wounds in our relationship? Somewhere along the line am I willing to talk about renewing our couple goals, dreams, meaning, finances etc., for our future together?)

Our Story

The description of the Velveteen Rabbit sounds quite familiar to me (Paula). The part about losing one's shape especially rings true! Looking at old photos we scarcely recognise in our young selves who we have become. But despite feeling "old and shabby" we are becoming more "real".

Reflecting on our recent African sojourn, a friend remarked that many of our blogs reveal times of deep distress and sometimes grief from our overseas ME events. He asked the obvious: Why don't we just stay home? Believe me, I've asked myself the same question, but why would we stay at home when our travels have been the source of our greatest growth?

So, while "nursery magic" makes the Velveteen Rabbit real, I believe it is the courage to step out of the nursery that makes us more real, for it requires profound bravery. Learning to love well is hugely risky. Little did I know my false self would entrap me and become a substitute for authenticity. For years I lived with lingering self-doubt, unable to trust my inner voice or believe that I was valuable and had a right to take up space in the world. The longer I failed to address this false self, the more my real self periodically vented through destructive acting out behaviours that sabotaged my close relationships.

This occurred on a trip to Kenya and Uganda to conduct several ME events with missionary couples. Towards the end, I was depleted, both physically and emotionally. Sometimes my behaviours do not make much sense to me and I became frustrated with myself over my responses to distress. Unexpected bursts of negativity and rage punctuated the already stressful situation on the mountain in Jinja, Uganda, when my legitimate needs threatened to rise to the surface. Attempts to contain this internal split sucked all my energy and then I beat myself up all over again. I can now see this as a coping mechanism to survive without annihilating my real self. I am weary of the defensive reactions in me that fight, judge, deny or rationalise my emotions, my highly sensitive responses and my hurtful behaviours.

After our African trip I entered into a kind of wilderness, not knowing what my distress was about and how to move forward. Even though the last marriage retreat with missionaries in Jinja was life-altering for them, it left us reeling. Three marriage retreats in a short time plunged us into an intensely vulnerable, painful and disconnected space. As with every married couple, our innate need for connection during stressful times makes the outcomes of disconnection painful and precarious. Perhaps this is worse for us because our ministry involves facilitating connection for other couples. Yet, we found ourselves dancing the destructive dance of disconnection and painfully stepping on each other's feet. I sent out distress signals but Barry was emotionally unresponsive to my distress. At the time, this dance was unknown to us. We thought we were just exhausted from being the "helpers".

Upon our return home I decided to do a spiritual retreat in order to understand this destructive pattern that we keep returning to. The spiritual retreat involved meeting with a spiritual director on the first day to ask for direction on how best to use this creative space in attending to my soul. I hoped time alone with God would halt my painful lack of connection from myself and each other and that the function of being in the wilderness – to stop fighting it and face life stripped down to its essence – would let the necessary shedding happen.

During my spiritual retreat I discovered how a conversation between us on the second marriage retreat in Kenya unearthed a profound level of pain. The pain emanated from my perception of messages received by me from a family member during a very vulnerable and painful time as a young wife and mother. In my heart I heard: "You can't cut it. You are a failure as a wife, a mother and a person. You are totally unacceptable. We don't want you, as you just don't measure up. What you are doing does not please God. What you have done will cost you dearly." When these messages washed over my shattered soul I believed them and they became who I deemed myself to be. I tried to build a false self to be acceptable but failed in that, too. In our early marriage, my husband also chose this style of relating that he learnt in his family home.

Similar to the character Javert in Victor Hugo's novel *Les Miserables*, the family member in question lived by the motto "Honest work. Just reward. That's the way to please the Lord." Javert's character is defined by his legalism and lack of empathy for anyone who does not live by his creed. Reflective thought is "an uncommon thing for him, and singularly painful". I now see how this person's creed is harmful and destructive to self and relationships. To survive I had to lock the wounded, needy young person away, because she could not stand being beaten up anymore. The lie I buried deep in my heart and that the enemy reinforced was, "No one will ever come for your heart. You are alone. You are on your own."

I realise now how the painful message influenced the essence of me and how I still try to live up to the "shoulds" that were passed down. When I can't (because it is not the real me) I project it onto my dear husband and hurt him. Sadly, my younger self also held compassion for me, but I shut it down to survive. Over many years I repressed any anger, my perceptions and my voice to fit in with family norms at the expense of my integrity. After the mountain, I realised that there are still parts that need healing, especially the lie that when I am distressed I will always be alone. I do not want to be who I am not and I do not want to punish those closest to me. In order to thrive, I am seeking to understand and honour the preciousness of my unique life path of high sensitivity. I want to learn to celebrate this uniqueness and listen to my heart. I want to live authentically and with integrity. Like the Velveteen Rabbit, I want to become more real.

I laid all this down and found that to experience my real self will lead to a generous life that is continually filled to overflowing from an Infinite Source. My ongoing spiritual journey involves coming out of numbing, of waking up and coming to life, of learning to trust the spontaneous appearance of my inner being where the Divine lives. I will grieve the past – "She held herself until the sobs of the child inside subsided entirely. I love you, she told herself. It will all be okay" (H. Raven Rose). I will imagine asking my younger self: What do you need? What is your biggest fear? What is your biggest desire?

Rather than drown in regret, I chose to ask forgiveness of God, Barry and myself. Turning first to my Creator, my Lover, my Rescuer, I heard Him tenderly tell me I am never alone: "Do not yield to fear, for I am always near. Never turn your gaze from me, for I am your faithful God. I will infuse you with my strength and help you in every situation. I will hold you firmly with my victorious right hand" (Isaiah 41:10 TPT).

Turning to my husband, I wrote a letter stating what I was forgiving him for. Returning from the retreat, I handed him the letter and asked his forgiveness for the things I said, the things I believed and the things I ended up doing during our time in Uganda. I told him I was sorry for not seeing and valuing him over the years, for shutting down my heart, for substituting unhelpful behaviours, for ignoring my reality and for not loving him enough to challenge his behaviour towards me.

God had the final word. The ending of John 10:10 reads: "I have come that they may have life, and have it to the full." After my retreat I purposed to show up and open my heart. Like the Velveteen Rabbit and the Boy in the nursery, we both long for the kind of connection that Brenè Brown defines as "the energy that exists between people when they feel seen, heard and valued; when they can give and receive without judgment; and when they derive sustenance and strength from the relationship".[10] Seen, heard, valued... three little words with huge significance. Together, Barry and I are changing the steps of our dance to the dance of connection. Choosing the brave path to step out of the nursery, we are becoming more real for each other.

Chapter Summary

- The third foundational principle of ME is a commitment to personal growth. Marriage, like a garden, needs tending and attention.
- Our commitment to personal growth can help to heal each other's wounds and enable us to be personally present. A commitment to personal growth can prevent the marriage from breaking, but repair takes effort, energy and attention.
- Personal growth involves a search for the realness.
- Spiritual by-passing can distract us from personal growth and difficult feelings and avoid seeing the big picture.
- Every marriage goes through predictable passages that need to be negotiated. Marriage presents an inevitable dilemma of settling for less or making a commitment to personal growth.
- When a leader couple brings their personal growth journey to ME, they offer inspirational hope to other couples.

Notes to Chapter 4

1. Margery Williams, *The Velveteen Rabbit*, first published 1922; quoted in T. Raiten-D'Antonio (2004). *The Velveteen Principles: A Guide to Becoming Real*. Health Comminciations Inc., p. 162.
2. R. Rohr (2013). *Immortal Diamond: The Search for Our True Self*. Jossey-Bass.
3. J. Welwood (2000). *Toward a Psychology of Awakening*. Shambala Publications.
4. I. Clayton (2011). Beware of spiritual bypass: Why do we avoid rather than accept? *Psychology Today*. Retrieved from https://www.psychologytoday.com/au/blog/emotional-sobriety/201110/beware-spiritual-bypass
5. D. Schnarch (2011). *Intimacy and Desire: Awaken the Passion in Your Relationship*. Beaufort Books.
6. Ibid.
7. D. Schnarch (2012). *Passionate Marriage: Keeping Love and Intimacy Alive in Committed Relationships*. Scribe Publications.
8. Ibid.
9. Ibid.
10. B. Brown (2012). *Daring Greatly: How the Courage to Be Vulnerable Transforms the Way We Live, Love, Parent, and Lead*. Avery.

CHAPTER 5

FOUNDATIONAL PRINCIPLE: A COMMITMENT TO FLEXIBILITY

Overview

This chapter explores a foundational principle of ME – a commitment to flexibility. The chapter is organised under the following headings:

⇒   The Challenge to Bend Without Breaking

⇒   Enemies of Flexibility

⇒   Characteristics of leader couples

The Challenge to Bend Without Breaking

A commitment to flexibility is foundational both within the leader couple's relationship and when preparing for or conducting ME events. The dictionary meaning of the word "flexible" is "capable of bending easily without breaking; of being bent repeatedly without injury or damage".[1] How can we bend easily without injuring our spouse or other couples?

The desire to become a leader couple is an indication of a sense of mission. You have already experienced the value of ME in your own relationship and want to help other couples develop their potential as well. Leading ME events requires a commitment to flexibility. Some of our most exhilarating times as a couple have been in our facilitation of ME experiences. We have the privilege of helping couples celebrate their relationships, communicate more effectively, manage conflict so it becomes a *means to* intimacy rather than an *enemy* of intimacy, revitalise dormant areas and blossom more fully as individuals and as couples. We know the joy of dreaming together, planning, caring, teaching, listening, encouraging, nudging, waiting, laughing, celebrating and sometimes crying together.

> "Anyone who has never made a mistake has never tried anything new." (Albert Einstein)

Nevertheless, some of our most exasperating and painful times as a couple have been in our facilitation of ME experiences when our differences frustrate and embarrass. There have been times when we have been tempted to quit and wondered why we got involved. At times, power struggles, conflict and anger have been our companions. We have wondered, "Where in the world is my spouse coming from... Mars? Venus?" A commitment to flexibility is required. We encourage the celebration of times of exhilaration and grasping ME skills in times of exasperation. Our experience tells us that when we renew our connection to each other, our zeal is renewed, we recommit to our mission and we become more effective as a team!

Enemies of Flexibility

In what areas are leader couples required to be committed to flexibility? What is the source of the challenges couples face as they share leadership? Often it is a combination of factors as shown in the figure below.

```
Personality
strengths and
differences

Communication
difficulties

Differing
expectations
```

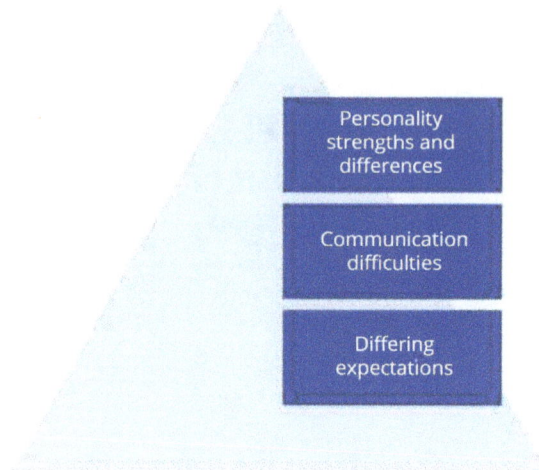

Each of these will be addressed from the perspective of a commitment to flexibility.

Personality strengths and differences

> Couples need us to appreciate and be ourselves.

Our relationship is the main resource we bring to leading ME experiences - comprising two individuals, each of whom has a unique personality, approach to life, to relating and to leading. In short, each spouse has a special individual style that is needed in ME. There will be those we lead who will especially identify with one of us because of who we are! Couples need us to appreciate and be ourselves.

We also have a unique couple style, a special way about us as a couple and how we relate to each other and to others. Our special "coupleness" makes a unique contribution to other couples. If we continue to work on and grow in accepting, appreciating and affirming our differences, the outcome will be flexibility in ourselves, our relationship, and our couple leadership style.

Communication difficulties

> Heart-to-heart communication involves open, honest sharing on a deep personal level.

Along with flexibility in our personality strengths and differences, communication difficulties present a further area of growth. Communication provides access to vulnerability and intimacy. The word "intimacy" can be phrased "into-me-see". Essentially, heart-to-heart communicating is open, honest sharing of primary feelings on a deep personal level. Feelings "serve a protective purpose"[2] but "[t]he most damaging feelings are those that are not discussed".[3] However, "wholesome experience and expression of feelings [are] necessary for mental health, peak performance, and relationships that go deeper than mere superficiality".[4] In fact, couples tend to communicate on a superficial level as a means of hiding from each other.[5] What makes us hide? The following is a (by no means exhaustive) list; reflect on those that generally apply to you.

- Holding things inside for fear of ridicule or appearing dumb or stupid.
- Not wanting to hurt or offend.
- Childhood influences.
- Sharing feelings represents weakness.
- A poor self-image or feeling ashamed of who I am – "Who really cares what I think or feel?"
- Fear of being ignored or rejected.
- Fear of intensity and feeling out of control.

- Fear of feeling exposed or vulnerable.
- Fear of betrayal of confidentiality.
- Fear of changing the relationship in some way.

It is in our feelings that we differ most from each other, but most couples have difficulty expressing them, often due to early messages – for example, don't cry, don't be angry, don't get upset – which protect the parents' own feelings. Yet, not saying what we feel, or ignoring small offences, eventually leads to a style of life in which we gradually lock one door after another and live in only a few of the rooms. We never get to enjoy genuine intimacy. Expression and acceptance of feelings is the key to an open and intimate relationship.

Differing expectations

In the beginning our differences attract us, adding mystery, romance and excitement. As we progress through different passages in our relationship, the

> Expression and acceptance of feelings is the key to an open and intimate relationship.

"little things" begin to disappoint and irritate us and prevent us from feeling authentic and comfortably "at home" with each other. For example, one spouse has poor self-worth, so they yield (give up themselves) to preserve harmony and avoid conflict, thereby building resentment. They see the difference as something their partner "does to me" rather than something they "give to me" to heal and complete me.

Pause for Reflection

- Try writing your name with your preferred hand.
- Now try writing it with non-preferred hand.
- Notice the difference.

If we try to make our spouse be more like us, we will only build dissatisfaction (it will be like writing with our non-preferred hand). It can also lead to a marriage crisis.

Marital crises present us with invitations. Someone aptly said, "You have been offered 'the gift of crisis'". The Greek root of the word "crisis" means "to sift; to shake out the excesses and leave only what's important".[6] Sometimes we lose touch with the sifting process. But here is the good news – the sifting process is an invitation to understand, empathise and heal our own and each other's feelings and childhood wounds. "Sifted" couples have conversations, while struggling couples have

> "There is a secret of the demands of marriage, a reluctance to give way any more than is absolutely necessary. There is a constant temptation to pull back from the full intensity of the relationship, to get along on only the basic requirements. But set against this is the constant challenge to give more and more of oneself, at deeper and deeper levels, and to see the outpouring of the grace of God into one's life."
> (M. Mason, The Mystery of Marriage, p. 27).

arguments or withdraw from each other. Successful couples accept and delight in each other's unique differences. They accept the "sifting" process rather than being defeated by their differences. "A great marriage is not when the 'perfect couple' comes together. It is when an imperfect couple learns to enjoy their differences" (author unknown).

Structure

Although flexibility is important, it should occur within structure, as structure, especially in the early stages of an ME event, reduces couples' anxiety and increases feelings of security. Leaders need to

> "The function of leadership is to produce more leaders, not more followers."
> (Ralph Nader).

communicate a sense of knowing where they are going and how to get there. The basic structure of the ME event should be developed in a way that overcomes the fear of the unknown and lets couples know the objectives and guidelines. These may be objectives for an entire event or a particular section of an event.

It may also beneficial to provide a basic timetable of the event. A detailed accounting is not necessary, but an overview including general times for sessions, meals, free time etc., is helpful. Even in a two- or three-hour ME group session, people want an idea of how time is to be used.

Characteristics of Leader Couples

Certain characteristics of leader couples facilitate flexibility and the ability to create a safe place for couple vulnerability and exploration. It would be beneficial for prospective leader couples to have a commitment to lifelong learning in the areas of human development, marital interaction and group process. The following characteristics are optimal for ME flexibility. Reflect on those that generally apply to you and those that need work.

> Leader couples represent themselves as vulnerable, human, and struggling with the same issues as the couples in the group.

- The couple are committed to marital growth and are currently working effectively on their own marriage.
- The couple are able to function well as a team, co-operating smoothly and not competing or getting in each other's way.
- The couple can communicate in a warm and caring attitude to other couples in the group.
- The couple are prepared to share from their own experience through dialogue and by example (more on this later). They represent themselves as vulnerable, human, and struggling with the same issues as the couples in the group. Trust commences when leaders expose their hearts to the group through the generous sharing of their experiences and honest dialogue with their own expressions of the need to keep growing.
- The couple are sensitive to others in the group and perceptively aware of what is occurring in the present.
- The couple are committed to promoting healthy marriages with fervour and enthusiasm, recognising that enriched marriages make a tremendous contribution to others and to society.
- The couple embraces a vision of enriched marriages for their country. They are not discouraged by family breakdown in society, but are mobilised by this vision into continuing to dream and achieve.
- The couple are encouragers, inspirers, teachers, facilitators and guides. Their style of leadership can be described as:
  - Facilitative
  - Respectful
  - Supportive
  - Safe.

Traditional patterns tend to rely on inflexibility; for example, authority, power, invulnerability and superiority in knowledge and understanding. None of these are appropriate in the ME process.

Support and follow-up for leader couples

Leader couples need ongoing support, follow-up and encouragement to remain flexible and optimal in their leadership style. The following are some ideas to accomplish this.

- Supervision.
- Co-leading with another leader couple.
- Writing a newsletter.
- Attending conferences and professional development workshops.
- Attending an annual leader couples' retreat.

Pause for Reflection

Our Leadership Style...

Complete the following questions alone, then share sensitively.

- The most important things for me in leading a ME event are...
- When I plan for a presentation or group experience I like to start with...
- One thing I think I can contribute to our leading together is...
- One thing I think I may have problems with is...
- Some things I look forward to in our leading together are...
- Some things I am worried about in our leading together are...
- I need to be more flexible in...

Discuss together.

Considering our answers to the previous questions, the areas we need to discuss and monitor as a leader couple seem to be...

Our Story

We are different in our styles. Barry is agenda-focused and likes to keep things on track, needing sessions to start and end on time. He provides a sense of stability and predictability. Paula is very aware of what is occurring in the group and will follow the issues that surface with gentle honesty. She makes room for pain when it appears, tears are welcome and she is prepared to risk exploring below the surface of issues.

The two styles embrace a wider audience than one style alone. Barry holds the group in the crucible and Paula is able to stir the issues for a greater sense of refinement.

Chapter Summary

- Involvement in ME consists of exasperating and exhilarating experiences that require a commitment to flexibility.
- Three areas of challenge for leader couples are dealing with their strengths and differences, communication difficulties and differing expectations.
- Structure is important, especially in the early stages of a group, to reduce anxiety and increase feelings of security.
- Leader couples can grow towards optimal characteristics of flexibility.
- Leader couples need to plan ongoing support, follow up and encouragement.

Worksheets on Flexibility and Differences

Reflections on My Uniqueness

- What do you like about being you?

- What is tough?

- What word describes you?

- What happen when under pressure?

- What is your greatest need?

- What is your greatest fear?

Share sensitively with your spouse.

Reflecting on Our Differences

Do alone.

1. I consider my strengths to be...

2. I consider my weaknesses to be...

3. I consider my spouse's strengths to be...

4. I consider my spouse's weaknesses to be...

5. The situation that would be most threatening to my spouse is ...

6. If I were to use my uniqueness as a male/female to support my spouse, it would look like...

7. The following is likely to be stressful for me in the near future ...

8. I need you to support me in ...

Share sensitively with your spouse.

WORD LIST OF ABILITIES, GIFTS AND STRENGTHS

Adventurous	Friendly	Patient
Ambitious	Generous	Peaceful
Analytical	Grateful	Perseverant
Appreciative	Helpful	Persuasive
Artistic	Honest	Persistent
Assertive	Hopeful	Practical
Athletic	Humble	Precise
Authentic	Humorous	Problem-solving
Caring	Idealistic	Prudent
Clever	Independent	Quick-witted
Compassionate	Ingenious	Resourceful
Charming	Industrious	Respectful
Communicative	Inquisitive	Responsible
Confident	Inspirational	Self-assured
Considerate	Intelligent	Self-controlled
Courageous	Kind	Serious
Creative	Knowledgeable	Spiritual
Curious	Leading	Spontaneous
Decisive	Lively	Social
Dedicated	Logical	Straightforward
Deliberate	Lovely	Strategic
Detail-oriented	Merciful	Tactful
Determined	Modest	Team-oriented
Disciplined	Moral	Thoughtful
Educated	Motivated	Thrifty
Empathetic	Observant	Tolerant
Energetic	Optimistic	Trustworthy
Entertaining	Open-minded	Versatile
Enthusiastic	Orderly	Visionary
Fair	Original	Warm
Fast	Organised	Welcoming
Flexible	Organised	Wise
Focused	Outgoing	

Notes to Chapter 5

1. Dictionary.com (2002).
2. G.R. Schiraldi (2000). *The Post-Traumatic Stress Disorder Sourcebook: A Guide to Healing, Recovery and Growth.* Lowell House, p. 92.
3. D.R Catherall (1992). *Back from the Brink: A Family Guide to Overcoming Traumatic Stress.* Bantam Books, p. 160.
4. Schiraldi, *The Post-Traumatic Stress Disorder Sourcebook,* p. 93.
5. J. Powell (1969). *Why Am I Afraid to Tell You Who I Am?* Fount Paperbacks.
6. Kathleen Norris, cited in G. Melton (2014). *Carry On, Warrior; The Power of Embracing Your Messy, Beautiful Life.* Scribner Book Company, p. 27.

PART B

A SAFE PLACE

CHAPTER 6

CREATING A SAFE PLACE

Overview

This chapter explores creating a safe place through community building. The chapter is organised under the following headings:

⇒ Aspects of Community Building

⇒ Creating a Meaningful Opening Exercise

In order to create a safe place for couples in a ME group, certain aspects need to be fostered, the first of which is community building. An overview of the three necessary aspects, community building, modelling and designing, is presented below.

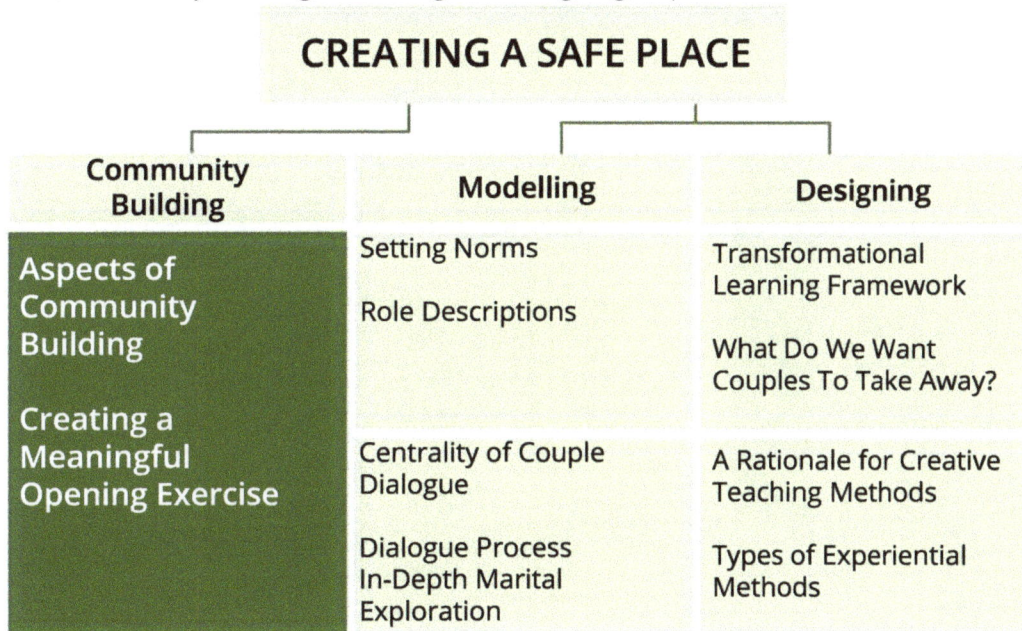

CREATING A SAFE PLACE

Community Building	Modelling	Designing
Aspects of Community Building Creating a Meaningful Opening Exercise	Setting Norms Role Descriptions	Transformational Learning Framework What Do We Want Couples To Take Away?
	Centrality of Couple Dialogue Dialogue Process In-Depth Marital Exploration	A Rationale for Creative Teaching Methods Types of Experiential Methods

Aspects of Community Building

The first aspect of creating a safe place involves community building, beginning as soon as the ME event commences. In the first couple of hours, the leader couple welcomes everyone, gives a short introduction, shares the aims for ME, sets group guidelines and asks about hopes and concerns for the time together. These will be expanded in the following sections.

Welcome and introduction

In the welcome and introduction, the leader couple share what brought them to ME and inform participants of housekeeping essentials.

Aims

> Marriage enrichment involves being intentional about giving time and attention to our relationship.

Aims are an expression of a purpose to be achieved over the life of the group and carried into the ensuing years. These should be stated near the beginning of the ME event. At the close of an ME event, participants can be asked to gauge if the aims have been met. Some overall aims of an ME event for participants might be:

- to be intentional about giving time and attention to our relationship;
- to take an honest look at our relationship as it is now;
- to sharpen our focus, and gain new insights and skills to make growth possible; and,
- to decide the directions in which we want to grow together.

Group guidelines

Group guidelines are intended to establish an agreement from couples that will form the guidelines for communication and interaction within the ME group. The guidelines also assist couples to become involved in the decision-making process. It is important to establish this group contract near the start of a group. The agreed guidelines are written on a large sheet of paper and pinned to a wall to allow the group members to refer to them during the progress of the group. If the group deviates from the guidelines, the leader couple can draw attention to the agreement. Some ideas for basic guidelines are listed below.

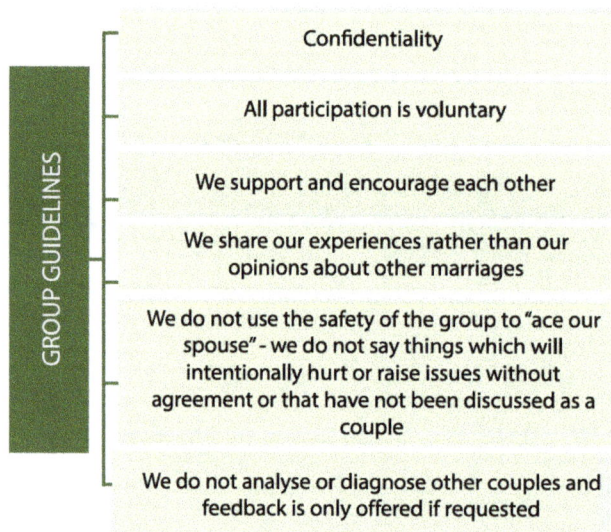

GROUP GUIDELINES

- Confidentiality
- All participation is voluntary
- We support and encourage each other
- We share our experiences rather than our opinions about other marriages
- We do not use the safety of the group to "ace our spouse" - we do not say things which will intentionally hurt or raise issues without agreement or that have not been discussed as a couple
- We do not analyse or diagnose other couples and feedback is only offered if requested

> The most valuable time will be spent talking with each other.

The following are some basic helpful hints to convey to couples to help them to feel safe and comfortable during the ME event.

- If you want to take your shoes off, lie on the floor et cetera, then do it!
- Over the ME event, you will have time to talk about topics with your spouse. Feel free to go outside, walk or go back to your room to talk. If you are in middle of a meaningful conversation, do not feel pressure to return, as we can catch you up later. The most valuable time will be spent talking with each other.
- You will receive handouts (show one) with questions to complete. First, complete alone. Second, share your reflections with your spouse. Try not to deliberate over each question. Rather, do them quickly. Usually the first thing that comes to mind is the most accurate.
- We encourage you to use the exercises, handouts et cetera to talk with your spouse.

The temptation will be to talk with others in the group. There will be plenty of time to socialise, so we encourage you to use this unique opportunity to talk to each other.

- During our time together, you may get irritated or angry, or may not feel like talking to your spouse. We encourage you not to sit with it! Be courageous and tell your spouse or us.
- There are *Dragons* (those who want to be here and pressured their spouse to attend) and *Dragees* (those who felt pressured to come) in the room. If you are a *Dragee*, we want to acknowledge your courage in being here.
- You may hear voices in your head from influential people in your life, past or present (mum, dad, church, teacher et cetera) that berate you with words like, *"What am I doing here?"* or *"I don't need this".* Muzzle them! You are here, so use the time well.

Hopes and concerns

Near the beginning of an ME event, it is beneficial to ask participants what they expect and to name their concerns. The purpose of extracting these hopes and concerns is:

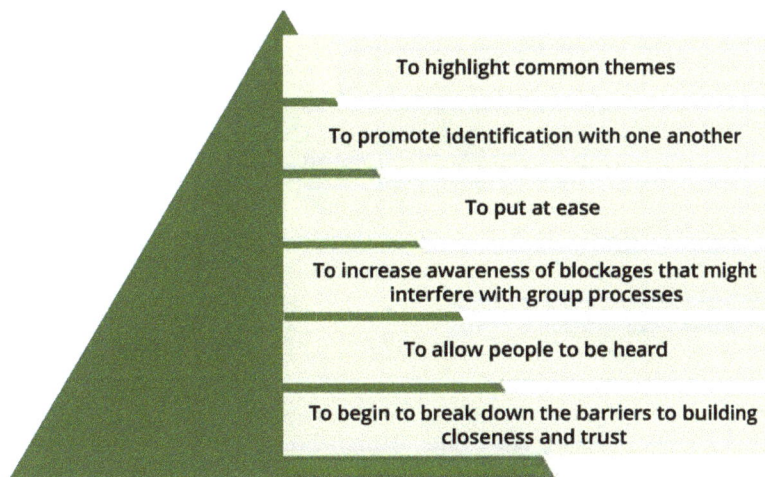

To highlight common themes

To promote identification with one another

To put at ease

To increase awareness of blockages that might interfere with group processes

To allow people to be heard

To begin to break down the barriers to building closeness and trust

Give each couple a sheet of paper and instruct them to draw two columns with headings. The first column is titled HOPES and the second column is titled CONCERNS. Encourage couples to talk together and record their hopes and concerns. Some examples of questions and responses of hopes and concerns are listed below.

> "[T]he two will become one... this is a profound mystery." (Ephesians 5:31-32).

Hopes	Concerns
What do you want to gain from this ME event? Also, how do you want to be different at the end of the ME event? An example might be that we would like to learn to communicate better.	What are you afraid may or may not happen? This might include physical concerns or comfort, or being able to leave behind things at home or work. Concerns may also include understanding content or concerns about one another.

Debrief couples' hopes and concerns in the larger group by recording them on a whiteboard and highlighting common themes.

Creating a Meaningful Opening Exercise

Pause for Reflection

What makes a good opening exercise?

The opening exercise is perhaps one of the most important over the time together. As indicated in the diagram below, there are specific purposes in this seemingly innocuous exercise. Leader couples need to be reading the group as they meet for the first time and refining the choice of exercise. The exercise is best tailored to the size of the group, time available for the retreat/event, a feel for the introvert/extrovert balance of the group and the themes that are common to the group. Such things as the age of most couples, common beliefs or values and the cultural setting also have an influence. The purposes of a good opening exercise are:

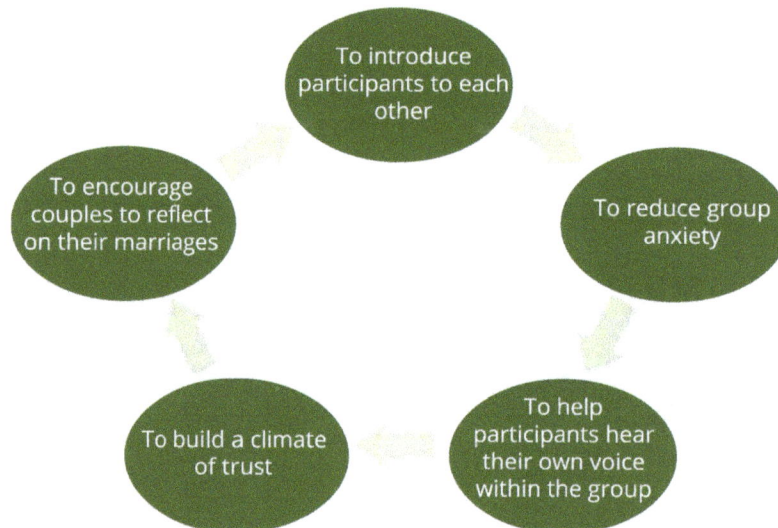

To introduce participants to each other

To reduce group anxiety

To help participants hear their own voice within the group

To build a climate of trust

To encourage couples to reflect on their marriages

In practice, the leader couple selects an introductory exercise or activity, explains the process and gives couples some check-in time with each other and time to prepare their response. The leader couple then begins by modelling their response to the group.

Creating a Meaningful Opening Exercise

Opening exercises are significant and can powerfully influence the time together.

Choose and Prepare an Opening Exercise or Activity

Answering Questions

The following questions are written on a whiteboard or flip chart, couples are given time to confer, and then spouses are encouraged to take turns to answer them. To conserve time the list can be shortened or couples can be asked to answer any four questions.

- Where do you come from?
- How did you meet?
- How long have you been married?
- What made you come to this retreat/event?
- What was one funny experience as a couple you could share with the group?

Three Words to Describe Our Relationship as It Is Now

Each spouse jots down their choices, the couple confers and presents their joint choice of three words to the group; for example, support, fun, boring etc. Leaders write these (preferably in different colours and at various angles) on a flip chart.

Symbols

As a couple, select a number of items you have with you (keys, hanky, credit card etc.) that symbolise your marriage. Select one or more to share with the group.

Present Issues

Each couple lists the major issues that are happening now in their marriage. Share these issues privately as a couple, then select one to share with the group.

Joyful Events

Individually list several joyful events that have occurred since you first met. Share them privately and then agree on one to share with the group.

Newsletter Headline

Hand out newspapers and scissors. Ask couples to cut out a headline that best represents their marriage. Alternatively, ask couples to make up their own headline from cut-outs in magazines (you will also need paper and glue sticks).

Alphabet Letters

Pick 3 random alphabet letters and write them down. Choose 3 unique things about yourself that start with each letter, e.g. A = aim is to...; R = enjoy romance; B = love ballroom dancing.

Preferences

Divide group in terms of preferences, e.g. night people/morning people; mountain/river; sweet/savoury etc.

Lolly Intro

Pass around a bowl of sweets. Ask people to take a few but not to eat them yet. Ask everyone to introduce their spouse and tell us as many things about them as the number of sweets they have taken.

Gathering Information

Give each person a 10 x 15 cm card or piece of paper. Ask them to write their name in large letters in the centre. (It is helpful to show them a sample.) The four corners of the name tag are then to be completed with answers to the following:

Top left-hand corner: My leisure interests include...	**Top right-hand corner:** My favourite food is...
Bottom left-hand corner: Three adjectives that describe my marriage are...	**Bottom right hand corner:** I decided to come here because...

Getting Acquainted

Together, answer the following questions.
- How did you first meet?
- What were your very first impressions of your spouse?
- How long have you been married?
- What is one of the funniest events you recall from your marriage?
- What is one of the most interesting things that has happened to you since you have been married?

How Well Do We Know Each Other?

Choose three to five of the questions below beforehand for this activity. Each spouse answers the questions alone, then compares the answers with those of their spouse.
- How would you describe yourself?
- What is the worst thing that has happened to you?
- What makes you laugh?
- What is your nastiest habit?
- What makes you angry?
- What do you find attractive in people?
- What repels you in other people?
- Do you have a most treasured memory from childhood?
- What do you think happens when you die?
- Is there a time in your life when you were happiest?
- What do you dream of?
- What scares you?

- What has been your biggest regret?
- If you weren't doing what you are doing, what would you like to do?
- How do you waste your time?
- What do you like most about yourself?
- How would you like your children to remember you?
- What would you write as your own epitaph?
- What five items are most essential to you?

Our Story

My most memorable opening exercises involve three men, all of whom rarely speak in the group. In response to our request to bring an object from home that represents their current status, the first man arrives with a candle that is set in a beer mug showing a frothy top layer of wax and a rich amber-coloured wax beneath. He holds the mug and speaks to his selected object. "This is me – a lot of froth on the outside but the best part is underneath." The exercise is successful. He speaks to the object, which takes the focus off him. He hears his voice within the group. He provides some powerful insights into how he sees himself and tacitly gives permission to gently explore the "amber" layer within.

Another time we invite couples to find an object from the garden that represents them in their relationship. One man chooses a rose bud with the green petals enclosing the flower within. "I am like this bud. I feel that it is time for me to blossom. I have been hiding behind these petals for too long." Needless to say, his declaration sets the norm for that group, which moves quickly into the deeper issues of relationships.

The third man is me. We are asked to take out our wallet/purse and select something that represents an aspect of our self that no one else would necessarily know. I share how the wallet reveals me. I have always chosen slim, no fuss or bulk, high-quality leather wallets. I usually have them for many years because of the quality. I share with the group that I get great enjoyment out of quality accoutrements that others may not recognise, but I delight in knowing that they are part of how I present. I spend quite some time thinking about what this says about me. I realise that this "secret" gives me comfort when I feel attacked, especially for something I have done or not done. It represents a proud response to feeling belittled by resorting to the knowledge that I have special, quality things. Undoubtedly this is a corrupt viewpoint and a transformative journey begins.

Opening exercises are significant and can influence the time together powerfully.

Chapter 6

Chapter Summary

- In order to create a safe place for ME couples, community building exercises and activities are employed. These include welcome, introduction and information about the aims of the ME event.

- Group guidelines form an agreement negotiated by the ME couples that guide group behaviour and interaction.

- Hopes and concerns help a couple to collaborate and articulate their expectations of the ME event.

- Community building occurs by using meaningful opening exercises that the leader couple model.

CHAPTER 7

CREATING A SAFE PLACE: MODELLING THROUGH SETTING NORMS

Overview

This chapter explores creating a safe place through modelling by setting norms. The chapter is organised under the following headings:

⇒ Setting Norms

⇒ Role Descriptions

While the first aspect of creating a safe space is community building, the second is leader couple modelling. An overview of how modelling fits into creating a safe place is presented below.

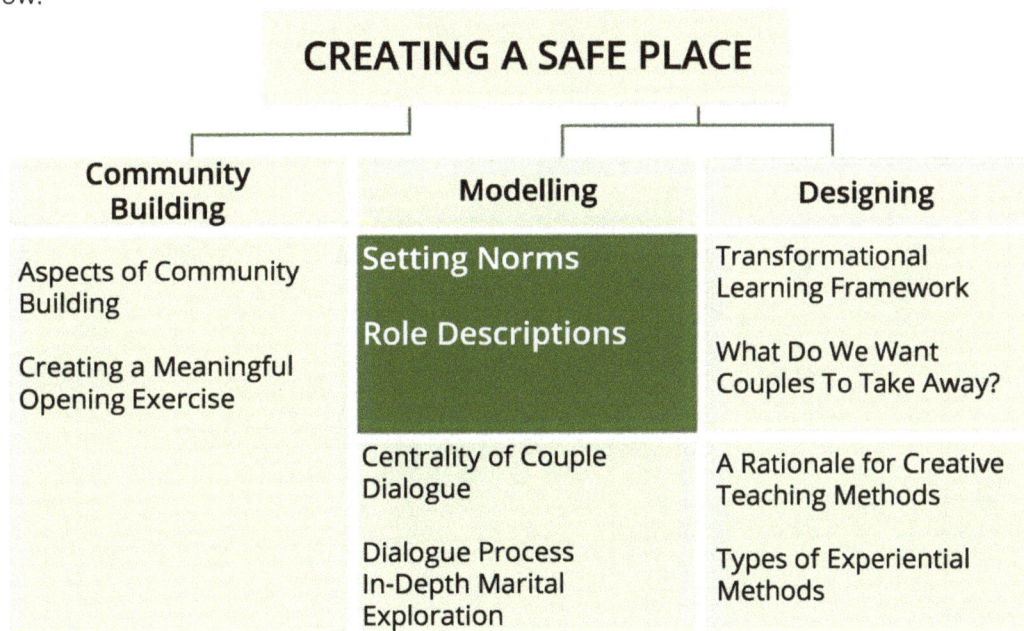

CREATING A SAFE PLACE

Community Building	Modelling	Designing
Aspects of Community Building	Setting Norms	Transformational Learning Framework
Creating a Meaningful Opening Exercise	Role Descriptions	What Do We Want Couples To Take Away?
	Centrality of Couple Dialogue	A Rationale for Creative Teaching Methods
	Dialogue Process In-Depth Marital Exploration	Types of Experiential Methods

Setting Norms

Leader couples deliberately set norms early in the group and monitor them throughout.

What are group norms?

Norms are codes of behaviour (usually unspoken) that guide the interaction of a group. Every group encounters them, even though the members may lack awareness of them. Norms are constructed from the expectations of group members and the explicit or implicit directions of the leader couple (or other highly influential group members). For example:

- in mixed groups, women do not speak first;
- group discussion remains on a rational level – emotions are not revealed; or,
- anger and conflict are not allowed to be acknowledged or expressed.

Once established, norms are very difficult to change. Leader couples exert the most influence over norms, whether consciously or unconsciously. Hence, it is important to deliberately establish group norms early in the ME event.

How does a leader couple set norms?

Norms *must* be introduced by personal example; therefore, it is essential that during responses to group questions and interactions, the leader couple start the process, perhaps with a personal dialogue. This will very quickly set the tone, depth of vulnerability and sense of safety in the group. These desirable, intangible group norms do not occur unless they are modelled. Opportunities may be provided for each spouse to tell their story, beginning with their hopes and concerns. Search for similarities among group members and tentatively state those you observe; for example, wanting to grow, wanting to be known et cetera.

What norms should a leader couple establish?

The group process benefits from leader couples intentionally establishing the following norms.

- A flexible agenda that is open to the needs of couples.
- Spontaneity of expression.
- Personal honesty leading to deepening relationships, intimacy and vulnerability. Levels of honesty must occur at each spouse's pace. Personal honesty is appropriately modelled but accompanied by restraint and responsibility. If personal honesty is discouraged, fear of further expression will be reinforced.
- Honest self-exploration and evaluation using open-ended questions (questions that place the content of conversation within the context of a couple's relationship) versus closed questions (only talking about content and details). In faith-based groups, the norm of responding to Scripture in an honest, self-exploratory way is an essential norm to encourage.
- Emotional expression; if emotion is stifled, the group will be lifeless and become like a lecture series, not a life-changing experience.
- Non-defensiveness.
- Genuine interest in others.
- Here-and-now focus.
- Divest the leader role of expertise by encouraging mutual responsibility and helpfulness. It is the group's responsibility to make group decisions. Create an interactive network (a social microcosm) in which spouses freely interact across the room, rather than directing all comments through the leader couple.

> Personal honesty leads to deepening relationships, intimacy and vulnerability.

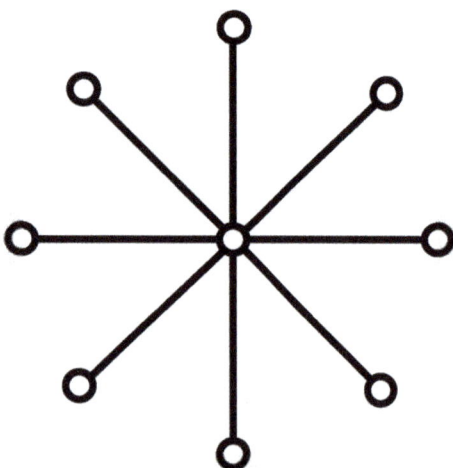

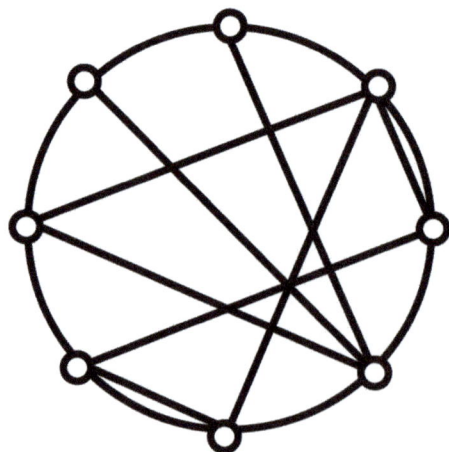

Yalom describes this type of interaction:

> A jazz pianist, a member of one of my groups, once commented on the role of the leader by reflecting that very early in his musical career he deeply admired the great instrumental virtuosos. It was only much later that he grew to understand that the truly great jazz musicians were those who knew how to augment the sound of others, how to be quiet, how to enhance the functioning of the entire combo.

- Become an observer and commentator on group processes;
- Genuine desire for growth; and,
- Encourage group members to support the group.[1]

Johari Window as a model for norm setting

The Johari Window is a useful tool for norm setting, as it offers increasing awareness and understanding of self and others. It was named after Joseph Luft and Harry Ingham[2] and was first used in an information session at the Western Training Laboratory in Group Development in 1955. A visual representation of the Johari Window is below.

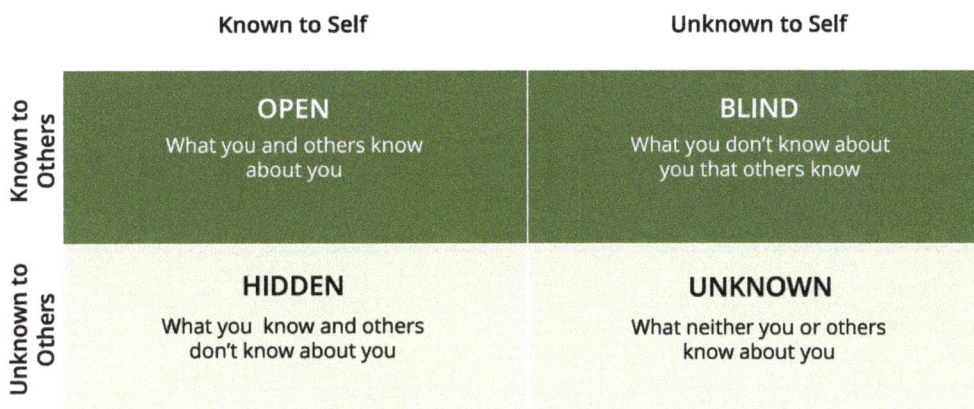

	Known to Self	Unknown to Self
Known to Others	**OPEN** What you and others know about you	**BLIND** What you don't know about you that others know
Unknown to Others	**HIDDEN** What you know and others don't know about you	**UNKNOWN** What neither you or others know about you

The four panes of the window represent the following.

Public	The open area is that part of our conscious self – our attitudes, behaviour, motivation, values, way of life – of which we are aware and are intentionally conveyed to others. We move within this area with freedom. This is my basic public personality. We are open books.
Hidden	Our hidden area is what we keep to ourselves. It cannot be known to others unless we disclose it. What we freely keep within ourselves, and that which we retain is often out of fear. The degree to which we share ourselves with others (disclosure) is the degree to which we can be known.
Blind	There are things about ourselves that we do not know, but that others can see more clearly; or things we imagine to be true of ourselves for a variety of reasons but that others do not see at all. When others say what they see (feedback), in a supportive, responsible way, and we are able to hear it; in that way we are able to test the reality of who we are and are able to grow.
Unkown	We are richer and more complex than that which we and others know, but from time to time something happens – is felt, read, heard, dreamed – something from our unconscious is revealed. Then we know what we have never known before.

It is through self-disclosure and feedback that our Public window is expanded, leading to an increase in *what others know about us* and a reduction in the Hidden window. Similarly, when we receive feedback about ourselves from others, there is a reduction in the Blind window. Self-disclosure is the pathway to becoming less hidden. The person in the Open window is usually the most relaxed. They are comfortable with themselves and not ashamed or troubled by the notion of other people seeing them as they really are.

Role Descriptions

Leader couples play many crucial roles in an ME group. Roles include the following.

Gatekeeper	Ensures that everyone participates and no one monopolises
Encourager	Offers words of praise, support, friendship, and creates a warm atmosphere
Reflector	Summarises the feelings, ideas, and reactions that are coming from the group
Listener	Pays keen attention to what individuals and couples are saying and responds appropriately
Clarifier	Asks questions to make sure couples understand one another; invites sharing of experience; explains content or processes that may be confusing
Follower	Allows the group to make decisions and to offer ideas
Standard Setter	Reminds couples of covenants or other guidelines that keep the group functioning at its best
Consensus Tester	Invites ideas about where the group should be heading or how it should function
Harmonisor	Mediates conflict between couples and helps people move toward compromise and reconciliation
Tension Reducer	Brings perspective and context to stressful situations

Some leader couples make the mistake of being too controlling. They tend to look upon their group members as people who need to "shape up". These leaders soon fade from the scene for lack of anyone to lead! They discourage and drive away those whom they wish to influence. In contrast are the leaders who operate from hearts of encouragement. Couple leaders who love the couples in their group tend to have hope and a vision for how every couple (including themselves) can be transformed. They have the courage to let go control of the group instead of trying to control it themselves. This leader couple usually remains effective for a lifetime.

Pause for Reflection

Reflections on Our Leadership Style

As a potential ME leader couple, answer the following questions (these questions should give you a feel for your heart as a leader couple). Do alone, then share sensitively.

- How do you push people in the direction you want them to go?
- When do you become easily frustrated with the people you lead or how do you patiently bear the "baggage" of your group members?
- How are you jealous of others in your group: their gifts, talents, looks, leadership skills? When do you find yourself competing with them?
- How do you listen to those you lead or do you find yourself thinking of what you're going to say while they are talking?
- What accomplishments and abilities do you tend to brag about and how do you use your position of leadership as a platform to build yourself up?
- When you are misunderstood by someone in your group, when do you find yourself hotly defending your rights?
- What is your unshakeable hope and vision for your group?
- How committed are you to persevere in leadership despite problems, discouragement and frustration?

Our Story

Sri Lanka Journal Entry Extract: 12 August 2014

It is the second day of our first workshop. One of our goals is to create a safe place for couples to share their stories without judgment, shame or blame. It has been tough going against the long-held fear of heart-to-heart sharing... the secrecy... the silence... the holding in... the shame of being seen as weak.

But we bare our vulnerable selves... the broken bits exposed... the impossible somehow has become possible... something breaks open and permission to break open is inhaled... slowly at first in long monologues that are stilted and boring until tears crack the heart and pain leaks out unconstrained... unfurling like a butterfly struggling to become that which was intended. The room is pregnant with grief... with seeds of hope. We stand in sacred space... the miracle of it washing over us.

One lady later declared that she had never encountered such depth of sharing in her entire life. They even decide to continue to meet regularly in their areas and every month or so as a group. Our interpreter is humbled and ecstatic.

Chapter Summary

- Norms are codes of behaviour that guide the interaction of a group.
- Norms are constructed from the expectations of group members and the explicit or implicit modelling and directions of the leader couple.
- Leader couples intentionally establish norms early in the group by personal example and monitor them throughout the ME event.
- The Johari Window is a model for norm setting designed to increase awareness of self and others.
- Leader couples play a variety of roles in a ME group.

Notes to Chapter 7

1. I.D. Yalom (1985). *The Theory and Practice of Group Psychotherapy* (3rd ed.). Basic Books, p.116.
2. J. Luft & H. Ingham (1955). The Johari window, a graphic model of interpersonal awareness. *Proceedings of the Western Training Laboratory in Group Development. Los Angeles: UCLA.*

CHAPTER 8

CREATING A SAFE PLACE: MODELLING USING COUPLE DIALOGUE

Overview
This chapter continues to explore leader couple modelling using couple dialogue as part of creating a safe place. The chapter is organised under the following headings: ⇒ Centrality of Couple Dialogue ⇒ Dialogue Process ⇒ In-Depth Marital Exploration

While a safe place is created by community building and by modelling through setting norms, another aspect is modelling using leader couple dialogue. An overview is below.

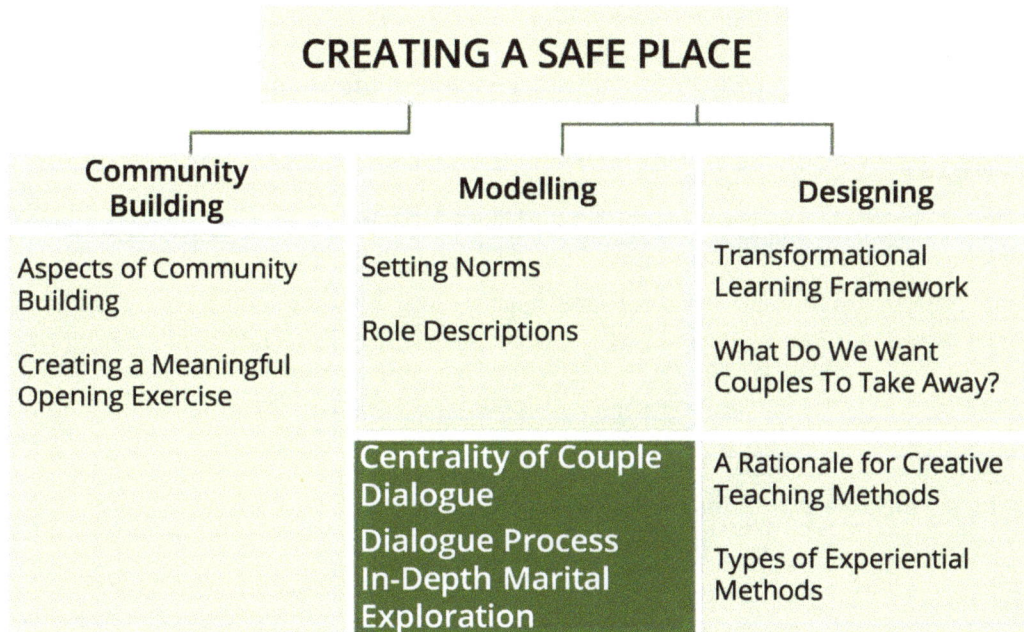

CREATING A SAFE PLACE

Community Building	Modelling	Designing
Aspects of Community Building Creating a Meaningful Opening Exercise	Setting Norms Role Descriptions	Transformational Learning Framework What Do We Want Couples To Take Away?
	Centrality of Couple Dialogue Dialogue Process In-Depth Marital Exploration	A Rationale for Creative Teaching Methods Types of Experiential Methods

Centrality of Couple Dialogue

Vulnerability is the essence of a place of safety. The very first dialogue of the leader couple will convey the message of whether this is a safe place to be vulnerable. This dialogue will establish a group norm of safety. Both private and shared couple dialogue is foundational to ME. One of the primary goals of ME, as stated by David and Vera Mace, is to develop a system of interaction between a couple to the degree necessary for that relationship to reach its full potential. At the heart of the system is couple dialogue – that is, the experience in which spouses communicate with each other. The following statements represent the basic elements of couple dialogue in ME groups.

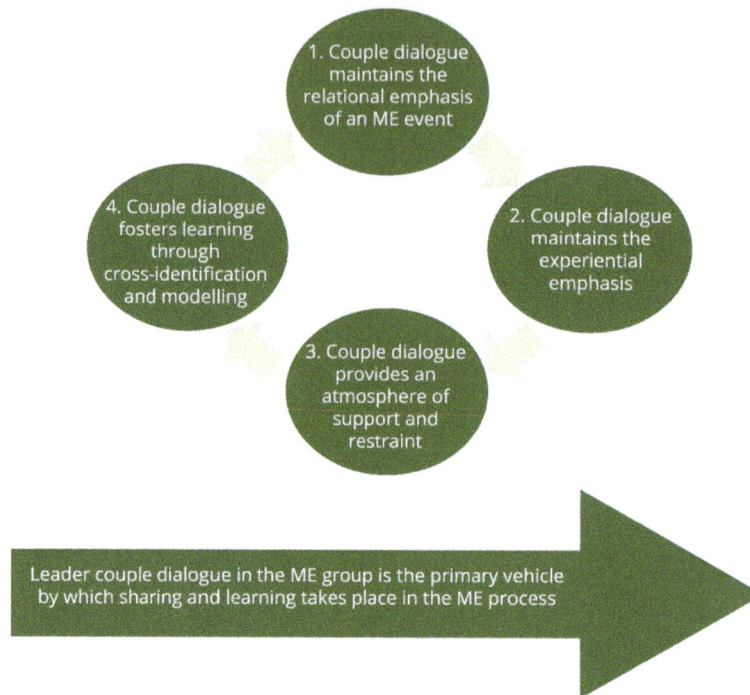

Leader couple dialogue is a transformational element of the ME process. The leader couple reflect on their own experience as a pathway to opening up the topic or issue in question for other couples to explore. ME focuses on experience rather than sharing opinions, thereby facilitating cross-identification with the experience of others. It becomes a source of great encouragement as couples learn that others face the same difficulties. Additionally, it enhances a connection that is beneficial for relationship healing.

Couple dialogue is communicated responsively through the social engagement system (tone of voice, body language, warmth, compassion, and openness) while affording couples dignity and control. This allows for the development of healing narratives in which the couples are enabled to live in the present moment.[1] Couple dialogue is a beneficial tool in enhancing couples' engagement during a ME event, stimulating their desire for attachment, facilitating self-disclosure and increasing their optimism and hope that healing can occur through building stronger relationships.

"Half the world is composed of people who have something to say and can't, and the other half who have nothing to say and keep on saying it." (Robert Frost)

Additionally, couple dialogue focuses on spouses as a couple rather than individuals with shared needs. The approach relies on the demonstration of the dynamic of the couple dimension rather than one person sharing their insights. This translates into a movement away from facts, opinions and principles towards the genuine experience of a living relationship that the couple is able to offer together. Facts, opinions and principles will not carry much weight if they exist in a vacuum removed from lived experience.

"The single biggest problem in communication is the illusion that it has taken place." (George Bernard Shaw)

To complement couple dialogue, the leader couple can offer some basic understanding of principles arising from their experience, often in the form of information and/or exercises designed specifically to focus on the topic or issue at hand. These help couples to further explore their needs and responses. Couples are also encouraged to set personal and couple goals, a practice sometimes referred to as *intentional marriage,* as couples are led toward the formation of a growth plan to guide them in the future. This becomes a powerful and enjoyable aspect of the ME process.

Dialogue Process

David and Vera Mace explain the key to couple dialogue as occurring in three stages.[2] These are outlined below.

1. Couple dialogue is embedded in a personal encounter between the husband and wife.

2. Couple dialogue in the group is the most effective way of sharing experiences; that is, "The couple's private dialogue gains a new validity when they can relax the intra-marital taboo and share their communication with the group. Again, and again, things begin to happen when couples dialogue aloud so that the others can hear them. As long as the couple are describing their situation, they can only be partially heard. When they begin to dialogue together, the authentic situation comes through." It is when the couples are able to dialogue in each other's presence that the real experience, sharing and learning often happens.

3. Couple dialogue is a testimony. It takes courage to dialogue with each other in a group with other couples. This is a learning process and as couples develop experience, they become skilled at ascertaining the appropriateness of their dialogue. In summary, dialogue can indeed be powerful testimony of a couple's journey.

The dialogue process involves the following steps.

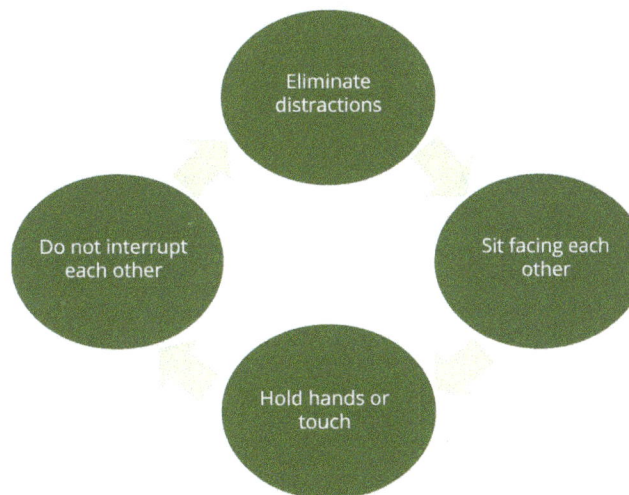

Eliminate distractions

Sit facing each other

Hold hands or touch

Do not interrupt each other

Couples in their first experience of dialoguing sometimes feel uncertain, even if they are eager to try the technique. In *Close Companions*, David and Vera Mace suggest that couples can be eased into dialoguing in a number of ways.[3]

"Nine tenths of education is encouragement." (Anatole France)

- Invite couples to turn to each other and discuss together just why they feel hesitant to dialogue!
- Suggest that the couple talk together about exactly how they are feeling right now.
- A good positive way of beginning a dialogue is for them to exchange their views about what they like most about their marriage.
- Sometimes couples are more comfortable about dialoguing for the first time with one other couple.

At first dialoguing may feel contrived. It takes practice to feel comfortable because:

- we are not used to talking about our marriage in the presence of other people;
- we sometimes do not have good communication skills and get into an argument instead of a dialogue; and,
- a complex problem may be simplified when only two people interact.

Dialoguing is more effective than group discussion because:

> "You can change your world by changing your words... Remember, death and life are in the power of the tongue." (Joel Osteen)

- the marital relationship is the focus;
- it promotes more intimate conversation with your spouse;
- it aids in self-disclosure;
- dialoguing with a spouse demands a high degree of honesty and authenticity;
- it encourages a response from a spouse rather than from the group; and
- the close physical contact tends to encourage positive responses.

Couples are able to communicate with each other through private dialogue, often a precursor for a commitment to change. In the emergence of a growth plan, the couples can focus on three particular areas.

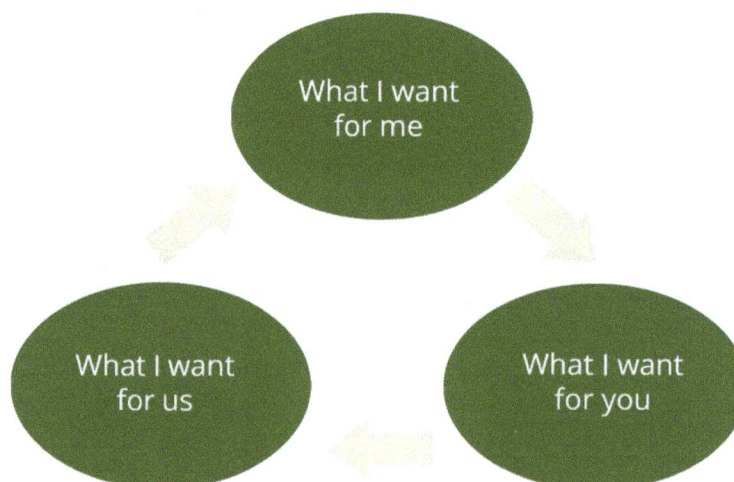

What I want for me

What I want for us

What I want for you

Skills in dialogue

The skills required in Dialogue are 1. Active listening, and 2. "I" statements about "My point of view". Chapter 2 explored active listening. "I" statements are a tool for the sender of a message to use to convey to the other person how they feel about an issue without blaming or demanding change. Dealing with conflict and/or anger requires more than love. It includes the hard work of learning and practising certain skills that enable us to express our thoughts, feelings and needs and to speak up for our rights and limits without violating the rights and limits of our spouse.

No one talks in "I" statements all the time, but they are particularly important when dealing with anger because anger evokes a sense of being under attack. Usually, we are tempted to attack in return, launching into a series of "YOU" statements. The urge to blame, accuse, and criticise can allow us to feel quite powerful. However, this usually evokes more of the same and simply escalates the conflict. This is where the work of love takes place. Can we get through the hard places where we are tempted to blame and attack and instead use language that describes our experience of the issue?

"It is not enough to show people how to live better: there is a mandate for any group with enormous powers of communication to show people how to be better."
(Marya Mannes)

An "I" statement is a message about us – owning what is happening for us in an open, honest way. We may say, "You made me angry". This is impossible because the anger is ours. It can feel risky to own our anger, let our spouse know about it and then invite them into our world to deal with it. It can seem offensive, even aggressive, when we first begin to communicate in this way. Nevertheless, it really opens communication.

The Conflict Resolution Network claims that "I" statements are not about being polite, soft, nice or rude, but about being clear. They are a conversation opener rather than resolution. The aim is to build relationships, rather than destroy them with harsh words and blame. If we expect the "I" statement to be the answer and to fix what is not working straight away, our expectations may be unrealistic. If we expect our spouse to respond immediately as we wish them to, this is also an unrealistic expectation. What we can realistically expect is that when we offer an appropriate "I" statement that is made with good intent, it:

- is highly unlikely to do any harm;
- is a step in the right direction;
- may change the current situation in some way; and,
- may open up to possibilities we may not yet see.

Sometimes we do not know what to say, yet a clean, clear statement of honesty about how we feel can often change things. The key to the success of an "I" statement is that we are direct, clear and non-attacking. "I" statements contain the following elements.

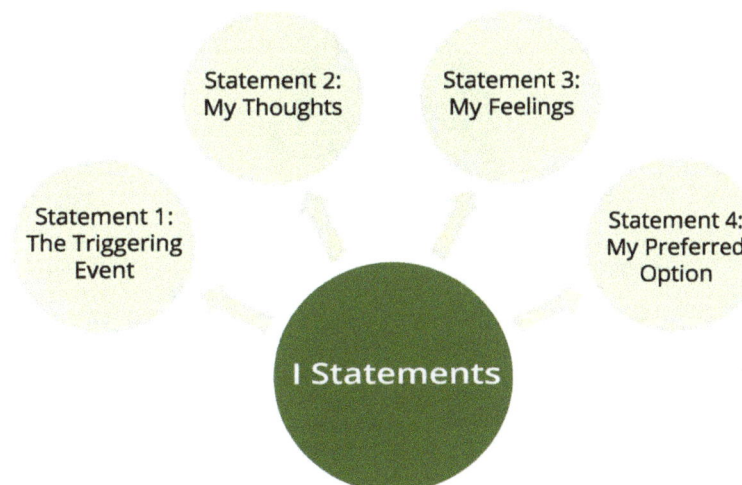

Statement 2:
My Thoughts

Statement 3:
My Feelings

Statement 1:
The Triggering
Event

Statement 4:
My Preferred
Option

I Statements

Example 1: My neighbour lets her dog roam in my vegetable garden. First, I will analyse and say what happened; secondly, I will describe what it says about me; thirdly, I will share my feelings about what happened; and fourthly, I will share my preferred option. So, I say:

Statement 2: what I think is that I am unimportant and powerless

Statement 3: and I feel really upset and angry

Statement 1: "When your dog tramples my vegetables

Statement 4: and what I would like is for your dog to be on a lead."

I Statements

Example 2: My mother calls me repeatedly at work. I say:

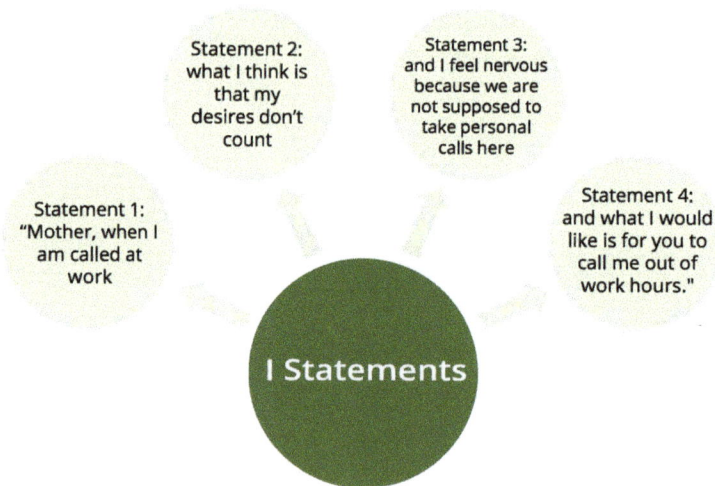

Statement 2: what I think is that my desires don't count

Statement 3: and I feel nervous because we are not supposed to take personal calls here

Statement 1: "Mother, when I am called at work

Statement 4: and what I would like is for you to call me out of work hours."

I Statements

Example 3: My son returns my car without petrol. I say:

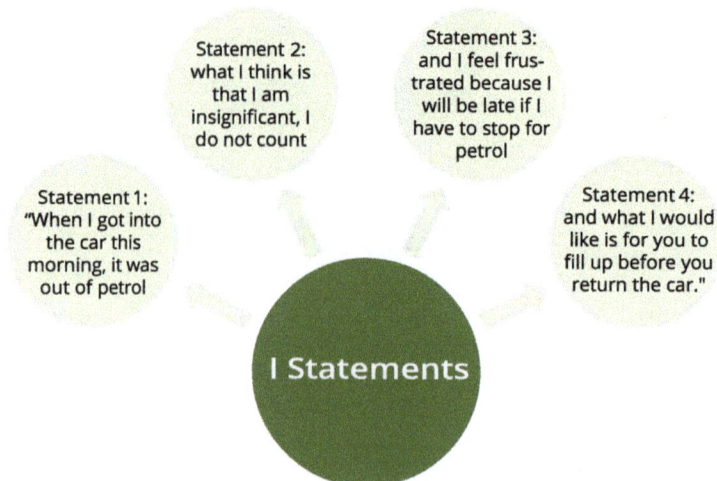

Statement 2: what I think is that I am insignificant, I do not count

Statement 3: and I feel frustrated because I will be late if I have to stop for petrol

Statement 1: "When I got into the car this morning, it was out of petrol

Statement 4: and what I would like is for you to fill up before you return the car."

I Statements

Example 4: When my spouse tries to fix me, I say:

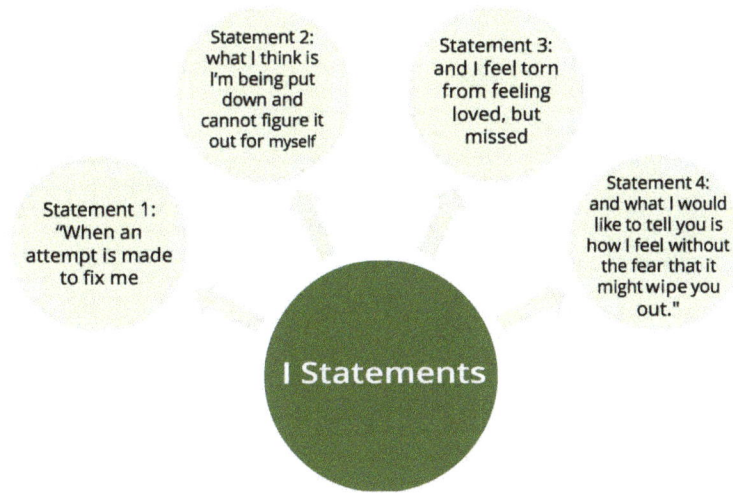

Statement 2: what I think is I'm being put down and cannot figure it out for myself

Statement 3: and I feel torn from feeling loved, but missed

Statement 1: "When an attempt is made to fix me

Statement 4: and what I would like to tell you is how I feel without the fear that it might wipe you out."

I Statements

Example 5: My spouse makes changes and decisions without consulting me. I say:

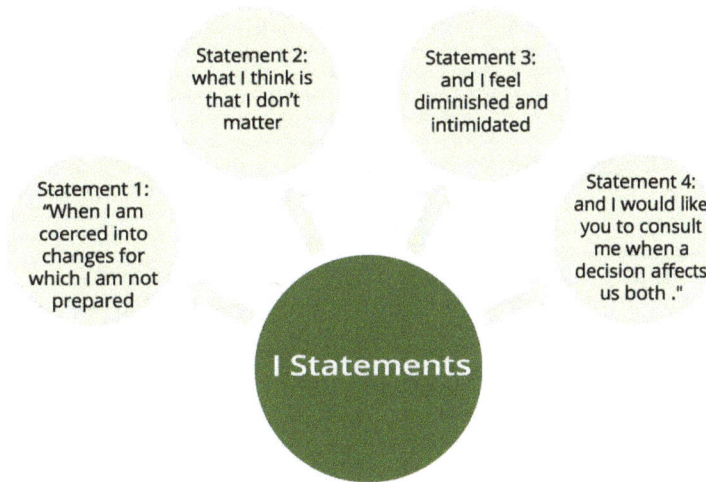

Statement 2: what I think is that I don't matter

Statement 3: and I feel diminished and intimidated

Statement 1: "When I am coerced into changes for which I am not prepared

Statement 4: and I would like you to consult me when a decision affects us both ."

I Statements

Example 6: My spouse pressures me to have sex. I say:

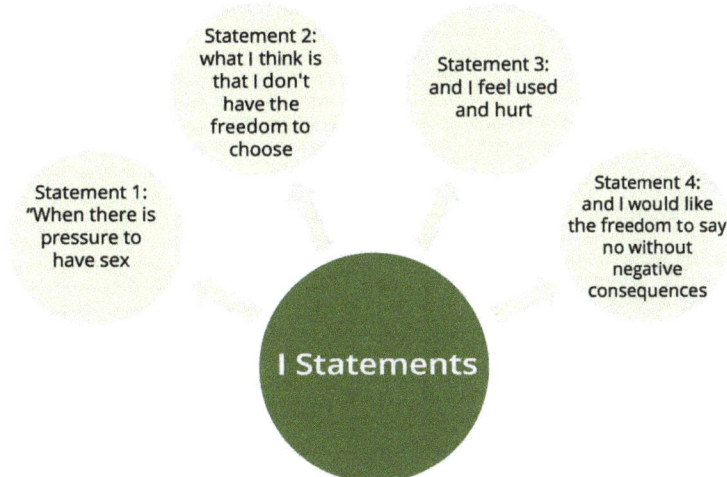

Statement 2: what I think is that I don't have the freedom to choose

Statement 3: and I feel used and hurt

Statement 1: "When there is pressure to have sex

Statement 4: and I would like the freedom to say no without negative consequences

I Statements

Pause for Reflection

"I" STATEMENTS

Do alone, then share with your spouse.

When...	I think...	I feel...	But what I would like is...
I am left by myself at a function...			
I see you go quiet...			
Something special is done to please me...			
I am not listened to...			
I sense you really care how I feel...			
There is a "no" to sex...			

In-Depth Marital Exploration

In-depth marital dialogue is a part of training for potential ME leader couples. It presents an opportunity for prospective leader couples to examine their relationship in-depth in the presence of a small group of other trainee couples and at least one of the trainers.

Why do this?

Evidence shows that a key factor in the effective leadership of couple groups is the willingness of the leader couple to be vulnerable by revealing something of their own humanity and their struggles during the growth process. More than anything else, it helps to create an atmosphere of openness and trust in the group of couples. **This is the key to creating a safe place**. If a leader couple acts defensively about sharing their relationship, they will not be fully effective.

If prospective leader couples choose to opt out of the in-depth marital exploration, they will miss experiencing a very powerful learning opportunity. If they have difficulty dealing with this requirement they should talk it over with the leader couple as soon as possible during their training.

The process of in-depth marital exploration

The process of in-depth marital exploration during training takes place in a protected situation where confidentiality is assured and where all the couples present (including the leader couple) have themselves undergone, or will undergo, the same experience. Each couple is given an agreed-upon group time for dialogue, including time for feedback. They do not address the group, but sit facing each other and

"Who you are is speaking so loudly that I can't hear what you' resaying."
(Ralph Waldo Emerson)

dialogue together. During the dialogue there is no interruption, unless the trainer couple need to offer guidance. Only when the dialoguing couple indicate that they are finished does any feedback from the group take place.

Should the couple prepare in advance? It is not necessary to rehearse what you will say. However, it may be helpful to talk over in advance what areas of your own relationship you will cover.

Pause for Reflection

As a couple, turn to each other and, through dialogue, explore in depth what makes you feel hesitant to dialogue.

Our Story

When we visit India to conduct ME events, we often ask whether participants' marriages were a love match or arranged. Even though a spouse is chosen for a variety of reasons across cultures, we have found that there is a universal need for closeness and connection.

Couple dialogue is a foundational part of any ME event, even in events where marriages are arranged. In Indian ME events, if we begin with a vulnerable dialogue, it very quickly creates a counter-cultural, safe space to open up; for example, in India a couple conveyed their reluctance to attend because they thought we would be like everyone else and give them more information that made them weary. However, during the opening session, our dialogue about a conflict we experienced in getting to the venue connected with a similar struggle. The couple expressed how they knew then that this would be different to any events they had previously attended. In their evaluation they wrote:

> Heart to heart sharing [dialoguing] is really a new thing for us. Most of us are sharing that we had a good experience. We are sharing heart to heart and are able to see new things and longings when we were able to do a few exercises. We were happy about the sharing... I hope when we go home there will be a difference and we will be different in our lives in the way we react and how we are sharing. I think there is going to be big change in our lives and it's going to remind us of what we have learned here and our lives are going to be changed actually.

Chapter Summary

- Vulnerability is the essence of a safe place.
- Both private and shared couple dialogue, is foundational to ME, as it facilitates the relationship to reach its full potential.
- Leader couple dialogue within the group is the primary tool by which sharing and learning takes place in the ME process.
- Couple dialogue focuses on spouses as a couple rather than individuals with shared needs.
- Dialoguing is more effective than group discussion.
- Skills in dialogue include active listening and "I" statements.
- A key factor in the effective leadership of ME groups is the willingness of the leader couple to be vulnerable by revealing something of their own humanity and their struggles together during the growth process. This vulnerability helps to create an atmosphere of openness and trust and is the key to creating a safe place.

Notes to Chapter 8

1. Fisher, J. (2014). Transforming trauma-related shame and self-loathing [PowerPoint slides]. Delphi Training and Consulting, Australia.
2. David & Vera Mace (1980). *How to Have a Happy Marriage: A Step-by-Step Guide to an Enriched Relationship.* Abingdon Press.
3. Ibid., p.142

CHAPTER 9

CREATING A SAFE PLACE: TRANSFORMATIONAL DESIGNING

Overview

This chapter explores creating a safe place by designing transformational marriage enrichment sessions. The chapter is organised under the following headings:

⇒ Transformational Learning Framework

⇒ What Do We Want Couples to Take Away?

While a safe place is created by community building and by modelling, a further aspect is designing engaging presentations that lead to transformational learning. An overview is provided below.

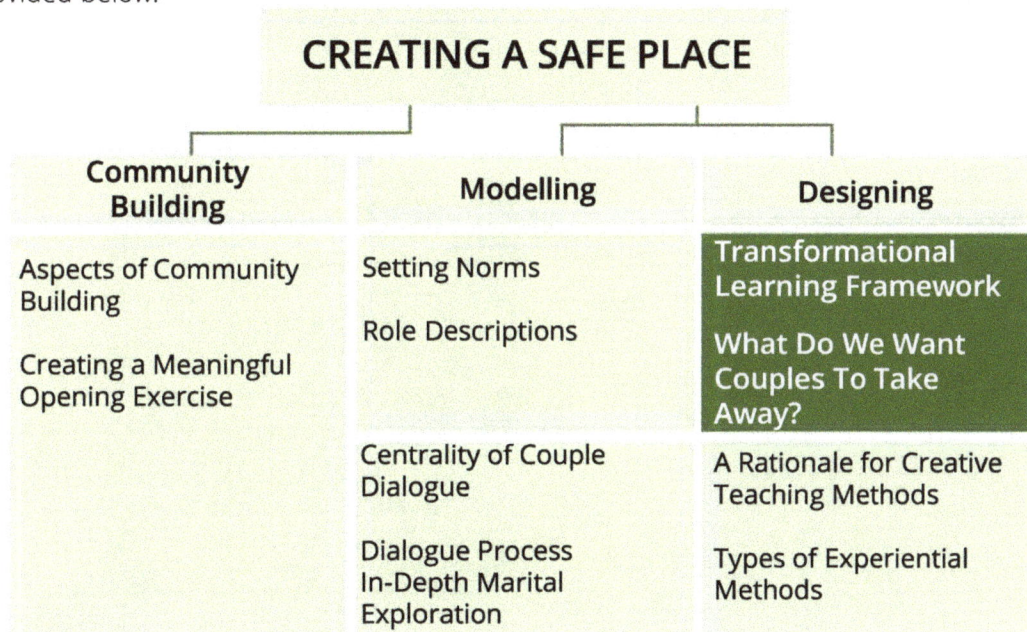

CREATING A SAFE PLACE

Community Building	Modelling	Designing
Aspects of Community Building	Setting Norms	Transformational Learning Framework
Creating a Meaningful Opening Exercise	Role Descriptions	What Do We Want Couples To Take Away?
	Centrality of Couple Dialogue	A Rationale for Creative Teaching Methods
	Dialogue Process In-Depth Marital Exploration	Types of Experiential Methods

Transformational Learning Framework

Designing a session for an ME event involves the consideration of several elements. They are as follows.

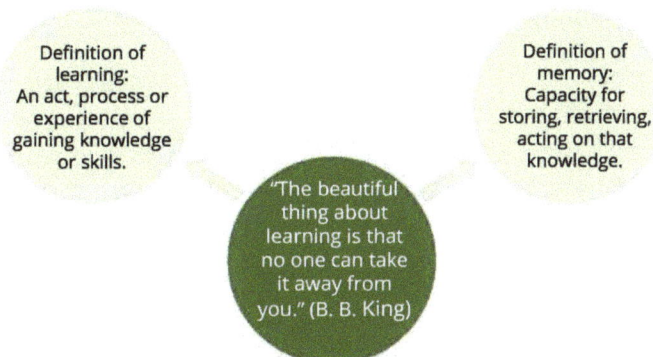

Definition of learning: An act, process or experience of gaining knowledge or skills.

Definition of memory: Capacity for storing, retrieving, acting on that knowledge.

"The beautiful thing about learning is that no one can take it away from you." (B. B. King)

The learning pyramid

> "You can teach a student a lesson for a day; but if you can teach him to learn by creating curiosity, he will continue the learning process for as long as he lives."
> (Clay P. Bedford)

The leader couple has a great deal of control over what occurs in a workshop. The choice of teaching methods can suggest the degree of involvement of the participants. Leader couples often select the easiest method of delivery without thinking through how that might impact learning for the participants. The choices we make affect the learning opportunities of our participants.

Teaching has been described as a creative activity. There are numerous ways to structure information in order to make it interesting and easy to understand. *The Learning Pyramid*[1] illustrated below depicts the importance of employing participatory teaching methods. This enables couples to experience and retain more of what we are attempting to convey. We tend to learn by doing. The illustration below depicts the type of learning activities that are the most helpful to include in a presentation if we want our participants to retain concepts.

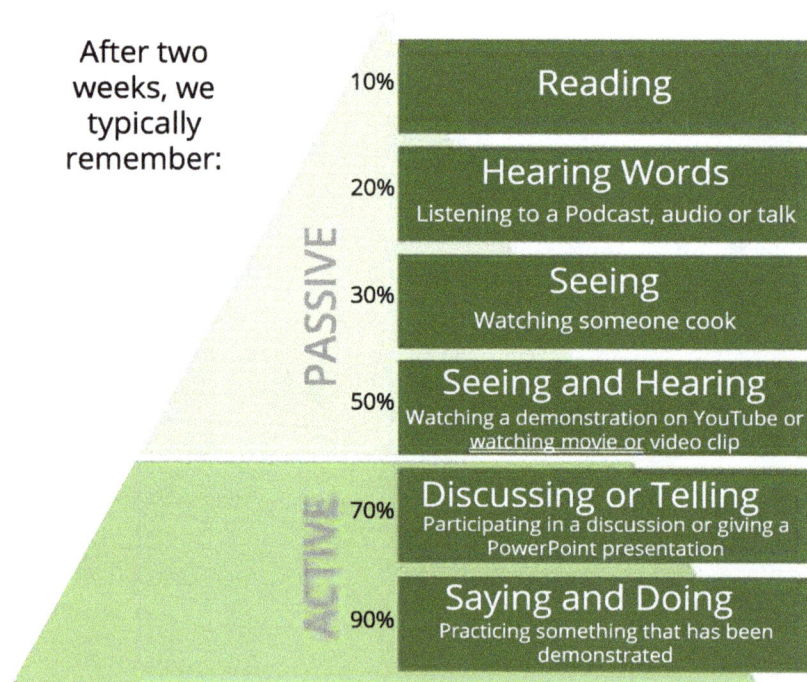

After two weeks, we typically remember:

10%	**Reading**
20%	**Hearing Words** — Listening to a Podcast, audio or talk
30%	**Seeing** — Watching someone cook
50%	**Seeing and Hearing** — Watching a demonstration on YouTube or watching movie or video clip
70%	**Discussing or Telling** — Participating in a discussion or giving a PowerPoint presentation
90%	**Saying and Doing** — Practicing something that has been demonstrated

PASSIVE — ACTIVE

(cited by L. Brissel, L. Morel & L. Dupont, Contribution to setting up a sustainable learning, 2013 International Conference on Engineering, Technology and Innovation)

Therefore, it is important to use creative media, handouts, exercises and/or activities to vary our teaching style for maximum retention.

Listening, seeing and doing maximise retention

> "I am not a teacher, but an awakener."
> (Robert Frost)

We learn much more effectively if we *see* and *listen* at the same time, than if we just listen without visual support. This means that it is important for a leader couple to help participants to learn by using visual aids. The most powerful visual aid in ME is the leader couple modelling how to have respectful, productive conversations about things that matter.

Doing or active participation is even more important if we want beneficial learning; for example, in a session on communication skills, an exercise in dialoguing:

- makes the information easier to understand;
- fixes it more firmly in couples' memories;
- asks couples to think about how the information might be used; and,
- asks couples to make plans to use it.

An *activity* is important but it still might not achieve anything if your participants:

- do not know why they are doing it;
- are not sure what they have learnt; and,
- do not know where their learning might take them next.

There is no point in going on to the next part of the program if the couples:

- do not understand *why* they have been doing the things you have asked them to do;
- have not really learnt anything; or,
- are not really clear about what they were meant to learn.

This means that each couple activity has to be followed by a *debriefing* session that provides opportunities for participants to ask themselves some important questions like:

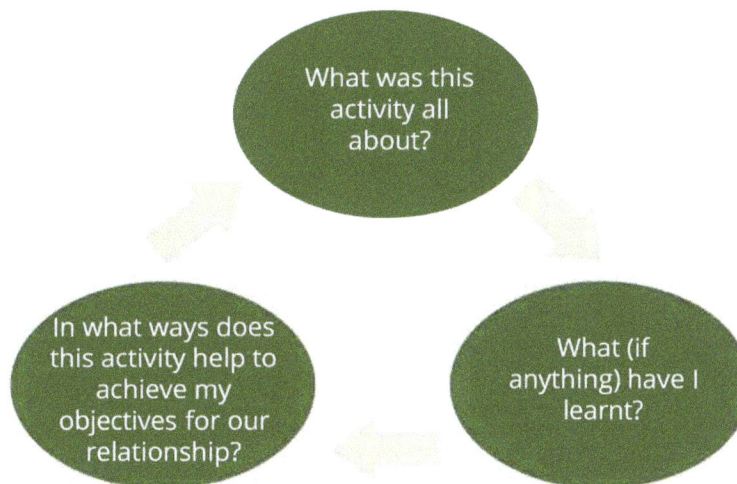

The suggested format of a session is illustrated below.

The suggested weighting of a session is illustrated below.

TELL	SHOW	DO	PRACTICE	REVIEW
Information Delivery Couple Dialogue		Couple/Group Handout or Activity		Debriefing

Tell and Show: This part of the session involves information delivery and couple dialogue. Couple dialogue can be a powerful way to teach and model respectful communication in the context of a relationship.

Do and Practice: This part of the session involves either couple or group activities or handouts.

Debriefing: This part of the session asks two questions:

1. What was the point of all this?

2. How did the activity relate to the information given in the session?

(Adapted from D. Malouf (1994). *How to Teach Adults in a Fun and Exciting Way*. Business and Professional Publishing.)

Information alone inhibits transformational learning

To many who lead, teaching equals lecturing. Yet there are countless other ways to help people learn. Do you find yourself talking for most of each session? Here are some good reasons to experiment with different teaching methods, such as dialogue, group discussion, role-play, and exercises.

"A good teacher can inspire hope, ignite the imagination and instill a love of learning." (Brad Henry)

"Educating the mind without educating the heart is no education at all." (Aristotle)

1. In her book, *Learning Styles*, teaching expert Marlene LeFever reports that only a small percentage of learners in Western culture learn best by listening to a lecture.[2]

2. Without feedback or interaction, you cannot gauge whether the material in your presentation is too basic for your group ("been there, done that"), over their heads ("huh?"), irrelevant to them ("so what?"), or hitting them where they live ("yeah!").

3. When you lecture, people hear from only one member of the group – you – and miss the benefit of others' insights and experiences.

4. When you lecture, you do most of the work.

5. Togetherness and community-building does not occur during a lecture.

6. You miss out on the chance to learn from the people you are teaching.

7. People learn best when a variety of teaching methods are employed.

There is the continuing danger in a retreat or similar event of slipping into a *telling* style on the part of the leader couple rather than sharing from an experience focus.

Transformational learning accesses right brain

Effective creative teaching methods are experiential in nature. Experiential learning accesses our right-brain. Metaphors, diagrams, exercises and activities bypass information that uses only the left-brain. There is a huge difference in how each side of the brain processes information. Lecture style (information only) appeals to the left-brain, as it involves the rational, including logic, reason and thinking. It is more verbal, analytical, linear and orderly, often called the digital brain. Conversely, the right side of the brain involves imagination, non-verbal cues, intuition, creativity and emotion. Experiential exercises tend to bypass the rational part of the brain. To be effective, adult education should appeal to both sides of the brain.

> "Change can be hard. It requires no extra effort to settle for the same old thing. Auto-pilot keeps us locked into past patterns. But transforming your life? That requires courage, commitment, and effort. It's tempting to stay camped in the zone of That's-Just-How-It-Is. But to get to the really good stuff in life, you have to be willing to become an explorer and adventurer."
> (John Mark Green)

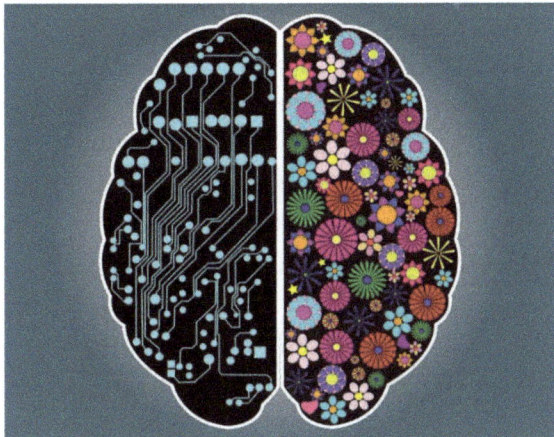

Adult education principles must underlie the design of ME sessions to be relevant, otherwise learners will lose motivation and interest. Adult learners bring to ME a rich history of knowledge and experience. They are seeking meaningful learning experiences for personal and couple growth and development. We assume that couple learners like to find their own way and can make their own decisions, are self-motivated, self-directed and desire to manage their own learning. They prefer ME content to be useful to them and tend to be drawn to two-way communication that involves interaction between the leader couple and other learners.

There is a range of experiential exercises and activities available on the Internet that combine both left- and right-brain learning. These can be effective in a ME session to help couples to very quickly understand the matters we seek to address. There are some samples included at the end of each chapter and also in the last two chapters. Leader couples can think about developing some of their own as well. A good metaphor, diagram or exercise is like a good picture. It may communicate more than a thousand words and will make the task of sharing much easier; for example, metaphors are a powerful way to convey complex, intangible concepts – they can be word pictures or literal images. Describing the concept of anger using a picture of a volcano appeals to both sides of the brain and clarifies and creates understanding.

> "You're transforming old patterns of your mind and letting go of thoughts you don't need to have around any longer."
> (Anonymous)

What Do We Want Couples to Take Away?

For a ME leader couple, a good starting point to design a ME session is to ask ourselves, "What is/are the main thing(s) we want couples to take away?" Structure the session around this; for example:

1. *Session Content – Creating a Need:* When designing a ME session, begin by creating a need. For example, in a session on communication, creating a need could involve handing out a rating scale and asking couples to rate themselves from 1 to 10 on how well they think they communicate in their relationship. Or you could ask, "Tell me about a couple you can relate to whose communication you admire. What appeals to you about the way they communicate?"

> "The teacher is no longer merely the one-who-teaches, but one who is himself taught in dialogue with the students, who in turn while being taught also teach. They become jointly responsible for a process in which all grow." (Paulo Freire)[3]

2. *Conveying the main concept(s):* This may sound obvious, but an effective event is something that is given by a confident leader couple with clean and simple visuals, which assist in telling the story or building the case the couple is trying to present. Not every person is a confident speaker. Try to gauge your comfort level as prospective couple leaders. Then, consider what needs to be built into the presentation to compensate.

Pause for Reflection

Where do we begin and what questions do we need to ask in designing a presentation?

The following questions will help us to begin preparing a session or presentation. There are five areas of focus questions to ask ourselves.

> "I cannot be a teacher without exposing who I am." (Paulo Freire)

1. From whom? Who's giving the presentation?

2. To whom? Who's the audience going to be?

3. In what venue? Is it going to be a small space or a large room or is it going to be a couple of people?

4. Through what medium? Is it going to be through dialoguing? Handouts or a flipchart? Experiential exercises?

5. What effect or goal are you hoping to achieve with this presentation?

Answers to these questions can tell you a lot about the content of your presentation and how long it should be. They help you build a base before you start placing the words on the slides.

Our Story

Right Brain

Over the years of my (Barry's) life, camping in the right brain has not been my preferred choice. My accountancy practice demanded a solution-oriented approach to problems and unfortunately, like a dominant hand, my left brain was most often in charge, becoming very comfortable in the dominant position. But I cannot recall ever reasoning myself to lasting change. Most of the significant changes have come about in a bed of pain and deep feelings. I have become an ardent advocate of experiential exercises that bypass the rational defences of my left brain. These are the ones that have given a voice to feelings and also practice in articulating my emotions.

Three couples sit with us in a little village in India. A sense of compulsion hangs in the air, as our host and translator apologises profusely for the numbers. The head of the organisation stands and welcomes us, then turns to the lovely couples and seems to harangue them for forty-five minutes. Very quickly audience connection disappears and eyes glaze into a practised look of "attention". I really don't think anyone is fooled. We step into the vacuum of limited expectations, minimal attention and a sense of endurance.

Immediately, we involve the couples in the process, switching between dialogues, cards and playdough. I can still recall the laughter when they model an animal that best represents their spouse when they are angry. That sharing this within a group is not a normal process in the culture is no impediment, as malformed bears, bulls, lions and turtles are displayed for all to see.

During the afternoon session, five more couples slip into the group. The next morning, we have six more couples and by the end of the workshop we have twenty couples. The power and attractiveness of transformational learning is evident in their feedback. They promise us that if we return our straw sleeping mat will be replaced with a "Hollywood" mattress. My left brain clicks in and I sigh – problem solved.

Chapter Summary

- A safe place is also fostered by designing engaging presentations.
- Participatory teaching methods enable couples to experience and retain more, as we tend to learn by doing.
- Information alone inhibits transformational learning.
- Lecture style appeals to the left-brain, as it involves logic, reason, and thinking while the right side of the brain involves creativity and emotion. To be effective, ME sessions should appeal to both sides of the brain.
- Couple activity must be followed by a debriefing session.
- A good starting point to designing an ME session is to ask ourselves, "What is/are the main thing(s) we want our participants to take away?"

Notes to Chapter 9

1. K. Letrud (2012). A rebuttal of NTL Institute's learning pyramid. *Education*, 133, 117-124.
2. M. LeFever (1995). *Learning Styles*. David C. Cook.
3. Paulo Freire (1993). *The Pedagogy of the Oppressed*. Continuum.

CHAPTER 10

CREATING A SAFE PLACE: DESIGNING USING CREATIVE TEACHING METHODS

Overview

This chapter explores creating a safe place by designing sessions using creative teaching methods. The chapter is organised under the following headings:

⇒ A Rationale for Creative Teaching Methods

⇒ Types of Experiential Methods

A safe place is created by community building and modelling, as well as designing engaging presentations that lead to transformational learning. Another aspect is designing sessions using creative teaching methods. An overview is provided below.

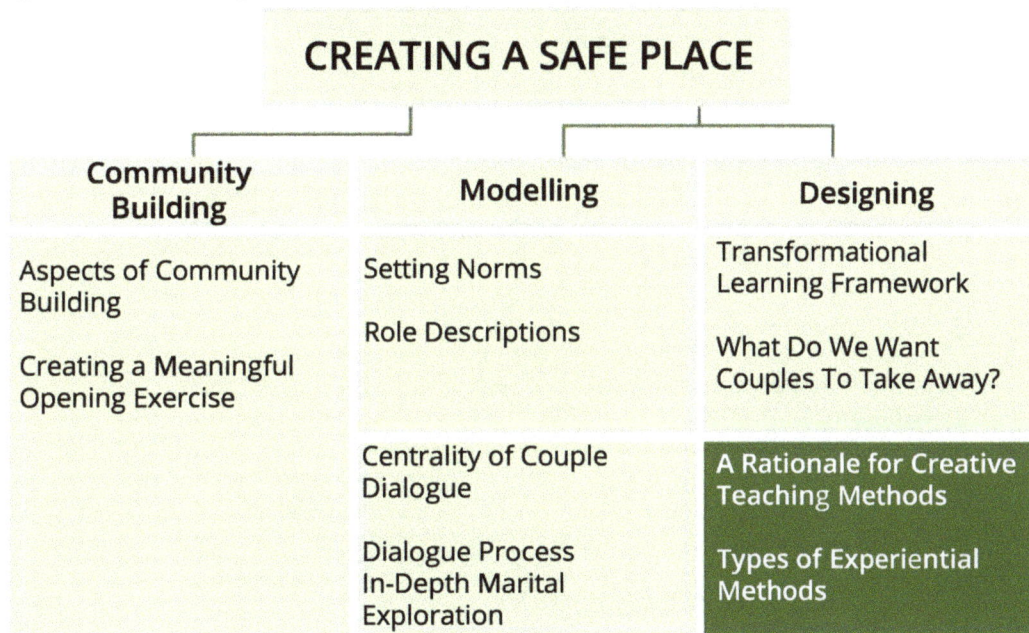

CREATING A SAFE PLACE

Community Building	Modelling	Designing
Aspects of Community Building Creating a Meaningful Opening Exercise	Setting Norms Role Descriptions	Transformational Learning Framework What Do We Want Couples To Take Away?
	Centrality of Couple Dialogue Dialogue Process In-Depth Marital Exploration	A Rationale for Creative Teaching Methods Types of Experiential Methods

A Rationale for Creative Teaching Methods

Creative teaching methods involve experience as the foundation of, and stimulus for, learning. Learning can only occur if the experience of the learner is engaged at some level. Learning always relates to what has gone before and seeks to integrate new meanings into old experience. Experience is the combination of a person's personal and cultural history, how it has influenced them and helped form the way they respond to the world. It is impossible to detach the learner from his/her context.

> It is a good idea to take time at the beginning to get a sense of the overall situation and mood of the group before digging immediately into the content of your presentation.

"Your work is not to drag the world kicking and screaming into a new awareness. Your job is to simply do your work ... sacredly, secretly, silently ... and those with "eyes to see and ears to hear' will respond."
(The Arturians)

Socialisation is the process by which our personalities are formed or constructed. We cannot undo what has happened to us, but we can find ways to reinterpret what has happened in the light of new knowledge and new ways of finding meaning. The extent to which we are able to accomplish this is often determined by the amount of support we have in our lives. Therefore, experiential learning, especially in groups, is one way to create a supportive environment for new learning. Experiential exercises are designed to do the following.

- Bring freshness, friendly interaction, and fun and to encourage a sense of "we". The role of a leader couple is to balance the needs of "I", "We" and "Task" of the group. A sense of "we" cannot be generated without couples knowing each other.
- Encourage couples to speak and be better understood. Everyone gets to hear the sound of their own voice in the group setting. Everyone is included and involved.
- Help create a comfortable environment. Using an object enables participants to talk about themselves in a less threatening way.
- Increase the depth of response and promote thoughtful reflection and self-awareness.
- Offer a way to talk about sensitive matters in a less threatening way, rather than simply saying them. For example, in a first meeting, when couples are asked to tell something about themselves that no one in the group knows, they can offer either a humorous or recent painful event.
- Assist couples to move from the vague and general to the specific, providing a beneficial way to clarify, prioritise and articulate thoughts and encourage creative thinking (moves away from the rational to right-brain activity).
- Facilitate tolerance-building of differences.
- Limit the intrusion of talkative participants who like to hold the floor and challenge them to talk in a different way. These participants often feel the most pressure – they talk to distance others.
- Lessen feelings of isolation and "I don't fit" mentality. People identify with others through the commonality of themes and issues.
- Allow comparison with other couples and promote support of one another. This occurs when barriers are broken down and trust and closeness are developed through the sharing of lives.
- Keep in mind that gathering exercises and resources is something that should be done on a continuing basis. The leader couple eventually find that they have a handout, exercise or activity for every occasion or issue. If one of them does not appear to work, discard it and look for one more suitable, or create your own.

What makes an exercise or activity effective?

A good exercise or activity facilitates transformational learning. It is:

- easily understood;
- uncomplicated and not excessively time consuming;
- reasonably completed within the available time frame;
- not demanding of a significant degree of literacy; not all couples will necessarily be articulate or able to work easily with words on paper, and the simpler the language used, the more appropriate the responses asked for, the better the outcome – the test of a good exercise is that it offers couples of all backgrounds a challenge at their own level without over simplifying matters or leading people to feel that it is all too much for them; and,

"The mediocre teacher tells, the good teacher explains, the superior teacher demonstrates, the great teacher inspires."
(William Arthur Ward)

- enjoyable. There should be some "kick" that couples can derive from actually doing the exercise and looking back on what they have learned from it. We are not inviting couples to engage in homework or boring assignments!

Cautions

Experiential exercises often bring up significant emotional material for participants. This can be helpful, as couples can learn about themselves and change. However, for traumatised individuals, experiential exercises may trigger traumatic memories that have not yet been understood and integrated. Therefore, it is extremely important that we know our audience and if we decide to use experiential exercises, choose ones that **do not trigger** traumatic memories if the person has not been adequately prepared, safety issues discussed and/or grounding exercises taught. Below are some guidelines for experiential exercises/activities.

1. Be aware there is no *right* or *wrong* way to tell a story.
2. Be careful not to touch drawings or symbols nor invade the storytelling space (physically, emotionally, cognitively).
3. Be careful not to name or label the drawing or symbol.
4. Listen from a position of *not knowing.*
5. Be careful not to interpret, intellectualise or confront.
6. Trust the process.

Sensitivity to group members and processes

One way to determine the success of a presentation is to monitor couple reactions while one is presenting or dialoguing; for example, signs of restlessness may indicate that the information is either too difficult to understand or just plain boring. We may need to simplify a difficult message, or maybe our presentation needs variety. We can increase audience participation by asking questions, small group discussion, couple dialogue, exercises, or by using other forms of media. Remember, "a picture is worth a thousand words".

The key to successful presentation is to know our audience. This means knowing something about their characteristics, needs and capabilities; for example, age, maturity, experience, gender et cetera. People from different cultural backgrounds, those who speak a different language, or those who are hearing impaired are unlikely to respond well if these factors are not acknowledged.

There are some practical ways we can prepare for a presentation. Below is a list of self-check questions. They are not exhaustive, but they suggest that leader couples should give serious attention to developing their expertise in interpreting and expressing non-verbal signals.

- ☐ Do we want couples to keep silent until question time?
- ☐ Should we invite couples to interrupt us so that we can deal with their inquiries on the spot?
- ☐ If the participants become restless, have we made any provision for this?
- ☐ Should we read from our notes or take the risk of improvising?
- ☐ Are our visual aids well designed?
- ☐ What will we do if we forget the point we are trying to make?
- ☐ What should we do if we sense we are losing our participant's attention?
- ☐ How do we overcome our initial fear of facing an unknown audience?
- ☐ Have we ensured that our presentation is free from judgments and prejudice?
- ☐ What kinds of persuasive appeals have we used; for example, humour, emotive language, fear etc.?
- ☐ Are these the most appropriate tactics for this type of presentation?
- ☐ Have we used plain language whenever possible, or is our presentation full of jargon?
- ☐ Do we really know our audience?

- Is our message tailored to our audience?
- Have we any safeguards in case we get side-tracked by too many questions from our participants?
- What if the technology fails?
- What if we get tongue-tied?
- What if we lose our notes?
- How can we be sure that our participants understand our presentation as we intended?
- How will our participants accept our line of reasoning?
- Has our information been well constructed? (Are we saying what we mean to say?)
- Is our information accurate?
- Are the chairs arranged in a circle?
- How should we dress for the presentation?
- Should we speak slowly or quickly?
- Should we speak loudly or softly?
- What other voice qualities should we use?
- What kind of facial expression should we adopt?

(Adapted from M. Kaye (1994), *Communication Management*. Prentice-Hall, pp.183-201)

Types of Experiential Methods

Experiential methods, activities and exercises create variety and appeal to all learning styles. In an ME event, they can include the following.

1. *Handout, activity, exercise:* Throughout this manual there are resources that can be used to begin your collection.
2. *Couple Dialogue:* It has been stressed that couple dialogue is one of the leader couple's greatest tools. The dialogue takes theory and places it in a real relationship. If we use it to create a need, we could position it near the beginning of a presentation. It can also be used if we want to explain a concept – for example, in a session on communication we could use a story from our relationship that couples can grasp.

Examples of experiential methods, activities and exercises include:

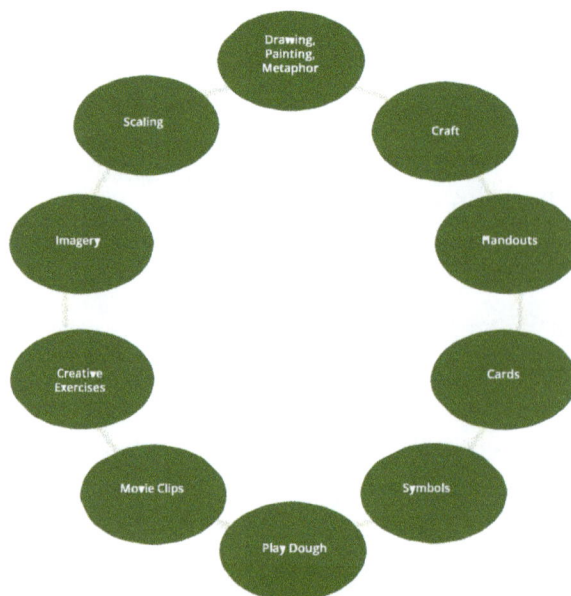

Drawing, Painting, Metaphor · Scaling · Craft · Imagery · Handouts · Creative Exercises · Cards · Movie Clips · Symbols · Play Dough

Drawing, painting, metaphor

People often say, "I can't draw". Emphasise that reflection through drawing is never about how good an artist we are. Effective use of this method has nothing to do with ability to draw. The appearance of the finished product is totally irrelevant, as it is an expression of the inner world. It may be helpful to provide a structure or a metaphor to stimulate the drawing; for example, "Every time I try to learn I feel like..." Resources needed are paper, crayons, felt-tipped pens, water-based finger paints et cetera.

Craft

Craft can be an individual or group exercise. It is symbolic, visual, non-verbal and a representation of meaning associated with experiences. Items for a collage can be stuck onto a sheet of large paper. Other items can be added by additional paintings or drawings. A collage can be produced after reflecting on personal experiences, as a way of making meaning from it, or as a way of communicating. Collages need time and should not be rushed. Resources needed are old magazines, scissors, glue, stickers, coloured paper; alternatively, couples may collect items of choice from the environment – for example, the garden.

Pause for Reflection

Together, make a collage of your relationship as it is now, depicting who you are, your different roles, aspects of your differing personalities, values and passions.

Handouts

There are a number of handouts throughout this manual and it is a good idea to continue to collect and maintain a selection covering the subjects most likely to be presented at an ME event. The questions need to be crafted carefully and designed to counter the tendency to stay with the rational. The idea is for each spouse to rate their response and then compare with each other. Differences will elicit conversation and possible areas of exploration. The participants should be encouraged not to dwell on responses – it is not a test, just a tool as a catalyst for communication. Usually the first response is most accurate. When appropriate, it is good to provide a rating for an anticipated spousal response, as this also opens doors to communication.

Picture or photo cards

Picture or photo cards come in various sets that can be purchased online and are aimed at emotions. Some have words below the pictures that represent character strengths or a description of the feeling evoked in the picture. Participants vary in their selection method, some being drawn to the words and others to the

> "It is essential to understand that battles are primarily won in the heart... [people] respond to leadership in a most remarkable way and once you have won [their] heart, [they] will follow you anywhere."
> (Vince Lombardi)

pictures. The cards are very effective in shaping words to describe how a participant is feeling. They are very helpful for someone struggling to name their feelings. Use of the cards in a group help to move couples into right-brain activity that tends to disarm the rational defences.

Symbols

Similarly to the cards, a symbol is used to open the pathway to the creative and emotional. The couples could be asked to go out into the surrounding area and chose an object that depicts their relationship as it is now or the place of spirituality in their life now. Individual spouses share and then an opportunity is given to share in the group. The benefit, especially for those not skilled in vulnerability, is that showing and addressing an object before the group removes the confronting vulnerability of sharing without the intermediary of the symbol. They talk about the symbol but reveal themselves. "Precious junk" from the kitchen, garage or markets and old toys are rich resources for accumulating symbols.

Playdough

Playdough can be used in many creative ways. Asking the participants to model an animal that best represents them when they are angry releases creativity, fun and a gentle vulnerability. This type of exercise is usually met with lots of laughter over a mixture of animals. The purpose is again to access the emotional, creative right brain. It is easier to talk about difficult feelings and acknowledge our anger when holding a hardly recognisable bear or lion. When we ask participants what animal best represents their father when he is angry, the playdough often becomes a channel to access pain and discomfort. The doorway to family of origin issues has been opened by a playdough key!

Movie clips

Short extracts from movies are a great way to introduce a topic or depict an issue. The poignancy or longings expressed in a scene can give participants words to describe their feelings and longings to each other. Two characters in conflict can be used to have the group unpack the scene using the "volcano" in preparation for couples doing the same on one of their conflictual issues. However, be aware of copyright issues.

Creative exercises

Leader couples need to be alert to creative exercises. Below are two examples of powerful activities to introduce a topic and create a desire for change.

- *Workshop on listening*. In a session or workshop on listening, ask participants: "What is the most precious, significant thing to you? Write on a piece of paper. No one will see what you have written so you can express your deepest heartfelt passion." The leader couple then collect the papers in a bowl and proceed to tear the pieces and let the fragments fall to the ground. Usually, the mood of the group visibly changes and an uneasy hostility begins to surface. Then ask, "What does it feel like?" The responses are often angry and predictable. Then say, "That is what it is like when we don't listen to someone, especially our spouse, and particularly when they are sharing some deep feelings and issues." The session is then ready to explore listening!
- *Numbers on the floor*. Write the numbers one to ten on pieces of cardboard about A4 size. Place them evenly spaced on the ground in a straight line. Ask the participants where they would stand for the purposes of the workshop; for example, a workshop on anger and conflict may have the word "express" at one end and "repress" at the other. Another example is a workshop on sexuality with the word "work" at one end and "play" at the other. The leader couple moves up and down the line engaging with participants by asking what made them choose to stand on their particular number. They can also be asked about their perceptions of the people at the other end. The exercise closes with participants noticing the number of their spouse and moving to stand on the number they would prefer. Couples are then encouraged to find their spouse and share their responses.

Imagery

Imagery is a powerful tool. An imagery exercise with an accompanying script that is useful in a workshop on family of origin or conflict is found in Chapter 15, *Additional Resources: When the Past Enters the Present.*

Scaling

Scaling helps couples break down their perception of their situation into gradations. It is a method that requires assigning a value to the rated object, as a measure of a rated characteristic or attribute. Usually this is numeric; for example, the pictured scale can be used to measure how well a couple resolves conflict, with zero being NOT WELL and 10 being VERY WELL. Participants are asked to plot where they perceive they fall on this scale by assigning a number to their response, which is then compared and discussed with their spouse. Couples are much more likely to take ownership of the issue when asked to rate their responses on a scale.

Leader couple participation in exercises

As participating leader couples, we complete each exercise in whatever way we have outlined to our couples. Then, as a way of further stimulating an open and vulnerable environment, we share what we have learnt or discovered in the process. This tends to stimulate the couples to share their own responses with the possibility of learning from each other.

> ""The meaning of life is to find your gift. The purpose of life is to give it away."
> (Pablo Picasso)

Remember, the gathering of exercises is something that should be done on a continuing basis so that we eventually we have an exercise for every occasion or issue. If an exercise does not seem to work, look around for another or create your own.

Demonstrating a skill

When teaching a skill – for example, reflective listening – the leader couple demonstrates the skill before the group. Below are some guidelines.

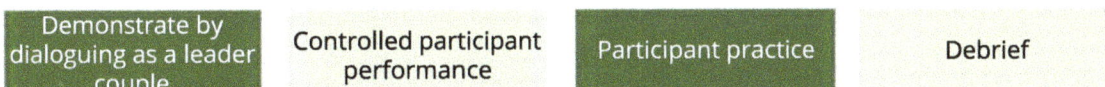

Demonstrate by dialoguing as a leader couple	Controlled participant performance	Participant practice	Debrief

- Demonstrate by dialoguing as a leader couple. Couples can then identify the big picture and what is expected from them.
- Controlled participant performance. It is difficult, and sometimes almost impossible, to counteract the effects of a skill learned incorrectly. Couples perform the skill under close supervision and at a controlled pace. The leader couple move around from couple to couple and intervene if necessary. It is essential to tell couples beforehand that this is going to happen so they are not surprised when you turn up!
- Participant practice. This should be about 50% of allocated session time. Be available during this time to answer any questions that arise. Do not take over from them, but get them to try to fix it themselves, while making suggestions.
- Debrief. Conclude the session by going over the main points and clarifying any areas of concern.

Careful use of humour

Times of violence and change can be times of extreme learning. The challenge is to make that learning positive, as there is a serious trap of falling into depression. Couples may be feeling that the doomsayers are right or they may be saying, "What's the point of learning something new as I don't know what tomorrow might bring?"

The leader couple can develop strategies for connecting current events to their ME content in relevant and constructive ways. A key to success is to meet these issues head-on and not pretend that they are external to our lives. Hope and optimism are foundational attitudes for learning and one of the keys to success is humour.

"Teach the way you'd want to be taught."
(Anonymous)

However, sometimes it is difficult for even the most adept humourists to find the "funny bits" in our world, and maybe we do not want to. Humour can come from our response to these events and our ability to de-mystify and de-mythologise the villains. One example of helping people cope with and survive adversity was shown in the *Changi* series on ABC Television, Australia. Australian soldiers interned in a Japanese prisoner of war camp during the Second World War learned to cope with the necessity of eating stray dogs by forming a "Dog Appreciation Society"!

Any attempt at humour will run the risk of offending someone, but the best humour reduces seemingly complex, frightening and paralysing issues to a childlike simplicity and clarity. So, as leader couples we can take issues that people find frightening and reduce them to a more realistic, proportional level. This serves to replace fear with relaxation in a way that enhances the learning environment and retention of the key content.

We can give examples that simplify the complex and highlight the obvious in a way that connects with our humanness. They can serve to diffuse anxiety and make daunting situations more manageable.

Pause for Reflection

What might be an example of humour in your relationship that you could use?

_____

_____

_____

_____

In times of dramatic change and uncertainty, our learners – and, indeed, all of us – need all the humour we can get. Look for examples, practise creating your own, take some risks. The reward will be a more relaxed and productive learning environment.

Our Story

Sangeeta pushes Raj into the circle of people greeting me. We are in the north of Sri Lanka for a reunion with Tamil workshop participants from previous years. Raj has a USB in his hand and pushes me toward our computer. He says something but I cannot understand. Using signs and gestures he gets me to load the USB. I pray there are no viruses.

I watch the images of Sangeeta and Raj conducting what is obviously a marriage retreat. They dialogue. They sit in a circle. They role play. They use cards that they have created from magazines and their own photo prints. It is humbling to watch what has been caught from our times with them. To see the smiling faces and hear the laughter of couples involved and the spontaneity and lack of boredom. Raj has been able to find a translator and he shares the experiences of the now many workshops he and his lovely wife have conducted and how well received they are in his community.

Sangeeta is with a group of women at the back of the hall, but she is not attentive to their conversation. Her interest is with us. I catch her looking and she smiles. I know the origin of the passion for what I am looking at. Their relationship was empty and dead when they came to our marriage workshop some years ago. Raj had been traumatised beyond belief during the war period and the 2004 tsunami. Tortured and broken, he had little to offer his wife and small children. Too much loss and grief. She cajoled him into that workshop and they found a way to talk about painful times. The cards opened him up to her gentle probing and gave voice to what had been suppressed for too long. No wonder their homemade cards featured in all their events.

Chapter Summary

- A rationale for creative teaching methods includes the drawing on learners' experience while seeking to integrate new meanings into old experience.
- Try to choose exercises and activities that do not trigger traumatic memories where the person has not been adequately prepared, safety issues have not been discussed, and/or grounding exercises taught.
- Experiential methods, activities and exercises create variety and appeal to all learning styles.
- Monitoring couples through observation of body language is essential.

PART C

MANAGING GROUPS AND EVENTS

CHAPTER 11

ELEMENTS OF ME EVENTS

Overview
This chapter explores the elements of ME events. The chapter is organised under the following headings: ⇒ Practical Elements of ME Events ⇒ Participatory Elements of ME Events ⇒ Format of ME Events ⇒ Practicalities of Planning a Group ⇒ Constructing a Timeline ⇒ Closing Activities ⇒ Evaluating the Effectiveness of an ME Event

Conducting an ME event necessarily involves certain elements that require attention. This chapter will address practical and administration matters involved in planning ME events.

Practical Elements of ME Events

Certain practical elements need consideration for ME events to be effective. It is optimal for ME events to be led by a trained married couple whose leadership is participatory. Ideally, the method is

> "Leadership is not about titles, positions or flowcharts. It is about one life influencing another." (John Maxwell)

basically experiential and dynamic, as opposed to didactic and purely intellectual. Time is allocated to both couple interaction within the context of the group and private couple dialogue. Structured experiential exercises are used to either initiate dialogue or in response to a couple dialogue within the group. Further practical elements are as follows.

- Group size should reflect a ratio of one leader couple to approximately eight to ten couples. The number of participants needs to be limited to prevent the experience becoming a traditional lecture exercise that would severely restrict the opportunity for participation and response.
- Participants should have some voice in determining the agenda for the event.
- Ideal session times cover at least fifteen hours through either a residential retreat or sequential weekly meetings.

It is a good idea to have a high point in a ME retreat, such as an evening "romantic" dinner. This presents a great opportunity for couples to dress up for the occasion and experience a romantic setting. Leader

> The purpose of a romantic dinner is to kindle memories of early times in couples' relationships and to reconnect with the feeling of first love.

couples will need to give due notice of this in any promotional material so that couples come prepared with the right dress for the occasion. The purpose of the evening is to kindle memories of early times in their relationships and to reconnect with the feeling of first love. A suggested program, together with resources, is included at the end of this chapter.

Participatory Elements of ME Events

There is a need for the leader couple to think carefully about how they will conduct themselves and use the time that is available to them in a ME event. A number of matters need to be kept in mind.

Body language

The body posture of the leader couple is extremely important when presenting. Closeness and distance convey messages that speak louder than words; for example, sitting slightly behind or away from a spouse during a dialogue or presentation conveys a message of awkwardness or discomfort. In addition, arms and/or legs crossed and leaning away from the audience are less likely to encourage participation or create a sense of safety.

Our Story

Sunil and his wife are waiting to say goodbye. They hold hands, very unusual in their culture. We have much affection for him, as he was our faithful translator and had weathered the storm of translating the sexuality section. I smile as I recall the intensity of expression, glistening sweat and quizzical look as I said "erectile dysfunction". He survived the session and is greatly relieved.

We hug each other, also culturally unusual, and linger in the emotion of departure. Paula asks, "What are you taking away?" Sunil blurts out that they want a relationship like ours. "What does that look like?", I ask. "We watched when the two of you were setting up for the sessions, how you were with each other. The little touches and chatter, each helping the other. We want our relationship to be like that."

Paula and I are relieved that we had experienced a run of "good" days leading up to the retreat and were connected. We acknowledge that more is caught than taught. It is sobering to realise that modelling as a leader couple occurs beyond facilitation.

Community building

An important task in any ME event, is to spend time in what is normally described as community building (see Chapter 6). Couples will attend an event, especially a retreat, with a variety of hopes and fears. Some will only be there because their spouse has insisted that they come.

> The leader couple's willingness to be vulnerable helps to create an environment where participant couples can risk being vulnerable with each other.

Consequently, it is essential to make the most of the community building opportunities at the beginning, realising that in the context of a weekend retreat, there will need to be a measure of ongoing community building throughout the event. While we may have had a very beneficial Friday evening experience of a weekend retreat helping people relax, we need to be prepared to also engage in more community building on Saturday and Sunday mornings. It does become easier, but some couples take a little bit longer to feel at home in a group. It is also helpful to have a range of exercises to assist in the community building task.

Agenda setting

It is necessary to make time for agenda setting. Leader couples do this in different ways. It is a matter of discovering a process that is comfortable and gives maximum opportunity for couples to identify their felt needs and concerns. Experience has shown that the building of an agenda in the group setting will produce one set of outcomes, while inviting couples to jot down subject areas on a piece of paper and submit these anonymously will produce another. A short assessment questionnaire can be emailed to couples beforehand, asking them to identify areas of interest and need. It is essential that agenda building be undertaken early in the process and, for the purposes of a weekend retreat, this should be done on the first evening or during the application process.

An inexperienced leader couple may find the process less daunting by preparing a number of sessions on meaningful topics (family background, communication, conflict, sexuality, differences, spirituality et cetera) and listing them for participants to choose the topics of most interest. The group could discuss the priority and order in which they are to be addressed, so that participants own the agenda. It is also a good idea on the following morning to spend time talking with the couples about the agenda items suggested so that all participants can see that their ideas and suggestions have been noted. This promotes ownership and sends couples the message that they have been listened to.

Alternatively, leader couples could describe the agenda as a *rolling agenda*, meaning that as particular matters are dealt with, they can drop off the agenda and new issues can be added. It lends a touch of dynamism to proceedings and sometimes other issues emerge as a consequence of what has been taking place within the dialogue process.

Leader couple input

It is important for leader couples to share basic principles on a topic, so that couples add to their understanding. Such material can be presented simply and informally. However, the passing on of helpful principles is of no value if there is not an

> Leader couples need to be alert for ways and means of offering exercises and activities that engage couples in applying what they have heard shared through dialogue and principles.

exercise or activity that seeks to capitalise on this input. Leader couples need to be alert for ways and means of offering exercises and activities that engage couples in applying what they have heard/shared through dialogue and principles. Therefore, there is a need to provide time for private dialogue and the undertaking of exercises as a very important component of the overall process of the ME event.

Private dialogue

Once couples have engaged with private dialogue and the completion of exercises, they will probably find increasing value in the use of time for themselves. Leader couples should feel relaxed if participants want a little extra time to talk over some matters. It is difficult sometimes to balance the emphasis between matters addressed in the larger group and what is undertaken on a spouse-to-spouse basis. Ongoing experience will help to reach that balance more quickly and effectively.

Participant expectations

If participating couples are drawn from a church congregation, there will be value in having brief times available for worship. Significantly, some religious groups of couples may attend expecting a Bible study weekend on family life. If this should happen, it can be easily explained that the intention of the ME retreat is to take a range of Biblical principles and apply these to the marriage relationship. On occasions, couples may come wishing to hide behind such activities, rather than addressing the issues that are actually before them.

Growth plan and closing

> It is not uncommon for a couple to report that they have had a huge let down upon their return home, because of the impact of children, the usual pressures waiting for them and endless other distractions.

Towards the close of the retreat, the practicality of allowing sufficient time for couples to draw up a growth plan requires a shift in orientation towards future intentionality. This process ought not to be hurried.

A closing session is necessary and includes a time of preparation for re-entry into the couple's world. It is not uncommon for a couple to report that they have had a huge let down upon their return home, because of the impact of children, the usual pressures waiting for them and endless other distractions. Time is well spent helping couples understand and prepare for the adjustment when returning to their everyday circumstances.

Format of ME events

The format of a ME event includes, but is not limited to:

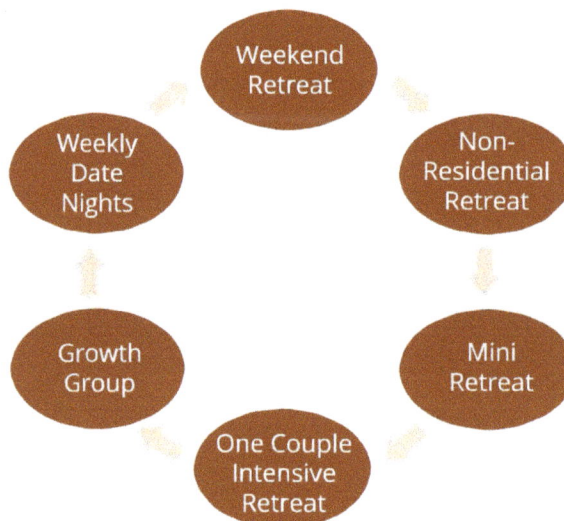

- weekend retreat;
- non-residential retreat;
- mini-retreat (one day);
- one couple intensive retreat;
- growth group meeting for six to eight consecutive weeks; and,
- weekly date nights for approximately six weeks.

Practicalities of Planning a Group

> "By failing to prepare, you are preparing to fail." (Benjamin Franklin)

ME events are usually planned months in advance, especially if booking a venue is involved. Careful planning in the early stages can avoid the stress of last-minute decisions. The following Pauses for Reflection might help us to think through the issues involved in conducting an ME event.

Practicalities of Planning a Group

Assume you are requested to run a ME event in your church or community. What would be important in your planning?

Discuss the following questions as a leader couple:
- How would you announce your ME event?
- How would you screen potential couples?
- Who might be excluded from your ME event and why?
- What would you use to help the couples to define what they want to get from the ME event?
- How would you attempt to engage the couples during the initial phase of your ME event?
- What might you do if the couples in your first session seem to be disconnected?

Constructing a Timeline

Assume you are requested to run a ME event in your church or community.

Discuss the question as a leader couple: When planning a ME event, how do we know what to do and when to do it?

Below is an example of a timeline.

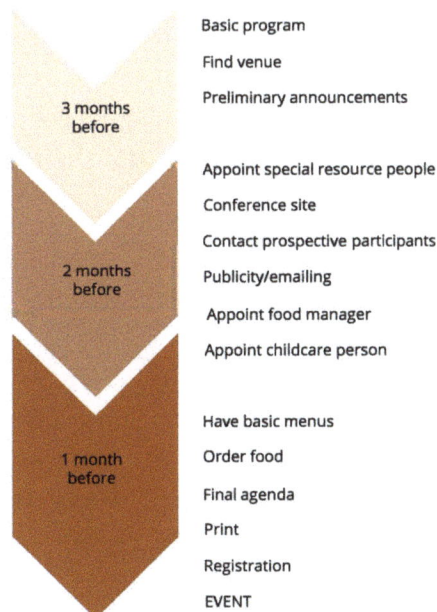

3 months before
- Basic program
- Find venue
- Preliminary announcements

2 months before
- Appoint special resource people
- Conference site
- Contact prospective participants
- Publicity/emailing
- Appoint food manager
- Appoint childcare person

1 month before
- Have basic menus
- Order food
- Final agenda
- Print
- Registration
- EVENT

Warning: We have arranged a number of retreats, booked venues and locked in numbers only to have couples withdraw after the final numbers have been submitted. Sometimes we have borne the cost of these late withdrawals because of friendships and preserving goodwill. Now we have the group organise the venue to avoid any misunderstanding and financial expense.

We have found it preferable not to have children accompany their parents to a retreat if at all possible.

Closing Activities

Pause for Reflection

What would constitute a good closing activity?

Closing activities are an important part of an ME event.

Following are some ideas for closure.

- Promotion of marriage enrichment.
- Plans for follow-up, support, or a growth group.
- Evaluations.

"The end is in the beginning and lies far ahead." (Ralph Ellison)

An informal evaluation should precede the final parting ceremony, so allow enough time. The final parting activity should be a simple ceremony of connection, affirmation and separation; for example:

- Holding hands in a circle to acknowledge each other and the contribution couples have made to each other.
- Embracing our spouses and thanking them as a final act of affirmation and appreciation.

Closure and sustaining marital growth

"The feeling is less like an ending than just another starting point." (Chuck Palahniuk)

The truth is that marital growth, even when understood for the first time, is not a process that continues automatically. A genuine discovery of the concept requires considerable discipline if there are to be any real, long-term benefits. Growth implies change, and even well-adjusted couples can find change difficult and unsettling. This is especially true if there is a need for communication and conflict-resolving to be developed and refined. It is all too easy for a couple, even with the best of intentions, to revert to old ways of relating after the enrichment experience has finished. In their hearts the couple may want to do better, but the environment will make it extremely challenging for those genuinely wanting to undertake significant changes in their relating patterns.

It is for this reason that leader couples must be wholly committed to change in their relationship. A leader couple that are basically settled in their approach to life and relationships will not be able to energise and bring about change in the lives of other couples. There needs to be an ongoing and genuine commitment to further refining and enhancing our own marriages as part of being a good model for others.

Planning for growth now

The *Growth Plan* is the genius of ME, as developed by David and Vera Mace. It is a time when individual couples bring together the possibilities for their futures in a way that has a measure of structure and intentionality to it. Devising the Growth Plan is more often than not surrounded by a genuine hope for better ways of relating in the future. In helping couples to draw up their Growth Plan, the leader couple also needs to acknowledge that this a working document and can be shaped and developed over the passage of time. The suggestion is that the plan may be reviewed as part of a couple's wedding anniversary celebrations or the anniversary of the ME event.

It is a good idea to suggest to couples that genuine change will come out of a genuine commitment to intentionality and change, and that long-term change may take as long as twelve months while new patterns become a part of a fresh lifestyle. The temptation to give up and revert to old ways is ever-present and couples need to be alerted to this – with the encouragement that it is worth pressing on to reach new heights, even though there may be setbacks.

The concept of ME Groups (MEGs) originated with David and Vera Mace, who believed that, ideally, a couple will find a support network very helpful in the process of ongoing marital growth. However, achieving this ideal can be quite difficult logistically. If couples attend events in different locations, experience has shown that it is almost impossible to direct them to a group that understands what they have experienced and can help them capitalise on the gains they have made. The exception is where a leader couple conduct a MEG on a regular basis, adding new members from events they conduct and integrating them into the group.

A strategy used by many leader couples is to arrange a reunion four to six weeks after an event as a way of following up. This may give rise to some or all of the couples committing to get together for a number of times over the next six months or more. The leader couple may attend the first of these sessions or give a longer-term commitment. Ideally, they can identify

> "Ends are not bad things, they just mean that something else is about to begin. And there are many things that don't really end, anyway, they just begin again in a new way. Ends are not bad and many ends aren't really an ending; some things are never-ending." (C. JoyBell C.)

one couple to act as liaison couple for the group and encourage member couples to take it in turns to introduce a topic followed by an exercise and dialogue in the group. *Time Together* (found on our website: connectingmaters.com.au), a six-week study booklet designed by Paula Davis, with some printed exercises, can set the new MEG on its way. In this instance, the leader couple could stay in contact with the liaison couple to support them.

If couples are participating in an event from an existing group, such as a church group, it is generally much easier to establish a support network. Most congregations are used to small groups for different purposes, so a couples' growth group is not a new concept in most churches. It is certainly ideal for the encouragement of couples who are committed to their growth plans. As mentioned above, there will be a need to suggest ongoing resources, as even the best-ordered MEGs can become little more than navel gazing or simply a socialising group unless there is some informed guidance regarding the future of the marriage journey.

Planning for growth in the future

As couples begin to lower barriers, they can take incremental action that builds and grows marital intimacy. David and Vera Mace defined intimacy as "shared privacy" or "being fully known and deeply loved". Intimacy has also been described as "INTO ME SEE". Gradually, the experience of intimacy can become more frequent and spouses tend to feel that their marriage is becoming an intimate relationship. Some ideas to get started on an Intimacy Plan are listed below.

1. *Start by recognising the intimacy we already have in our relationship.* Talk together about the satisfactions and pleasures we have enjoyed during times of closeness.

2. *Reaffirm our commitment to the growth of our relationship and our growth as individuals.* Make a list of the things we value in our marriage and the hopes and dreams we have for our marriage, our spouse and ourselves.

3. *Become partners in building self-esteem.* Express appreciation to each other and encourage each other's efforts and growth. Affirm each other as sexual partners.

4. *Build trust.* Re-examine our expectations of each other. Revise them as needed and renew our agreements, then carry through with what we agree to do, as this builds trust. If our agreements fail to work, renegotiate and try again.

5. *Learn skills for sharing feelings.* Share our own feelings using "I" statements and reduce "You" statements that create defensiveness. It is equally important that we learn to listen so we can understand our spouse.

6. *Work to clear up anger and resentments that occur in our relationship.* Avoid attacking or blaming our spouse, and begin looking behind the anger to discover the deeper feelings that triggered it.

7. *Help each other take risks.* Begin by sharing our own hurts, shortcomings, mistakes, or other sensitive topics. Then as we listen, try to understand rather than to judge.

8. *Nurture the joy and satisfactions shared in marriage.* Express these to each other. Allow time and energy for physical, sexual pleasure. Cultivate playfulness, humour and celebration.

9. *Search for ways to express love to our spouse.* Find out what actions help each of us feel loved by completing this sentence in several ways: "I feel loved when you..."

10. *Set aside time for each other.* Give our marriage priority. Arrange our commitments so that our relationship gets prime time and energy.

11. *Daily bonding rituals.* It is important to create rituals and activities couples can do to hold onto their connection. Bonding rituals begin at birth; for example, mother greets child, tells child where she is going, offers comfort on return. How many couples say goodbye in the morning and hold each other? One powerful bonding ritual is the ten-second kiss when one spouse leaves in the morning and returns in the evening.

12. *Identify a specific action each of us could take to create more intimacy.* This action should be *specific and immediate.* Make a date to check progress. Do daily check-ins, diary dates and heart talks. At the end of this chapter there is some helpful information and guidelines for establishing *Heart Talks* in the couple relationship.

Our Story

I am surrounded by loss. Recently, I sat with an old friend who just lost his wife to cancer. Last week I sat with another old friend who just lost her husband to cancer. I cry copious tears for these dear ones and for our broken world. But I love happy endings. We watched Cinderella at the movies this year. Predictable? Yes. Corny? Yes. During the movie I was thinking how Barry is probably about to throw up. I lean across his chair and ask if he is enjoying this. His answer surprises me. He tells me he is a sucker for a happy ending. Does it stir longings? Definitely!

In a blink it is the last day of a three-day trauma workshop for people-helpers held in Colombo, Sri Lanka. The participants tell us how they thought they would be receiving only information. Instead they are tender within, seeing the significance of their own inner work as an essential prerequisite to helping someone else. The Tree of Life drawing exercise has torn some asunder. As a metaphor for life, a tree is drawn to represent the many facets of a life. As couples draw, their faces reflect joy and pain, confusion and hope. Many come during the day to share their stories with us and request help to get unstuck. Some tell us they have been set free and we marvel. Others need to sit with difficult decisions and grieve profound pain. Growth flourishes and the blessings continue to shower us with fruitfulness and abundance.

Sri Lanka has burrowed into our hearts and connected us with what we desire most – to leave behind a sweet fragrance in this world. Scratch the surface and there is a deep hunger within us for something real like this that sustains life and brings meaning.

The air in the room is charged. Conversations flow freely. Honesty, vulnerability and authenticity wash over the room like the sea washes over rocks, a continual surging and receding, only to surge again. Hearts split open and healing and wholeness fall in. Our own hearts swell with love for these people. At the close we feel so alive, so vibrant, like a ripe flower opening her lips to collect life-sustaining raindrops.

We know in our depths that our small work in this country is bringing healing and freedom to many. Who could have known that our pain and struggle would be used in later years to deepen the mystery of personal healing? Our mess has indeed become our message. Our shared vulnerability opens doors to healing: "I have come to believe ... that what is most important must be spoken, made verbal and shared, even at the risk of having it bruised or misunderstood" (Audre Lourde). And, as Francoise de la Rochefoucauld so eloquently expresses it, "The passions are the only orators which always persuade".[1] Our brokenness has become a signpost of hope for other broken souls.

Evaluating the Effectiveness of an ME Event

Evaluations are standard ME practice and provide the basis for quality control. Evaluation will take place by couples whether or not it is planned. We believe it is best practice to complete formal evaluations as an integral part of the event. It is important to hand out an evaluation form at the end of a ME workshop, as it will tell you whether participants' expectations were met and whether they learned what they wanted and needed to learn. It will also let you valuating the Effectiveness of an ME event.

Pause for Reflection

As a leader couple, discuss:

How will we know we have accomplished what we set out to do?

Evaluation can be formal, informal or both.

1. Formal evaluation
   Areas to be evaluated are:

   - clarity of goals;
   - methods of attaining goals:
     - What did we learn?
     - How well did we work together?
     - What happened to us as individuals?
     - Was the leader couple competent enough?
     - Were we able to participate in decision-making?
   - venue and value for money.

2. Informal evaluation

   - Ask participants at the end of a ME event:
     - What did you find helpful?
     - What would you have liked to explore further?
     - What can we do to improve the event in the future?

It is also important for those involved in the ME event (leader couples, organisers, support people, etc.) to get together immediately after an event while the memory is still fresh and evaluate the ME workshop.

Start with the questions:

- Have we done what we set out to do?
- Did this activity meet its objectives?

Ask the comparative questions:

- What did we set out to achieve?
- What are the signs we have done this?

Ask the 'gap-filling' questions:

- What did we not do that we intended to do?
- What did we do that we didn't intend to do?

Ask problem-solving questions:

- How could we improve next time?
- How could we do more of what we did right?
- How can we let go the things we don't want to be doing?

Chapter Summary

- ME includes attending to practical elements; for example, leader couple participation, structured experiential methods designed to facilitate couple dialogue, session times, agenda setting and a romantic dinner.

- Participatory elements of ME include attention to body language, community building, leader couple input, private dialogue, participant expectations, a growth plan and closing exercises.

- ME format can consist of a weekend retreat, a non-residential retreat, a mini retreat consisting of one day, a one couple intensive retreat or a growth group meeting for six to eight consecutive weeks.

- Careful planning of a ME event in the early stages can avoid the stress of last-minute decisions.

- Is helpful to construct a timeline of things to do before a ME event.

- It is important to plan closing activities to include evaluation, planning for growth now and planning for growth in the future.

- Creating a Growth Plan is a time when couples bring together the possibilities for their futures in a way that has a measure of structure and intentionality to it.

- In the future, as couples begin to lower barriers, they can be encouraged to take incremental action that builds and grows marital intimacy.

- Formal or informal evaluation is necessary to gauge the effectiveness of an ME event.

Worksheet on Romantic Dinner

Romantic Dinner

Purpose of the romantic dinner

The aim of the romantic dinner is to rekindle memories and feelings around the period when the couples first met. The evening could begin with some connecting games and over dinner sharing some of the answers to the first three questions. After dinner we invite the husband and wife to give each other a simple neck, shoulder and head massage. This moves the memories and feelings to touch and we conclude the evening with private expressions of intimacy.

Program for the romantic dinner

Describe:

How you first met.

How you proposed.

Where you first kissed.

Where you spent your honeymoon.

What is one of the funniest events you recall from your marriage?

What is one of the most exciting things that has happened to you since you got married?

Massage video: Give each other a back and neck rub.

Ask couples to hold each other's hands. Express to each other: "What your hands mean to me …"

Complete these sentences:

- "I feel romantic when you …"
- "I feel good when …"
- "I feel intimate when you …"
- "I am saying I love you when I …"

Complete these sentences:

- "Something romantic I would like to do with you …"
- "Something romantic I would like to do for you …"
- "Something romantic I would like you to do for me …"

Share a fantasy about the future.

Worksheet on closure

Heart Talks

1 John 4:18 says: "There is no fear in love. But perfect love drives out fear, because fear has to do with punishment. The one who fears is not made perfect in love."

Fear of self-disclosure, sharing who I really am and what I really feel, blocks heart-to-heart communication. It is a well-known psychological principle that the best way to expand the capacity for love is to let go of fear. How do we overcome our fear of self-disclosure?

What sort of heart-to-heart conversations can we have that give us the ability to experience this capacity for love that lets go of fear?

In the book Lifemates, the authors develop a series of Love Fitness Workouts called Heart Talks.[2]

Time together is the foundation of every intimate relationship and instigating Heart Talks reinforces our couple connection. In the beginning, it helps to stay away from conflictual areas; in a later session we will learn how to talk about difficult areas in our relationship. Heart Talks establish a safe emotional environment of care and trust, allowing both spouses to:
- accept and enjoy the risk of self-disclosure;
- discover hidden parts of ourselves; and,
- develop new emotional connections.

Virginia Satir claimed that "Communication is to a relationship what breathing is to sustaining life." Heart Talks establish a safe emotional environment of care and trust, allowing both spouses to:
- accept and enjoy the risk of self-disclosure;
- discover hidden parts of ourselves; and,
- develop new emotional connections.

Heart talks can also serve to benefit our love relationship in the following ways.

1. **Emotional safety:** We can create safety and trust to talk about whatever might be disturbing one or both of us.
2. **Tension release:** Every love relationship will encounter rough points and accumulate frustration; Heart Talks are a way of clearing the air.
3. **Nurturing and connecting:** Heart to heart communication nurtures us in a way that no amount of physical sex alone can provide. Heart Talks provide a way to experience greater intimacy and connectedness on every level of our being.
4. **Learning more about myself:** Some people shy away from intimacy because they fear going deeper into themselves. A Heart Talk is a personal invitation to a lover to get closer to us and help us discover more about ourselves.
5. **Feeling affirmed, understood and accepted:** No matter how autonomous and independent we may be, it is important to be fully acknowledged and understood by those to whom we feel closest, particularly our lover. Heart Talks help to make sure that each of us gets the acceptance and acknowledgment we need.
6. **Fun, play and laughter:** Heart Talks are more than serious emotional conversations; they are also a means of having fun and experiencing the joys of intimacy.

7. **Rediscovering my spouse:** In the busyness of everyday life, it is easy to take our lover for granted and assume we know how he or she thinks and feels. Heart Talks are a way of rediscovering recent changes in our feelings, ideas and goals.

8. **Energising our love relationship:** By strengthening the bonds of intimacy, Heart Talks allow us to experience new heights of passion. We can discover new ways of enjoying each other that we might not have even thought possible.

9. **Healing myself:** Heart Talks are an opportunity to heal our self by reclaiming our "dark side". To love deeply, each of us must accept the feelings of hostility, fear, rage, confusion and helplessness that lie within us. Heart Talks allow for confession, forgiveness and understanding of the contradictory forces of love and anger. When we learn to embrace each other's dark sides, we also become more compassionate with ourselves.

Guidelines for Heart Talks

It is important to create appropriate environment for Heart Talks.
- Silence the phone and remove devices.
- Take precautions against outside interruptions.
- Set a time limit at first, at least 20 to 30 minutes, but not more than an hour per sitting. Aim for two half hour sessions per week at first, and an additional one-hour session per fortnight.
- Be aware that spouses are not alike in their tolerance of, or desire for. intimacy. Respect their pace and style of self-disclosure.
- The husband is the initiator, but both spouses need to take responsibility for maintaining mutual respect, honouring Heart Talk agreements and creating an atmosphere of safety and trust.

Guidelines are very simple. It is recommended that couples adhere to the following two guidelines to ensure maximum benefit.
- Try not to interrupt your mate.
- Listen: whoever holds a prearranged symbol (one method is to hold a pen, a Heart Talk pillow etc.) may speak without interruption, while the listener clarifies what they have heard and communicates, "Tell me more."

The guidelines are an essential element to creating the emotional safety and trust necessary to make Heart Talks work. However, both partners need to consider the following prerequisites and commit to honouring them.
1. I promise not to withdraw emotionally or to leave physically. I will not reject you for anything you wish to share.
2. I will be committed to creating a safe space for you to express your most intimate feelings, staying open and vulnerable to you.
3. I am committed to not using what you say against you or to provoke an argument later.
4. I will be responsible for my emotions and I will not blame you for how I feel.
5. I will share the truth from my heart as caringly, honestly and respectfully as I can.
6. I will remain committed to you and this process and use any block or conflict that may arise as a stimulus to more learning and greater love.
7. I will not try to manipulate, defend or control what you communicate.
8. I commit to dealing with and working through any barriers that come up in our Heart Talks until there is mutual understanding.
9. I agree that we can disagree. I will allow you your feelings, understanding and point of view.
10. I agree to finish each Heart Talk session with at least one embracing hug and a sincere, "I love you".

Conversation Starters for Weekly Heart Talks

Talk over the following questions with each other, attempting to keep within the Heart Talks guidelines.
- The one thing that delighted me most about you this past week is …
- If you had the power to change one thing about me during this past week, I think you would like to change …
- The best thing that has happened to me during this past week is …
- The best thing that has happened to us as a couple during this past week is …
- What I would like us to do together during next week is …

Love & War: Devotional for Couples by John & Stasi Eldridge is an 8-week devotional with short daily thoughts and readings that could serve as conversational starters.[3]

Our Growth Plan

What I want for me as a person for this coming year:

What I want for you as a person for this coming year:

What I want for us:

In the light of our discussion we commit ourselves to:

Future Hopes And Aspirations

What I like about our marriage:

What I think could be better:

A dream that I have had for a long time and have not yet fulfilled is:

A dream that my spouse and I share and hope to fulfil is:

What immediate, measurable goal (or goals) can I set for continued growth in our marriage?

Worksheet on Evaluation

Marriage Enrichment Event Evaluation

☐ Husband
☐ Wife

How satisfied are you with the retreat? Use the number ratings below to circle those that apply to you:

1 = Very Dissatisfied; 2 = Dissatisfied; 3 = Neutral; 4 = Satisfied; 5 = Very Satisfied

A.	Venue and meals	1	2	3	4	5
B.	Cost	1	2	3	4	5
C.	Amount of time for discussion with my partner	1	2	3	4	5
D.	Amount of time alone with my partner	1	2	3	4	5
E.	Group discussion	1	2	3	4	5
F.	Length of sessions generally	1	2	3	4	5
G.	Amount of information given	1	2	3	4	5
H.	Discussion questions	1	2	3	4	5
I.	Film clips	1	2	3	4	5
J.	Saturday night activities	1	2	3	4	5
K.	Feeling comfortable with content	1	2	3	4	5
L.	Opportunity to ask my own questions	1	2	3	4	5
M.	Relevance to me personally	1	2	3	4	5
N.	Relevance to my relationship	1	2	3	4	5

Overall how would you rate the retreat you have just attended?

Dissatisfied	Poor	Satisfied	Good	Excellent
1	4	3	4	5

Presenter's	- style	1	2	3	4	5
	- clarity	1	2	3	4	5
	- openness	1	2	3	4	5
	- warmth	1	2	3	4	5

How did the retreat match your expectations?

Marriage Enrichment Event Evaluation (Cont.)

What topics or activities were particularly helpful?

What topics were not helpful and how could the retreat be improved?

What are the three most important aspects of this retreat for your relationship?

1).

2).

3).

Further comments

Notes to Chapter 11

1. Retrieved from https://www.brainyquote.com/quotes/francois_de_la_rochefouca_151053
2. H. Bloomfield, S. Vettese & R. Kory (1992). *Lifemates: The Love Fitness Program for a Lasting Relationship.* Penguin.
3. John & Stasi Eldridge (2012). *Love & War: Devotional for Couples.* Waterbrook Press

CHAPTER 12

CULTURAL ISSUES

Overview

This chapter explores cultural issues that influence ME groups. The chapter is organised under the following headings:

⇒ Cross-Cultural Effectiveness of ME

⇒ The Danger of Cultural Encapsulation and Ethnocentrism

⇒ Issues in Collective Cultures

⇒ Culturally Competent Leader Couples

Cross-Cultural Effectiveness of Marriage Enrichment

ME has been found to be effective in every culture. As mentioned in Chapter 1, every couple in every culture finds that "nurturant solace" offered by close relationships can protect them from physical and emotional illnesses and improve their resilience.[1] However, ME couples from differing cultures bring disparate value systems, beliefs and prejudices that can surface early in the life of an ME group. Considerable psychological damage can occur if positive norms regarding cultural diversity and racism are not quickly established. "The term culture encompasses the values, beliefs, and behaviors shared by a group of people. But culture does not just delineate an ethnic or racial heritage; it also can refer to groups identified by age, gender, sexual identity, religion, or socioeconomic status."[2]

> The beauty of the world lies in the diversity of its people.

Culture will influence our behaviour and that of other couples, with or without our awareness. Increasing our awareness of cultural values and personal assumptions will help us to work sensitively with culturally diverse couples.

> "Culture is the name for what people are interested in, their thoughts, their models, the books they read and the speeches they hear." (Walter Lippmann)

Pause for Reflection

CULTURAL DILEMMAS

Discuss the following questions:

1. Are you aware of any cultural universals?
2. Try to identify five behaviours or longings you believe to be universal.
3. Try to think of two examples of each of the following, selecting one example from your own culture and another from the culture of another society:
   a. Folklores
   b. Laws
   c. Taboos
4. What are some dominant values of Australian society?

The Danger of Cultural Encapsulation and Ethnocentrism

Differences between cultures can be minimised or ignored by leader couples.

Cultural encapsulation is defined as "the lack of understanding, or ignorance, of another's cultural background and the influence this background has on one's current view of the world... The purpose of this encapsulation, or 'cocoon,' is to allow people to protect themselves."[3] Consequently, differences between the cultures can be minimised or ignored by leader couples, resulting in cultural encapsulation; for example, a ME leader couple may devalue differences through the use of stereotypes based on individual-based learned assumptions about culture.[4] Thus, cultural encapsulation may inadvertently permeate the philosophy and practice of a Western ME group.

Ethnocentrism is similar but not identical to cultural encapsulation. It is defined as "the belief in the inherent superiority of one's own ethnic group or culture; a tendency to view alien groups or cultures from the perspective of one's own";[5] for example, problems arise when leader couples assume shared values with group members from a different culture when, in actuality, they are different.[6]

"Cultural differences should not separate us from each other, but rather cultural diversity brings a collective strength that can benefit all of humanity."
(Robert Alan)

Clearly, cultural encapsulation and giving priority to Western concepts of marriage can be counter-productive in culturally diverse groups. Cultural disparities that arise must be acknowledged and addressed in order to maintain transparency and to avoid imposing our values.[7] Reflection is required by leader couples on what it means to live in, and belong to, Western culture, including how gender relationships are arranged, how foreigners are treated, how the culture delineates what is appropriate for public and private domains[8] and how our own culture accommodates the cultural and religious practices of ethnic groups.

Issues in Collective Cultures

Collective voice

"The crucial differences which distinguish human societies and human beings are not biological. They are cultural."
(Ruth Benedict)

Traditionally, cross-cultural approaches to groups have been predicated on individualistic constructs. In collectivist societies, groups are implemented around family/kinship social relations, cultural obligation and spirituality that may fall outside of conventional Western conceptions.[9] In collective cultures the value of social harmony is paramount, and "opinions and votes are predetermined by [the] in-group".[10] The "in-group" is usually the extended family and cultural tradition. We have found that across cultures, our vulnerability through dialogue facilitates openness and encourages self and emotional disclosure that leads to relationship healing.[11] Perhaps this is because the vulnerability modelled by a leader couple demonstrates how to disclose and express emotional needs to a spouse. If couples are encouraged to access and explore painful emotions in their relationships, exploration optimally takes place within the context of "a corrective emotional experience".[12] Couple dialogue is a powerful tool to facilitate norms of vulnerability, emotional disclosure and "a corrective emotional experience" during a ME event.[13] In fact, couple dialogue is a tool that is effective across cultures in facilitating self-disclosure, increasing optimism and hope and building stronger relationships.

Moreover, individualistic values dictate that individuals are autonomous and able to change their circumstances.[14] However, in the Aboriginal community, "people will present issues that have influenced and affected the collective family group, rather than the individual. The individual themselves may not have a direct experience with the said issues but she/he will speak from a plural form as if they have had such an experience."[15] Couples from collective societies tend to seek help from their collective experience rather than as individuals. Typical Asian cultural beliefs are "forbearance, endurance, and nonaction".[16] Additionally, a more directive, structured, problem-solving approach is preferred. Therefore, facilitating response to conflict in ME needs to reflect the group identity and relational focus of collective societies.

Age and Authority

In many cultures, elders or people in authority roles (including leader couples) are seen as the ones with the answers. Therefore, a participant who offers a suggestion within the ME group might appear disrespectful, resulting in the loss of face. Further, asking questions or requesting clarification might be seen as implying an individual is unable to make him/herself clear or does not know what they are talking about. The leader couple could take time early in the group to clarify cultural differences of this kind.

> "A nation's culture resides in the hearts and in the soul of its people."
> (Mahatma Gandhi)

Group discussion

Different cultures also hold different ideas about what constitutes a normal, civil discussion, with implications for ME groups. Raised voices and a robust tone of voice may be interpreted very differently by different cultures. What one person would see as a normal, another might perceive as

> "We may have different religions, different languages, different colored skin, but we all belong to one human race."
> (Kofi Annan)

an angry argument. On the other hand, a person who expects more feeling and passion in a discussion might mistake a restrained or soft-spoken delivery as a lack of enthusiasm. Processing is vital in these situations.

Affect

There may be differences in the display of affect and emotionality. Westerners tend to be more direct in their communication, whereas in Asian cultures:

- restraint is valued; and,
- silence that may be uncomfortable for Westerners equals respect.

These disparities may result in dissimilar patterns of communication arising in ME groups. An undesirable norm can be created if an "open and obvious display of prejudiced attitudes and behaviors" is ignored, leading to "discounting what may be a significant part of identity of minority group members" and interfering with the "working through of the unfinished business of racial problems for group members".[17]

Self-disclosure

Our Story

Paula's Sri Lanka Journal Entry Extract

After the conference another young man conveys how beneficial the sessions have been for him and his wife (married for a year). He expresses that he learned that he demonstrates his love for his wife in ways he likes to receive it. Now he desires to show his love for her in her way. He articulates how he is encouraged by Barry's tears and reveals that he too, is emotional when speaking of things close to his heart. It has granted him a sort of permission to come out of hiding and he cements the exchange with a warm hug (unusual for Sri Lankan men).

> "Difference is of the essence of humanity. Difference is an accident of birth and it should therefore never be the source of hatred or conflict. The answer to difference is to respect it. Therein lies a most fundamental principle of peace: respect for diversity." (John Hume)

ME is predicated on a couple's self-disclosure to each other as necessary for change and growth in a relationship. However, in a collective society, to self-disclose is to risk judgement for lack of emotional discipline. Hence, there are cultural limitations on self-disclosure. Internal discipline is seen to attract respect. Collective societies are supposed to look to those who have faced similar experiences and have acquired enough inner strength and resilience to suppress their emotions.[18] In fact, self-disclosure can be akin to leaving a person with an "open wound".[19] Pressure to share or disclose family dynamics in a ME event can cause couples from collective cultures to experience internal conflicts with their values, traditions and restrictions. When it comes to resolving conflict, collective cultures tend to value "saving face", avoidance and the use of mediators to intervene.[20] Conversely, individualistic cultures tend to value self-expression, assertive strategies and speaking out as ways of resolving conflict.[21] As a result, a leader couple may inadvertently experience cultural bias in the way self-disclosure is modelled and in the way conflict is managed.

Paula's Sri Lanka Journal Entry

Both women had to ask permission from their husbands to tell their stories. When it was given, they told their stories in tedious detail (for about 20 minutes) as a way to seemingly contain their emotions. But when they could no longer contain, they broke down in tears. This vulnerability opened the group to deep sharing. Two of the men had tears in their eyes. This was counter-cultural.

> "Keep your language. Love its sounds, its modulation, its rhythm. But try to march together with men of different languages, remote from your own, who wish like you for a more just and human world."
> (Hélder Câmara)

Likewise, in *shame-based* cultures non-disclosure tends to be a product of using the emotion of shame for behaviour regulation.[22] A strong emphasis is placed on loyalty to the extended family that is intended to act as "a major source of identity and protection against life's hardships".[23] Shame appears to play a pivotal role in ensuring social correction and conformity, thus strengthening and reinforcing social bonds and a couple's sense of collective identity.[24] A leader couple must take this into account when conducting a session on family background.

Notably, self-disclosure tends to be a by-product of trust, but this could create a dilemma as couples from alienated minority groups may find it difficult to trust.[25] If a couple does not feel they belong in society at-large, they may have difficulty feeing they belong in a group that is representative of that society.

Confidentiality

Collective cultures tend to consider relationships to be primary and confidentiality is not as highly valued. Cultures high on the individualistic dimension may find this attribute confusing, as privacy and confidentiality are valued. Working cross-culturally, we have found that lack of self-disclosure is often due to fear of lack of confidentiality, safety and trust. Therefore, a confidentiality agreement at the beginning of an ME event is a major part of creating a safe place.

Our Story

Paula's Uganda Journal Entry Extract

The women are reluctant to speak. When I ask about their shyness, one very brave woman conveys that they fear their words will spread through the village and their husbands will punish them. They are especially afraid as recently a brave woman told her husband how she felt about him and he beat her to death. The fear is real and palpable. I think about how to break the silence and facilitate self-disclosure in a safe way. It comes. We split into triplets and promise confidentiality with raised hands. I stand back and observe, as several groups break free from their silent prisons. My heart leaps.

Experiential learning

Picture cards offer a safe way to externalise sensitive matters in a less threatening way than direct self-disclosure.[26] Cards allow a space in time when the couple is separated from the problem and enabled to gain some control by disclosing how a problem influences and impacts them. In ME, picture cards can promote identification with other couples and support of one another by breaking down barriers and developing trust and closeness through the sharing of lives. Picture cards are available for purchase from St. Luke's Innovative Resources, Victoria, Australia (https://innovativeresources.org/), and have been developed using a strengths-based approach.

Our Story

Paula's Uganda Journal Entry

We try an exercise with Bear Cards – pictures of bears expressing different feelings. I immediately wonder if this was a mistake as chaos breaks out trying to choose a card. Eventually, we are able to form a line stretching around the room, culminating at the table where the bears lie exposed.

It turns out to be a great move as each person shares or attempts to locate within themselves and verbalise a feeling. This is so foreign to the Acholi. We must begin small. Lunch is an hour-and-a-half late as they take time to express emotions using the bears! I cannot convey how much they loved these cards. They deliberated over them and their faces lit up with recognition of the feelings depicted.

Everyone wanted to share their bear card and, even though there were peals of laughter, identifying a feeling was ground-breaking in a culture where emotional discipline reigns.

Paula's Sri Lanka Journal Entry

I bring a set of Photolanguage cards with me. We lay them on the floor. I tell the couples that yesterday we talked about trauma and that words have different meanings to different people because we are unique. I ask them to choose a card that symbolises what trauma means to them. The sharing begins with those who were present yesterday and swells to the new couples.

We are staggered, as it has been so difficult to obtain participation in this culture and this morning we cannot stop the sharing. The stories range from everyday disappointments to the horrors of war. For two hours the sharing continues, by both men and women. We just sit and listen as one after another of the participants pops up and self-discloses. Tears flow with the sharing of grief and I discern how they need this, they need to tell their stories. I feel we are on sacred ground and I'm overwhelmed with the sense of privilege in being a trusted listener.

Paula's Sri Lanka Journal Entry

We do the Tree of Life drawing exercise on the second day. Visually impaired spouses are encouraged to use inner visualisation (they were able to see before their war injuries) and local team members come alongside and assist in the drawing. It promotes talking between couples, something that is foreign to most Tamils, for whom marriage is an arrangement with the wife ending up like a servant to the man and the family. Normally, she has to swallow her needs and pain and there appears to be a lot of depression. However, some self-disclosed for the first time.

Our Story

Couple dialogue appears to overcome the negativity of shame and hiddenness in all societies by facilitating self-disclosure within a safe, non-judgmental group environment. It can be transformative when demonstrated and applied within a collective framework that values an interdependent social system; for example, couple dialogue communicates to the opposite sex that they are valued for their role and contribution to the social system. Couple dialogue leads to the breaking down of the barriers erected by women's reticence in sharing their experiences.

In the following quote Esther explains how this is achieved in northern Uganda. "Women are always bottling their issues. They can't open up with a man. But they [the leader couple] had a wonderful way of bringing it out. I think everybody was like: Wow, that can work! Especially the women. There was a statement, 'I feel this when you do this', and 'I feel like this when you...' It's not, 'I'm attacking you'. So that was a new way of talking. I believe these are things that we need to know that will drop our negative cultures though they are still very strange because women don't talk like that. But if it works, if it could bring the marriage together. Why not try it although it could be strange to the culture?"

Culturally Competent Leader Couples

"Traditions are the guideposts driven deep in our subconscious minds. The most powerful ones are those we can't even describe, aren't even aware of."
(Ellen Goodman)

Cultural competence essentially means awareness of cultural differences. "The word competence is used because it implies having a capacity to function effectively".[27] Livingstone claims that "relationship building is fundamental to cultural competence and is based on the foundations of understanding each other's expectations and attitudes, and subsequently building on the strength of each other's knowledge, using a wide range of community members and resources to build on their understandings".[28]

The first phase of making the most of diversity is to make a concerted effort to become aware of the dimensions of cultural diversity that exist within a ME group. When conflicts, ill feelings or stressful situations arise, it may be linked to cultural differences. Acknowledging and valuing the differences between individuals and groups of people is a crucial initial phase. It is important that diversity is not merely tolerated. Differences can be considered strengths.

The second phase of making the most of diversity is for couples to talk about difference. Diversity can cause force couples out of their comfort zones, but it need not cause division. Two things can be remembered concerning cultural diversity.

1. It is difficult to address cultural differences without resorting to stereotypes. In the purest form, there is no such thing as a stereotype. No person is exactly like another person and no individual is a clone of another member of a group.
2. As diversity in a ME group grows, so does the complexity of communication and the need to spend greater effort developing improved communication skills.

It is imperative to set norms and goals, such as:

1. We are committed to discovering new levels of communication; and,
2. We want to establish an atmosphere of sensitivity, understanding and trust.

People in groups from different cultures share universal longings for connection and closeness. An appreciation and acceptance of both commonalities

> "A person without a culture is a slave."
> (Swahili proverb)

and differences are essential to effective working relationships. A variety of ideas, talents, skills and knowledge are desirable attributes to any group. Providing a supporting and nurturing environment enhances other group goals by exposing group members to new issues, ideas, information and cultures. Diversity creates opportunities for character development by teaching tolerance and respect for people and by encouraging concern for equity. Such a group will flourish.

Additionally, awareness and discussion are integral to gaining a clearer picture of cultural diversity. Major barriers to communication that interfere with

> "Strength lies in differences, not in similarities."
> (Stephen R. Covey)

people from diverse cultures working together must be addressed. Following are some guidelines to consider.

- Learn to listen for the message beneath the words – listen for what is really being said, not what you want to hear.
- Learn to communicate clearly and fairly.
- Do not misjudge people because of accent or grammar.
- Test for understanding – ask questions to be certain you are clear on what is being said.
- Use language that fosters trust and alliance, rather than harsh words. Each person wants to succeed in this venture. Be calm and positive.
- Articulate pluralistic values for the group; show ways in which they are an integral part of the group's mission and vision.
- Demonstrate ethical commitment to fairness and to the elimination of discrimination in all its forms in the group.
- Value ongoing personal learning and change, solicit views and opinions of diverse people, invite feedback about personal behaviour and blind spots and be open to belief modifications and actions based on feedback.
- Empower diverse individuals and encourage others to do so as well.[29]

Leader couples need to work on creating a safe, non-judgmental ME environment that facilitates every participant's empathy for their spouse and others, in ways that decrease their shame and hiddenness.

Our Story

An example from our experience demonstrates how cultural issues can be surmounted. Our Indian audience looked stunned. We had set up an ice-breaker exercise which required each participant to introduce their spouse. This meant that the women were required to speak in the group. This was not their cultural norm and we were aware of a degree of discomfort. The ice did not break very well and we launched into our retreat with the thought that perhaps we were not going to hear much from the wives.

Using various creative exercises, we began to coax the women into fuller participation. The group was not used to this type of learning but soon began to enjoy the interactive format so much so that our group expanded after each break as news spread that this marriage workshop was not just about providing information but engaging with the principles and actually talking with spouses. We shared our own struggles and learning with dialogues that surprised our audience but created a safe place to be vulnerable and honest.

Our dear translator was sweating profusely and visibly uncomfortable as he faithfully followed us through the usually unspoken subject of intimacy. He said to Paula, "If you can talk about these areas and you are a woman I can do it. But some of the words have many options for translation and if I slip the result will be very crude." The session on intimacy proved to be the most crucial one and afterwards the women came to Paula and hugged her, some of them crying. The relief felt among all of the couples was palpable. Women now participated freely and their husbands were unthreatened. Sometimes cultural barriers need a little nudge.

Pause for Reflection

Personal Reflections On Culture

Making the most of diversity in a group requires the commitment of all involved. Changing prevailing attitudes and assumptions is not easy. Often the only hope is to change behaviours rather than deep-seated attitudes. Members of a group must be committed to what they are doing and address issues related to cultural difference. There may be resistance to disturbing the status quo, but it is no excuse for avoiding change.

Attention to cultural diversity may be the necessary catalyst for change. Groups that strive to address specific needs and issues have no chance of success, or even continued existence, unless they mirror, understand and make the most of their members' cultural diversity. It is helpful to reflect on your attitudes and behaviour using the following questions.

1. In what ways does your own culture influence the way you think, feel, and act?
2. How prepared are you to understand and work with couples of different cultural backgrounds?
3. Do you feel more or less comfortable working with particular groups?
4. How might you increase your comfort level and skills with these groups?
5. How is your ME program providing the awareness, knowledge, and skills you

need to work in groups with diverse couple populations?

6. What kinds of life experiences have you had that will better enable you to understand and mix with people who have different worldviews?

7. What are areas of cultural bias that could inhibit your ability to work effectively with couples who are different to you? What steps might you take to challenge your biases?

8. How familiar are you with how various cultural groups perceive or respond to couples from your cultural group as well as those from their own cultural and ethnic identity group?

9. How would you feel if a couple shared these reactions or stereotypes with you?

Chapter Summary

- Marriage enrichment has been found to be cross-culturally beneficial in terms of marital adjustment and happiness.

- Cultural encapsulation and ethnocentrism can minimise the differences and/or devalue other cultures or lead one to view one's own culture as superior.

- Issues in collective cultures include value differences in terms of the value of social harmony and how opinions and decisions are predetermined by the group.

- Other issues include a collective voice rather one's own, deference to age and authority, inferences made in group discussions, restraint of affect and self-disclosure, and different understandings of confidentiality.

- Facilitating experiential learning is a way to overcome disparities in cultural learning.

- Culturally competent leader couples display an awareness of cultural differences, make a concerted effort to become aware of the dimensions of cultural diversity that exist within a ME group and encourage couples to talk about their differences.

- Leader couples provide strong leadership by creating a safe place through setting a norm that values cultural diversity.

Notes to Chapter 12

1. P.A. Davis (2016). *A Culturally Responsive Education Program for Trauma Counsellors in Developing Countries* (Doctoral thesis, Australian Catholic University). Retrieved from h2p://researchbank.acu.edu.au/theses/617; S.M. Johnson (2004). *The Practice of Emotionally Focused Couple Therapy: Creating Connection* (2nd ed.). Brunner/Routledge; S.E. Taylor (2002). *The Tending Instinct: How Nurturing Is Essential to Who We Are and How We Live*. Holt.

2. M.S Corey, G. Corey & C. Corey (2009). *Groups: Process and Practice* (8th ed.). Brooks/Cole–Cengage Learning, p.17.

3. L. McCubbin & S. Bennett (2008). Cultural encapsulation. In F. Leong (Ed.), *Encyclopedia of Counseling* (Vol. 3). SAGE Publications, pp.1091-1092.

4. T.A.A. Portman (2007). Ethics and multiculturalism. In R. Cottone & V. Tarvydas (Eds.), *Counselling Ethics and Decision Making* (3rd ed., pp. 212–226). Pearson/Merrill Prentice Hall.

5. American Heritage® Dictionary of the English Language (5th ed.) (2011). "ethnocentrism". Retrieved from http://www.thefreedictionary.com/ethnocentrism

6. M.A. Sayed (2003). Psychotherapy of Arab patients in the West: Uniqueness, empathy, and "otherness". *American Journal of Psychotherapy*, 57(4):445–460.

7. D. Eisenman, S. Weine, B. Green, J. De Jong, N. Rayburn, P. Ventevogel, A. Keller & G. Agani (2005). The ISTSS/RAND guidelines on mental health training of primary healthcare providers for trauma-exposed populations in conflict-affected countries. Retrieved from https://www.rand.org/content/dam/rand/pubs/working_papers/2005/RAND_WR 335.pdf; C. Stampley & E. Slaght (2004). Cultural countertransference as a clinical obstacle. *Smith College Studies in Social Work*, 74(2): 333–347. DOI: 10.1080/00377310409517719)

8. R.A. Shweder, M. Minow & H. Markus (2002). (Eds.). *Engaging Cultural Difference: The Multicultural Challenge in Liberal Democracies*. Russell Sage Foundation.

9. B.C.H. Kuo, G. Roysircar & I.R. Newby-Clark (2004). Development of the Cross-Cultural Coping Scale (CCCS): The implications of collective, avoidance, and engagement coping strategies for counselling. *Measurement and Evaluation in Counseling and Development*, 39(3):161–181.

10. G. Hofstede (2011). Personalizing cultures: The Hofstede model in context. *Online Readings in Psychology and Culture (ORPC)*, 2(1). Retrieved from http://scholarworks.gvsu.edu/cgi/viewcontent.cgi?article=1014&context=orpc, p. 11)

11. Davis, *A Culturally Responsive Education Program for Trauma Counsellors in Developing Countries*.

12. G. Corey, M. Schneider & P. Callanan (2003). *Issues and Ethics in the Helping Professions*. Brooks/Cole/Thomson Learning, p. 48; R. Sarles (1994). Transference–countertransference issues with adolescents: Personal reflections. *American Journal of Psychotherapy*, 48(1):64–74. DOI: 10.1111/j.1745-8315.2012.00575.x, p. 64.

13. Davis, *A Culturally Responsive Education Program for Trauma Counsellors in Developing Countries*.

14. D.W. Sue, & D. Sue (2008). *Counseling the Culturally Diverse: Theory and Practice* (6th ed.). John Wiley & Sons.

15. N. Pattel (2007). Aboriginal families, cultural context and therapy. *Counselling, Psychotherapy and Health*, 3(1):1-24. Retrieved from http://www.cphjournal.com/archive_journals/V3_I1_Pattel_1-24_2007.pdf, p. 8

16. Kuo et al., Development of the Cross- Cultural Coping Scale (CCCS), p. 161.
17. "discounting what may be a significant part of identity of minority group members" and interfering with the "working through of the unfinished business of racial problems for group members" (Beaton 1974 as cited in I.H. Johnson, J. Santos Torres, V.D. Coleman & M. Smith (1995). Issues and strategies in leading culturally diverse counseling groups. *The Journal for Specialist in Group Work*, 20(3):143–150. DOI: 10.1080/01933929508411338, p.81.
18. K.M. Asante (1984). The African American mode of transcendence. *Journal of Transpersonal Psychology*, 16(2):167–177; Davis, *A Culturally Responsive Education Program for Trauma Counsellors in Developing Countries*.
19. M. Dwairy & T.D. van Sickle (1996). Western psychotherapy in traditional Arabic societies. *Clinical Psychology Review*, 16(3):231–249. DOI: 10.1016/S0272-7358(96)00011-6, p. 236.
20. Hofstede, Personalizing cultures: The Hofstede model in context.
21. Ibid.
22. M.R. Creighton (1990). Revisiting shame and guilt cultures: A forty-year pilgrimage. *Ethos*, 18(3):279–307. DOI: 10.1525/eth.1990.18.3.02a00030
23. S.L. Dolan, & K.M. Kawamura (Eds.). *Cross Cultural Competence: A Field Guide for Developing Global Leaders and Managers*. Emerald Publishing Group, p. 109.
24. Davis, *A Culturally Responsive Education Program for Trauma Counsellors in Developing Countries*.
25. Johnson et al., Issues and strategies in leading culturally diverse counseling groups.
26. J. Cooney & K. Burton (1986). *Photolanguage Australia*. Catholic Education Office; Davis, *A Culturally Responsive Education Program for Trauma Counsellors in Developing Countries*.
27. T.L. Cross, B.J. Bazron, K.W. Dennis & M.R. Isaacs (1989). *Towards a Culturally Competent System of Care: A Monograph on Effective Services for Minority Children Who Are Severely Emotionally Disturbed*. Child Development Centre, Georgetown University, p. 1. Retrieved from http://www.ncjrs.gov/App/publications/abstract.aspx?ID=124939
28. R. Livingstone (2014). *What Does It Mean To Be Culturally Competent?* ACECQU. Retrieved from https://wehearyou.acecqa.gov.au/2014/07/10/what-does-it-mean-to-be-culturally-competent/#_ftn1
29. M. Loden & J.B. Rosener (1991). *Workforce America: Managing Diversity as a Vital Resource*. Business One Irwin

CHAPTER 13

HANDLING DIFFICULT SITUATIONS

Overview
This chapter explores handling difficult situations in a ME group. The chapter is organised under the following headings: ⇒ The Spouse Who Advertises the Faults of Their Mate ⇒ The Enthusiastic Spouse with the Super Dragee Mate ⇒ The Persistent Latecomer ⇒ Preaching Through Dialogue ⇒ When Couples Refuse to Dialogue ⇒ The Couple Consistently Stuck in Dialogue ⇒ The Couple Who Need Counselling Rather than Enrichment ⇒ The Problem of Sub-Groups

It is acknowledged that from time to time there will be difficulties arising within the ME group situation. In order to create a safe place for participants, difficult situations need to be handled perceptively and considerately. In addition, feedback needs to be given thoughtfully and sensitively with well-chosen, well-timed words. We must refrain from giving pat answers. Following are examples of some of the difficulties that may occur, together with some possible strategies for coping with these situations.

The Spouse Who Advertises the Faults of Their Mate

This is not consistent with the agreed group guidelines. It may be possible to share a concern privately with the person involved during the next break. If this persists, ask the couple to turn to each other and dialogue about it. Alternatively, the group may be invited to share concerns and to work together towards resolving the situation. It is not an occasion for exercising authority or power.

The Enthusiastic Spouse with the Super Dragee Mate

It is almost certain that the enthusiast will be harming their "Super Dragee" mate by forcing them to come to ME. If the Super Dragee is inhibiting the group process, there may be a need for one member of the leader couple to suggest quietly to the difficult couple that they slip away from the group with them privately for a few minutes with the comment

> "The knowledge that [he] had passed a loveless, institutionalized childhood and had escaped from his origins by prodigies of pure intellect, at the cost of all other human qualities, helped one to understand him – but not to like him."
> (Arthur C. Clarke, *A Fall of Moondust*)

that "something has come up unexpectedly". If you cannot convince the Super Dragee to participate, it might be best if the couple leave. However, you might like to make a time in the future to discuss the Super Dragee's extreme reluctance so that they are not excluded from similar events in the future. Also, you may suggest counselling if there is significant resentment from either spouse.

The Persistent Latecomer

There is no point alienating the individual or the couple who arrive late for sessions. Indicate at the start of a retreat that they will be missing out on important orientation and information. It is important for a leader couple to build up a reputation for punctuality so that everything commences at the set time; most people will soon fall into line with this. Indicate in the letter sent to couples prior to any event that punctuality is essential. Consistent lateness may be indicative of a continuing problem in a marriage, or it may simply be a symptom of a disruptive, dominant approach to others.

Preaching Through Dialogue

Occasionally a person may use a dialogue as a vehicle for preaching some kind of sermon. The spouse who does this may over-ride the other spouse and not give them a chance to respond in any meaningful way. In this case, it may be helpful to say, "Thank you for making that point so clear. Perhaps your spouse might like to share their insights on this particular issue." Or, "We need two sides of the picture so we do need to hear the other side".

> "Feeling compassion toward a dangerous person will not lead you to submit to them or put yourself at risk or condone their actions. What it does simply, is relieve your anxiety – which immediately makes you stronger and more resilient."
> (Laurie Perez, *Breakthrough: How to Have Compassion for Those Who Do Harm*)

It may be possible to point out that the person is restricting themselves to one or two styles of communication. It could also be helpful to refer back to the ground rules regarding advice giving.

Another way for the leader couple to address this is to say, "It seems to me that you are... and I am wondering if this is coming through to other group members. I need your help to clarify this." Another approach is, "I am troubled by the image you are projecting as this may be doing yourself harm and I want to protect you from this". It could also be that the person "preaching" may see that he/she is turning people off but may not know how to deal with the situation. As a last resort, it could be useful to model an effective form of dialogue privately with the couple concerned.

If a couple are critical of the leader couple's leadership of the group, it is possible to request the permission of the group to let the couple take the leadership for the rest of the session. It is always important to point out when the group guidelines are being broken. We are missing the important features of leadership if leader couples act aggressively or defensively.

When Couples Refuse to Dialogue

First of all, this is acceptable within the ground rules of the weekend. If this problem is serious, the leader couple may take the following line: "It would seem that we have not yet created the degree of trust or the atmosphere conducive to dialogue. We need to review this and see what the problem is." Another line would be: "We feel badly that people are not feeling free to participate and we are just wondering if anybody is feeling left out, unhappy or uncomfortable." It is entirely possible that people may not be in a state of readiness.

The emphasis on concerns always has great potential. Concerns take priority and it may be possible through these to identify whether there is hostility towards any individual or couple. It needs to be remembered that groups become what they are encouraged to become, and leader couples should help a group to break through any negativity. The group needs to be aware that it is valued by the leader couple.

The Couple Consistently Stuck in Dialogue

In a couple dialogue, one or other spouse may get stuck, with all the destructiveness that this implies. The leader may choose to make a variety of statements to open this area up. "Excuse me, I feel the need to say something at this point. It seems that you may be having a difficulty in communicating with your spouse. I think Mary may be hurting. It is good that you are trying to say something to her but it seems that you may not be getting through. Perhaps there is a need to help you in this." This is not an attack on the person but, rather, a statement offering support in building effective communication. Another way is to ask, "Would you like some help to get your meaning across?" The most common response is "Yes". There may be a need to take the heat off if one spouse is obviously uncomfortable. This can be done in various ways including, "Mary doesn't seem to be getting through at the moment and I am wondering if someone else would like to take this issue up. We will come back to you after you have had a chance to relax."

This may be an opportunity to use a technique shared in a leader workshop facilitated by Ian and Gerlinde Spencer, the couple who wrote the foreword to the manual. They described the process and used us as volunteers to demonstrate how it could be employed.

We have "doubled" with other couples on a number of occasions when they have become stuck in the "dance of destruction" of secondary emotions. This technique, like parroting, helps remove the volatility and heightened emotion from the interchange. It allows the individuals to see the underlying feelings of the other and helps to formulate and convey their deeper issues.

The leader couple continue the conversation from the place where it became stuck. The couple do not talk to each other. They now speak through their "alter ego": the male leader for the husband and the female leader for the wife. In fact, the husband and wife become coaches of the leader couple, correctimg any misrepresentation, and are consulted prior to any compromise or solution that may be suggested. The leader couple continue the conversation searching for the underlying messages and acknowledging and validating feelings that have been ignored in the "dance of destruction". They constantly check with their "coach". The seating arrangement is a square with the spouses sitting opposite each other and their "alter ego" on the adjacent corner.

The conversation might sound like: "Can we come over and help you in this conversation? We will sit beside you and endeavour to try and speak for each of you. Tell us if you think we are saying what you are wanting to say and let us know if you think we are missing it." The leader couple can then take up the conversation in place of the couple in question by identifying the problem through dialogue via conversation on their behalf; for example, "Mary, I feel that I am not getting through to you and I need your help." The other spouse in the leader couple team can then respond, "Well, Tom, you're coming over as..."

After this kind of conversation has proceeded for a while, the leader couple can turn to Tom and say, "Tom, am I representing you adequately? Would you like to take this conversation over again? If it becomes too hard difficult, we will be happy to help you out again. We see that you want to get through to each other and all we want to do is help you." Doubling can alleviate conflict and "stuckness".

Hopefully the spouses are able to hear each other's pain, understand each other and be more in touch with their own pain and feelings. The leader couple are removed from the emotion and are not tied into the history of the issue. This usually enables them to move to an acceptable resolution and deeper understanding, which enables the couple to move through the conflict. The doubling ends when the couple are happy with the outcome.

The Couple Who Need Counselling Rather than Enrichment

A couple who need counselling can consume a great deal of time on a retreat. Other couples become counsellors instead of being enriched themselves. In this situation it is necessary to take the couple aside and explain that more time is needed to help and the support necessary is more than the group can provide.

It is important to pledge the help of the leader couple and then to welcome the couple back into the group. "We want you to feel a part of the situation but there is a need to allow people who have come to work through their situations." When a crisis does arise, it is often very helpful to have a period of silence to reflect and to talk quietly before moving on.

The Problem of Sub-Groups

There is always the possibility that sub-groups may emerge within a retreat group. This can be raised through concerns expressed by the leader couple in various ways – for example, "I have the feeling that some of you may be clinging together. Perhaps I am not right – but I am wondering if my feeling has any foundation. I notice that some of you have preferred to sit together, I am wondering if you would like to rearrange yourselves." Anything of this nature is an attempt to face a difficulty straightforwardly and lovingly.

If there is a need for a change or correction within a group, the situation has to be faced directly and not through manoeuvring, which would be duplicitous. A sub-group may not always be bad, but there is value in couples rotating at meals and avoiding consistent contact with friends who may have come with them on the retreat.

Our Story

The couples are dialoguing well, as chatter fills the room following a session on sexuality. A wife shushes the group, indicating that she has something important to convey. She asks, "Can a husband rape his wife in marriage?" Her husband leans back, crosses his ankles and puts his hands behind his head. The room grows eerily quiet, everyone eagerly waiting for a response. Time seems to be suspended. I (Paula) sense Barry's reluctance, as he waits for me to catch the ball that has been thrown into my court.

I reply, "I am wondering if you are talking about yourself. This forum is not suitable to answer your question, but I am happy to meet with you both over lunch and chat." Over lunch, she spills her story in the safety of another. It is a story of her husband's attempts to gain and maintain power and control over her through a wide range of abusive behaviours.

I listen without judging, offering validation of her courage and strength in sharing this information. To him I respectfully convey that he is responsible for the abuse and for stopping it. I let him know that he is actually damaging himself and that, if he continues, he will end up alone and lonely without the connection he craves. I refer him to health care professionals who conduct groups for perpetrators.

Difficult situations sometimes arise where it is especially tricky to convey acceptance for the person (not the behaviour) and remain free of judgement.

Chapter Summary

In order to create a safe place for participants, difficult situations need to be handled perceptively and considerately.

Several situations that may arise are:
- The spouse who advertises the faults of their mate.
- The enthusiastic spouse with the super dragee mate.
- The persistent late comer.
- Preaching through dialogue.
- When couples refuse to dialogue.
- The couple consistently stuck in dialogue.
- The couple who need counselling rather than enrichment.
- The problem of sub-groups.

CHAPTER 14

GIVING FEEDBACK

Overview
This chapter explores giving feedback to ME couples. The chapter is organised under the following headings:

⇒ What is Feedback?

⇒ People Perceptions

⇒ Statement of Values for Feedback Givers

What Is Feedback?

Feedback is the sharing of your thoughts and/or feelings about another's behaviour. It involves dealing with content that is related to either personal characteristics or performance in a skill area. For our purposes, feedback is divided into two categories.

> ### Positive Feedback

> ### Negative Feedback

1. *Positive feedback.* Deals with behaviours that we think are effective or about which we have positive feelings.
2. *Negative feedback.* Deals with behaviours that we think are ineffective or about which we have negative feelings (note: negative feedback is not necessarily bad feedback).

Examples:

- *Positive feedback.* "I am pleased that you had the courage to bring up ……. in the group. Did you notice how it was received?"
- *Poor Negative feedback.* "When you did ……., you disrupted the group."
- *Good negative feedback.* "When I heard that comment, I felt ……."

Why offer feedback to couples? Feedback is offered in order to:

1. help the recipient and others. When we give feedback, we are offering valuable information that can be useful in skill development and interpersonal effectiveness.
2. build and maintain closeness to others. Positive feedback helps couples feel good and increases the probability that behaviours that build closeness will be repeated. While it may be painful to hear, it makes it possible for couples to discuss and work through a problem area, rather than avoid the problem and grow apart.

> "We all need people who will give us feedback. That's how we improve."
> (Bill Gates)

Feedback and debriefing are crucial to assess if the intended learning has taken place. The purposes of feedback and debriefing include the following.

- To bring the couple back into the group.
- To clarify what happened during their time together.
- To dissolve tension or anxiety.
- To bring out assumptions, feelings and changes that occurred.
- To give participants opportunities to develop self-observation and self-awareness.
- To reflect on why things happened the way they did.
- To develop observational skills of other people.
- To draw conclusions about behaviour.
- To draw out new points for consideration.
- To reinforce good learning.
- To reflect on ways of improving couples' relationships.
- To help couples to apply learning to other situations.

Pre-feedback considerations

Before deciding to give feedback, especially negative feedback, consider the following.

- Good feedback is intended to help, not punish, put down, or create distance. Ask ourselves: Do we honestly want to help? Have we been asked for help? If not, do not attempt feedback.

- Giving feedback means becoming more involved with another person or couple by sharing our feelings and perceptions. In some cases, additional time is required to discuss the feedback and deal with the feelings provoked by the feedback. Are we willing to become involved and spend time? If not, we can postpone our feedback.

- In general, feedback should not be imposed on someone or a couple who does not want it. Sometimes the receiver explicitly asks for feedback. At other times there is an implicit agreement between two people about the giving of feedback. If we do not know how the person or couple feels, it is acceptable to tentatively ask: "I have some feedback for you. Would you like to hear it?"

- Effective feedback is best offered at a time when the receiver appears to be ready to receive it. When a potential receiver is preoccupied or experiencing deep emotions; for example, sadness, isolation et cetera, it is usually best to postpone.

- Good feedback is directed toward behaviour over which the receiver has some control. Frustration is only increased when someone is reminded of a characteristic that he/she cannot do anything about.

- Negative feedback is enhanced by specific suggestions for improvement. Before offering feedback, ask ourselves, "How can this person behave more effectively?"

(Source: David H. Johnson (1973), *Reaching out: Interpersonal effectiveness and self-actualisation,* Prentice-Hall)

Guidelines for giving non-threatening feedback

Guidelines for giving non-threatening feedback include checking perceptions and communicating them in a non-threatening way. Notably, feedback has two functions.

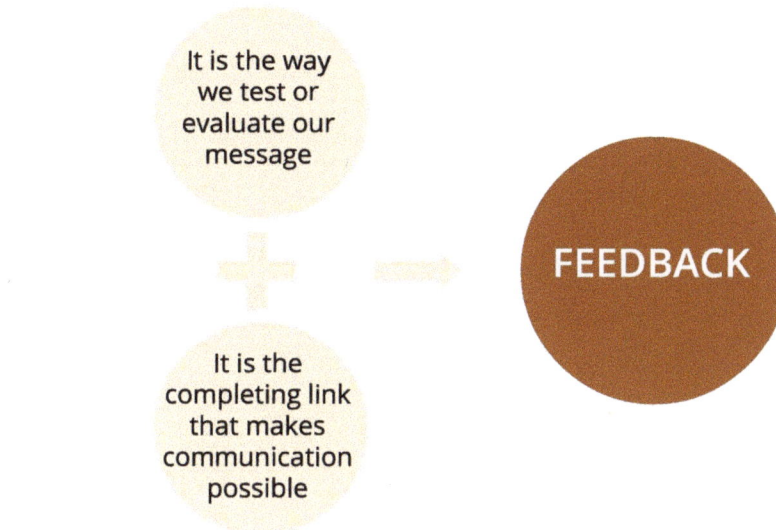

It is the way we test or evaluate our message

+ → **FEEDBACK**

It is the completing link that makes communication possible

Feedback involves self-disclosure about how we are reacting to how another person or couple is behaving. The purpose of feedback is to provide constructive information to help them become aware of how their behaviour affects us and how we perceive their actions. It is important to give feedback in a way that will not threaten them nor increase their defensiveness. The more defensive an individual or couple become, the less likely it is that they will accurately hear and understand feedback.

Once the decision to offer feedback has been made, the way in which feedback is given becomes important. Characteristics of helpful, non-threatening feedback include the following.

> "Criticism, like rain, should be gentle enough to nourish a man's growth without destroying his roots." (Frank A. Clark)

- Give feedback that is descriptive of what the receiver is doing, but not evaluative or judgmental about what he is as a person; for example, *do not say*, "You're stupid". This makes a judgment about the receiver as a person and is very likely to provoke a defensive response. A more effective piece of feedback is, "I think your last response missed the intensity of Joan's feelings. You said irritated. She sounded furious to me!"
- When giving feedback, share your observations and reactions, rather than giving advice or being judgemental (offering an evaluation in terms of good or bad, right or wrong, nice or not nice); that is, share your feelings and/or thoughts about the receiver's behaviour, rather than their personhood. This helps build trust. A good way to do this is to use phrases such as, "I noticed...", "I liked...", I didn't like...", "I thought...", "I felt..."; for example, "When you backed her up in the meeting today, I felt relieved". Or, "I liked your response to Jane. You picked up on the sadness in her voice." Or, "I was angry when I saw you controlling Janet".
- Be specific rather than general in your feedback; for example, avoid saying "Your responses have been pretty good", "You never ....", "You always ....". Instead, say "I especially like the way you confronted Bob. Your response to him was clear and accurate, yet respectful."

- State your feedback clearly and directly; for example, do not say "John, I have been sort of wondering, well, I have been thinking that maybe, perhaps, you know, well, remember when you were kind of talking today, and you know you said how you felt about Jane, well, I sort of don't know about that, maybe". Instead, say "John, when we were talking you said you were not too sure about Jane. I'm not sure Jane understand what you meant by that".
- Respect the couple's right to make the final decisions about their behaviour. Do not order people around or tell them what to do.
- Do not give a person or couple more feedback than they can handle at one time. This leads to information overload.
- In general, give feedback as soon as possible after the behaviour in question (depending on time factors and the receiver's readiness to hear feedback).
- In a group setting, feel free to check out your perceptions with other group members: "Is that OK with you?"
- Use honest, positive feedback freely. By pointing out strengths to capitalise on, you can help a person or couple as much as, if not more, than by commenting on ineffective behaviour.

> "What is the shortest word in the English language that contains the letters: abcdef? Answer: feedback. Don't forget that feedback is one of the essential elements of good communication." (Unknown)

People Perceptions

When receiving feedback, we tend to process incoming information in terms of our values, expectations and perceptions of people. These sets of assumptions affect the communication strategies we select. Virginia Satir writes in *Peoplemaking* that:

> This is how it works. You are face to face with me; your senses take in what I look like, how I sound, what I smell like, and, if you happen to touch me, how I feel to you. Your brain then reports what this means to you, calling upon your past experience, particularly with your parents and other authority figures, your book learning, and your ability to use this information to explain the message from your senses. Depending upon what your brain reports, you feel comfortable or uncomfortable – your body is loose or tight.
>
> Meanwhile, I am going through something similar. I too, see, hear, feel something, think something, have a past, have values and expectations, and my body is doing something. You don't really know what I am sensing, what I am feeling, what my past is, what my values are and exactly what my body is doing. You have only guesses and fantasies, and I have the same about you. Unless the guesses and fantasies are checked out, they become 'the facts' and as such can often lead to traps and ruptures.[1]

> "The difficult people who we encounter can be our greatest teachers."
> (Eileen Anglin)

By increasing our awareness of our internal values, we can identify our habits of communicating, examining them and modifying or extending them as appropriate. Interpersonal communication is effective when we have the ability to check the impressions we form of other people based on our own perceptions of their messages and signals. In this way we are, in fact, testing the accuracy of our perceptions and attributions.

The characteristics and motivations that we attribute to other people are based on our selective perceptions and assumptions and might indicate more about ourselves than they do about the other person.

Pause for Reflection

What helps communication?

_____

_____

_____

What blocks communication?

_____

_____

_____

Stereotyping and discrimination

Stereotyping occurs when we treat an individual as part of a group and ignore their particular characteristics. *Discrimination* occurs when the stereotype is acted upon. The stereotypes can be positive or negative but are usually irrational. Examples might be:

- "Men are aggressive."
- "Women are emotional."
- "Foreigners don't care about our plight/"
- "Educators are sensitive people"
- "Living standards in our country are lower than they were 50 years ago"

Pause for Reflection

What stereotypes tend to occur in marriages?

_____

_____

_____

How can we use communication principles to deal with these stereotypes?

_____

_____

_____

Statement of Values for Feedback Givers

"By sharing my perceptions and feelings about your behaviour, I want to help you – that is, if it is OK with you. I want to offer information called feedback that will be useful to you in making decisions about what you do. I want to let you know where I stand, what I like and what I do not like, not to put you off, but to build trust and closeness between us. I respect you. I acknowledge your responsibility for yourself and your right to make the final decisions about what you do and how you do it."

Our Story

Dominant

Paul dominates our group. He has an opinion and special knowledge on every question, even the rhetorical ones. Sharon, his wife, says nothing. We try a number of muzzling type manoeuvres, like asking for a response from someone who hasn't said anything, even requesting that a wife share her thoughts. It doesn't work: his presence abates very little. Our question to the group is too juicy for him to resist, and I see him ready to interject. Paula says, "How about you turn to Sharon and talk to her about this issue". His energy diffuses and he mumbles a few words to his wife. Paula then asks Sharon if she would like to respond. She does and the balance of the group is restored.

Sharon and Paul are committed to working on their marriage and inclined to explore becoming a leader couple. Their practice dialogues are still dominated by Paul and this will need to be addressed by some feedback. Group feedback is incredibly valuable, because it is not just the opinion of one person and must be handled carefully. Paul and Sharon would benefit from leader couple feedback; for example, "Paul, have you noticed that in conversation your words appear to fill the majority of the space? I am wondering how this works for you? Is this something you are aware of?"

To his credit Paul allows the questions to lodge in his heart and with his eyes on Sharon he shares how habitual this is. He knows he is doing it but can't seem to draw back. "If my words fill the space then I don't have to receive your words. I am afraid", he tells his wife. He then shares some of the details of a troubled childhood filled with caustic and constant words tearing at his worth and the misery of knowing that what he is doing actually creates animosity in his frustrated listeners. He is ready to begin the hard work of change.

Chapter Summary

- The characteristics and motivations that we attribute to other people are often based on our own selective perceptions that might indicate more about ourselves than they do about the other person.
- The accuracy of our perceptions and attributions about people need to be tested.
- Stereotyping occurs when we treat an individual case as part of a group and ignore the particular characteristics of the individual.
- Discrimination occurs when the stereotype is acted upon. The stereotypes can be positive or negative but are usually irrational.
- Feedback is the sharing of your thoughts and/or feelings about another's behaviour.
- It is important to give feedback in a way that will not be threatening and increase defensiveness.
- Giving non-threatening feedback includes providing constructive information to help couples become aware of how their behaviour affects us and how we perceive their actions.

Notes to Chapter 14

1. Virginia Satir (1990). *Peoplemaking.* Souvenir Press, p. 72.

PART D

ADDITIONAL WORKSHEETS AND RESOURCES

CHAPTER 15

ADDITIONAL WORKSHEETS

Overview
This chapter includes additional resources for use in a ME event. The chapter is organised under the following headings: ⇒ The Sexual Connection ⇒ When the Past Enters the Present ⇒ The Spiritual Connection ⇒ Future Hopes and Dreams

A. The Sexual Connection

Sexual problems present a powerful opportunity for growth. Difficulties in the sexual area are often about disconnection rather than personal defects. Sexuality can become reactive and cause painful, lonely disconnection. Then we might settle for less and ignore the scary, painful pursuit of connection and intimacy. Nevertheless, "sexual healing... comes through the process of reclaiming our sexuality in relationship with our spouse".[1]

The leader couple will benefit from learning about the basics of sexual desire – how often is normal, the effects of pornography, male and female differences in arousal, impotence, menopause and premature ejaculation. Couples often crave this information and it can be conveyed in a respectful, safe environment. However, we caution couples that what is said about sexuality is in no way intended to be prescriptive. There is tremendous variation between and within genders. We convey that we will speak in generalities and do not wish to stereotype.

Husband and wife love languages

This is an area of generalities and often it is reversed, especially if there has been unwanted past sexual activity. Nevertheless, generally, a husband's sex drive tends to have a huge influence on his life. For many men the desire to have sex with their wives is beyond strong. Being desired sexually is one of his deepest needs – he will feel close to his wife, in love, confident and like a man. His need for regular, passionate touch and sex is hard-wired into him and is directly connected to his mental health.[2] Closely aligned is his need for respect. If his wife does not meet his need for physical intimacy, he will not feel respected. It is a man's love language. Being desired, respected and honoured are three of his deepest needs.[3]

Generally, a wife needs to feel loved through emotional connection. Agreeing to sex is different from desiring sex. A husband wants his wife to desire him sexually. If a wife sees sex as just another chore, it is better to have no sex than to strip away his manhood and humiliate him. Yet, a wife needs to be loved unconditionally and completely by her husband in order to desire him sexually; this is her love language. She needs to feel provided for and fought for to feel secure. Before the physical bonding can occur, she needs a strong emotional bond. When a husband consistently meets her need for emotional intimacy, she will feel closer to him, be drawn to him physically, and will likely be responsive sexually and tend to pursue her husband sexually.[4]

Fostering a safe emotional bond

Fostering a safe emotional bond is crucial for good sex. If the husband initiates and meets his wife's need for emotional bonding, she feels safe and confident in his love and can then meet his sexual needs. If the wife desires her husband and respects him, he willingly gives his love to her and protects and honours her.

Our Story

The silence in the room is palpable, as we began a session on sexuality in India. The women draw their veils across their faces, becoming increasingly bashful as we introduce the session. Nevertheless, everyone is riveted.

The interpreter stumbles over words. Later, he tells us how in his language, there are about six meanings to one word. If he chooses the wrong one, it will come across as vulgar. He is only able to relax into it when he tells himself, "If Paula, a woman, can talk of such things, it is OK for me to translate it".

Those in our group have little or no information about sex, as it is a taboo subject in their homes and society. During our session, there is no group interaction, even from those who have been vocal in other sessions. As we dialogue about past and present areas of struggle for us, we sense the alertness and listening in the room.

Later, as we stand in a circle and ask what they are taking away from this session, the women come to me, falling on my neck, some with sobs and relief at knowing they are not alone. With no language, empathy is conveyed through eyes and touch. It is a moving finale to a sensitive topic.

Worksheets on Sexuality

Unlocking Intimacy In Our Relationship

- How satisfied are we with our sexuality and/or sexual relationship? If this could be improved, how might we raise our level satisfaction?

- How satisfied are we with the level of space and closeness in our relationship? What could make a difference?

- How hidden are we with each other? If we could be less hidden, what might make a difference?

- Is the frequency and style of our love making satisfactory to us? If this could be improved, what might make a difference?

- Can we talk about affection and touch honestly? If this could be improved, what might make a difference?

- Is there enough touch in our relationship outside of sexual situations? If this could be improved, what might make a difference?

Reflections On Intimacy In Our Marriage

Complete alone. Using a 0 – 10 scale, rate the following areas in your relationship as honestly as possible. Then sensitively share your perceptions with your mate.

0 = none   10 = highly satisfied

1. Emotional intimacy

0----1----2----3----4----5----6----7----8----9----10

2. Sexual intimacy

0----1----2----3----4----5----6----7----8----9----10

3. Intellectual intimacy

0----1----2----3----4----5----6----7----8----9----10

4. Communication intimacy (sharing all types of intimacy)

0----1----2----3----4----5----6----7----8----9----10

5. Work intimacy (the closeness of sharing jobs/tasks)

0----1----2----3----4----5----6----7----8----9----10

6. Recreational intimacy

0----1----2----3----4----5----6----7----8----9----10

7. Crisis intimacy (closeness in sharing/support in problems and pain)

0----1----2----3----4----5----6----7----8----9----10

8. Conflict intimacy (facing and struggling with differences)

0----1----2----3----4----5----6----7----8----9----10

9. Spiritual intimacy (the connection from sharing core values/concerns)

0----1----2----3----4----5----6----7----8----9----10

10. Commitment intimacy

0----1----2----3----4----5----6----7----8----9----10

What are my thoughts and feelings about this?

What areas could be improved and how might we improve them?

My Sexual Biography

- How do you think your parents felt when you were born?

- Can you remember your parents touching you as a child (e.g. tickling, cuddling, wrestling, etc)?

- When did either of them stop?

- Do you recall your parents saying "I love you" to you?

- What were your parent's views on pleasure and play?

- Were they affectionate towards each other or was there an undercurrent of tension and aggression?

- What was their attitude to nudity?

- When did you realise your parents had sex together and how did you feel about it?

- Looking back, how would you rate your parents' sex life?

- When did your parent(s) first speak to you about sex? How did this feel?

- What kind of hidden messages do you think you received from your parents with regard to sexuality?

- How and when did you first learn about sex?

- Were there any early sexual experiences that were uncomfortable, embarrassing or humiliating for you?

- What was your earliest sexual experience?

- How did you feel about the changes in your body at puberty?

- What messages did your teenage friends and peer groups give you about sexuality?

- What kind of attitudes to sex do you consider you acquired during childhood?

- Which of these do you not feel safe sharing with your spouse?

- What kind of attitudes to sex do you consider you acquired during your developmental years?

- My thoughts and feelings as I complete this are...

- Which question do I NOT want to share with my spouse?

Sensitively share one or two questions with your spouse as time allows.

Sexual Satisfaction Inventory

How satisfied am I with...

	None	Not Satisfied	Could Be Better	Mostly Satisfied	Highly Satisfied
Preparation for Love-Making					
Expression of love, tenderness and affection					
Romance in our marriage					
Time commitment to sex					
Time away together					
Bathing, perfumes, body oils					
Privacy for love-making					
Build-up to love-making					
Atmosphere for love-making					
My spouse's interest in sex					
Initiation of love-making					
Love-Making					
Overcoming our inhibitions					
Communicating sexual needs/desires					
Loving caressing of body					
Tuning in to what my spouse wants					
My spouse tuning in to what I want					
Sensitivity to moods and feelings during love play					
Connection during love-making					
More prolonged love-making					
Achieving satisfactory orgasm					
Frequency of love-making					
After Intercourse					
Sharing closeness and warmth to each other					

My Sexuality

- I feel good about being a man/woman when...

- I dislike being a man/woman when...

- Which is nearest to my own attitude:
    - ☐   I feel good about my body.

    - ☐   My body is not perfect but it is ok.

    - ☐   I try not to think much about my body.

    - ☐   I wish my body were different.

- Sharing my body with my spouse is...

- I like to be touched...

- I dislike being touched...

- When my spouse shows affection in public I feel...

- Most people have sexual fantasies. I feel about mine...

- What I want most out of our sex life together is...

- If there is any "unfinished business" (sexual trauma, abuse, other sexual partners, etc.) about my past sexual experiences, how can I set about sorting this out?

- Which of these responses do I not want to share with my spouse now?

Sexual Inventory

	Yes	No	Maybe
I would like to make love sometimes in the morning.	—	—	—
A sexy nightgown would add to our intimate relationship.	—	—	—
We have been overcome with passion in our lovemaking.	—	—	—
I would like us to kiss in a crowded lift (or do adventurous/romantic things together).	—	—	—
It would really make me happier if we were more playful in bed.	—	—	—
I think my spouse would really like me to show more interest in sex.	—	—	—

I think our lovemaking is		Yes	No	Maybe
	positive	—	—	—
	relaxed	—	—	—
	pleasant	—	—	—
	physically satisfying	—	—	—
	emotionally satisfying	—	—	—
	spiritually satisfying	—	—	—

B. When the Past Enters the Present

This session is about breaking free from those patterns in our parents' marriage that we have unknowingly accepted as our relationship model.

We bend and twist like a windblown tree

On a recent trip to Rottnest Island, we noticed that when the wind constantly blows from one direction, the trees grow under that influence and bend and twist. That happens in our lives, too, in that sometimes people grow up bent and twisted. We bend and twist in a certain direction due to the pressures applied to us by our families. We learn to do what we are shown.

Sometimes this is positive, but at other times it may be an injustice, or even abuse; for example, quickness to anger, substance abuse, chauvinism, sexism, racism, physical or sexual abuse. Family systems pass these negative traits down from generation to generation. The only way to break this transgenerational bondage is to deal with it.

Family of origin influences everything (FOOIE). In the beginning of a relationship, couples often tussle over whose family of origin is going to set the template for their relationship. We need to encourage couples to break free from patterns in their parents' marriage that they have unknowingly accepted as their relationship model and instead intentionally create their own.

Key Exercises

There are a few key exercises that are effective in this area. They can be adapted for your ME purposes. The first involves inviting couples to engage their imaginations. We then ask them to imagine the following.

> "I believe God takes the things in our lives – family, background, education – and uses them as part of his calling. It might not be to become a pastor. But I don't think God wastes anything." (Eugene H. Peterson)

- Your parents are behind a screen.
- You are watching their relationship.
- How do they model marriage?
- Do you want your marriage to look like theirs?
- What do you want to take from theirs into your own relationship?
- What do you want to leave behind?

While couples are still imagining, we move on to the second part of the exercise.

- Now, you are both behind a screen.
- Your children are watching your relationship.
- How do you model marriage?
- Do you want your children to have a marriage like yours?
- What might they want to take from yours into your own relationship?
- What might they want to leave behind?

The second imaginative exercise involves providing large sheets of butcher's paper and crayons. We read from the following script.

> Sit comfortably... close your eyes... take a few deep breaths... and breathe out any tiredness... relax...
>
> Visualise the house or flat you lived in that was most important to you before you were 10 years old... If you lived in many... choose the one that was the most significant... Imagine yourself as a child again standing outside that house... Now...

recall the neighbourhood around the house where you lived... take a walk around the neighbourhood... walk to your school... walk in the gate... look around...

Now... leave the school and walk to the place you would hang out... walk to the house or flat you lived in... notice the front garden if there is one... walk to the door... open it and step inside... take a tour of your house or dwelling... notice the different rooms... Try to recapture the sights... and sounds... and smells... of each room... Try to capture the experiences and feelings you associate with each... Walk around the living room... the kitchen...your siblings room... your room... your parents or caretakers rooms... where your family spent most of their time... where you spent most of your time... and so on...

Then, we invite each person to draw a floor plan of their house or dwelling and complete the handouts, *Family Background* and *Family Roles* handouts (see below). We invite them to take their spouse on a tour of their house or dwelling, explaining each room and sharing their answers to the questions on the handouts.

The third exercise is about family memories. It involves the following instructions.

- Draw one or two early childhood memories.
- Create a title for each memory, as if you are writing a pithy newspaper headline that captures its essence.
- What important themes does the memory capture about your past and your present marriage relationship; for example, conflicts, emotions, attitudes, values etc.? The title of the story often helps to clarify this.

Our Story

The first time I (Paula) tentatively ventured into looking at my past was in the first ME retreat we attended. We were given sheets of butcher's paper and crayons and asked to draw a floor plan of our home (or the home that influenced us most) from our childhood. An accompanying handout had questions about living in that house. Then we were asked to take our spouse through a guided tour of our floor pan.

Tears caught me unawares. In fact, the depth of pain surprised and scared me. Unable to contain the depth of my grief, I exited the room and went for a walk in an attempt to soothe the storm within.

This is an example not only of how experiential activities reach previously defended hard places, but of how the past influences the present. In time, I was able to open this previously locked door and find hope and healing. Yet, it was this activity that began the long journey.

Worksheets on When the Past Enters the Present

Family Background

Do alone, then share with your spouse.

- What was your house like?

- Who lived there?

- Where did each of you spend the most time?

- How were the chores divided?

- Which particular rooms were special for you?

- Who did you talk to about your concerns and problems?

- What things were <u>not</u> safe to talk about?

- Remember a time when something good happened to one of your family.

- What was said or done to celebrate and express joy?

- Remember a time when there was a cause for weeping because of a loss or family trauma. What was said or done to express sorrow?

- How was touch and affection expressed?

- How was privacy handled?

- How was anger and conflict handled?

- In what ways am I like my mother/father?

- Something from my childhood home that I want to transfer to my current home is...

- Something from my childhood home that I do <u>not</u> want in mine is...

Family Roles

Who took the initiative or the primary responsibility for the following activities?	Father/Carer	Mother/Carer
Ironing		
Preparing meals		
Shopping		
Cleaning the house		
Washing		
Budgeting		
Paying the bills		
Managing the finances		
Mowing the lawn		
Repairing the house		
Servicing the car		
Disciplining the children		
Spiritual training		
Leader in spiritual things		
Head of the house		
Remembering birthdays		
Buying gifts		
Replying to couple emails		
Feeding the pets		
Laughed the most		
Crying the most		
Inviting guests home		
Offering help to others		
Making major decisions		
Talking the most		
Settling family arguments		
Showing the most affection		
Showing the most sensitivity		
Encouraging the most		
Planning major events (holidays, etc.)		
Listening to family member's concerns		

What does this reveal to you?

My Family History

The person who influenced me most outside of my family was...

The nicest thing about my family was...

One thing that was not so nice...

The ways I am like my mother are...

The ways I am different from my mother are...

The ways I am like my father are...

The ways I am different from my father are...

The person in my family with whom I had the most difficulty was...

A problem from my childhood that keeps coming back is...

If I could change one thing about myself as a result of my upbringing, it would be...

Something I have overcome from my family background is...

The major differences between our family backgrounds are...

The nicest thing about my spouse's family is...

One thing I am not comfortable with in my spouse's family is...

The areas that could provoke possible conflict in our relationship are...

The feelings I am aware of as I do this are...

Pleasure And Pain

Together, write down:

The 5 most pleasurable memories in our relationship.

-
-
-
-
-

The 5 most painful memories in our relationship.

-
-
-
-
-

Which has had the most impact?

Which has influenced you the most in how you feel about yourself?

Discuss together.

My Childhood Messages

Use the diagram below to begin to reflect upon your childhood messages (both positive and negative) and how they still influence you, especially in the ways you relate to your spouse. These messages can be spoken or unspoken ones that were built into your sense of yourself as you grew up. For this activity, use the arrows to enter the name of the person sending the message and record the details of the essence of the message (either implicit or explicit).

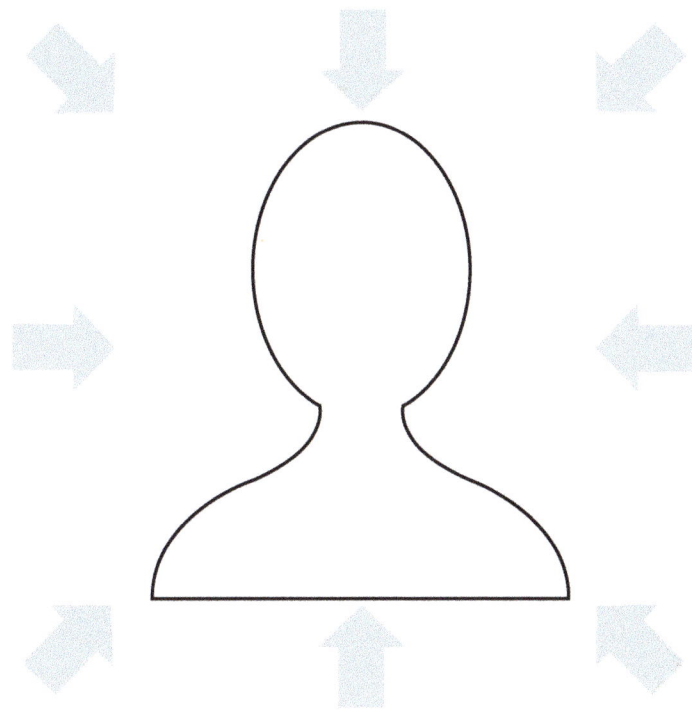

What I tell myself now is...

What I have transferred from these previous relationships (list the names) to my spouse is...

Childhood Influences

Complete alone. Answer the following question relating to my childhood family:

Pain was handled by ....

Anger was handled by ....

Affection was ....

Disapproval was handled by ....

Feelings were ....

Communication was ....

Safe topics were ....

Unsafe topics were ....

Laughter and fun were ....

What I learned about life from my family was ....

....

Something about my childhood family that I like best and want to happen in our home is ....

....

Something in my family that I don't want to happen in our home is ....

....

....

The feelings I have now about answering these questions are ....

....

Share sensitively with your spouse.

Evaluating My Family History

What do I wish my mother/female caregiver had done differently?

What do I wish my father/male caregiver had done differently?

What I wanted most as a child (apart from things) and didn't get was...

I responded to this by...

The main area of struggle for me as a result of my upbringing is...

My spouse can support me in...

Healing My Hurts

1. What is difficult or frightening for you about remembering a past hurt? (Recall a specific hurt.)

2. What might give you the courage to face past hurts?

3. What losses can you identify from your past?

4. Which loss has influenced you the most in how you feel about yourself?

5. What past hurts/events arouse feelings of anger within you?

6. How do you think and feel about yourself when you are angry with the person who hurt you?

7. What does forgiveness mean to you? (Think of a specific person and event.)

8. What would make it difficult for you to forgive a past hurt/pain/loss? (Recall a specific person/event.)

9. What would make forgiveness possible?

C. The Spiritual Connection

This area of our life is intensely personal. God knows all about us, even the secret, hidden things. The way we feel about ourselves, the struggles we have, the messages that run in the background of our life. To share our conversations with God with our spouse is to invite them into every area of our life. This is a searing intimacy. Connecting in spirituality is vital to our relationship health. Emotional health is essential to spiritual health.

> "I am never in control of what happens around me, but I am always in control of what happens within me." (Fearless Soul)

> "Nothing glows brighter than the heart awakened to the light of love that lives within it." (Guy Finley)

Emotional bond as a sacred place

Emotionally, we function best when the elements of conflict resolution, friendship, the lack of negativity and a sense of purpose and meaning inform the core of our being.

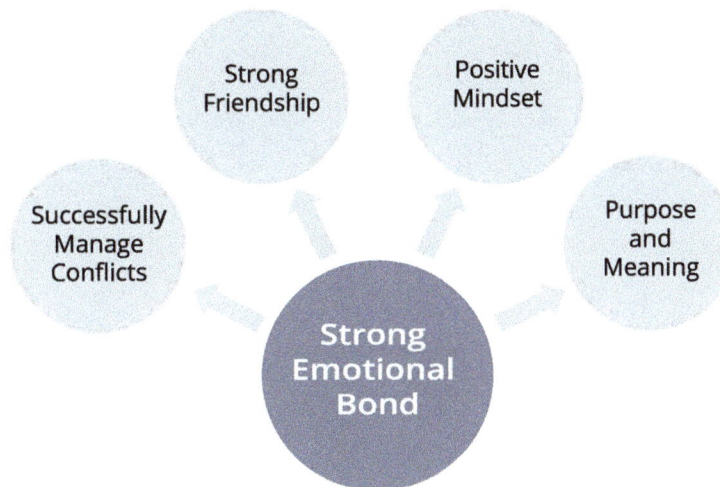

Keeping our emotional bond safe

Four suggestions to be intentional about keeping our emotional bond safe:

- sharing a common dream or vision for life;
- talking about your shared vision can foster attunement;
- implementing your shared goals can help you to be a stronger couple with a purpose; and,
- creating daily or weekly rituals will enable you to spend quality time together.

Our Story

The second three-day workshop in Sri Lanka leaves us speechless. We are prepared for blindness but how can we prepare for missing limbs, facial injuries and the ugliness of an almost 30-year war? These are the people who have to go on living, surviving, coping. They are the weary and the lame. In Australia, we live in an appearance-obsessed society. What would it mean for us to have one side of our face blown away, to lose our sight, to have no hands to hold a child, to be unable to attend to bodily functions or to need to be fed by another? Bearing witness to all this is extremely confronting and humbling. How on earth do we begin this workshop? What can we offer the bruised and broken of this world?

Yet, this is a spiritual, sacred space. In our humanity, how can we avoid seeing their pain and horror? We cannot close our eyes to these hurting people (even though we want to) and pretend their wounds do not exist. We are helpless in the face of such suffering. All we are certain of is that there is hope and unless pain is faced it is always transmitted, for hurt people hurt people. We silently pray that we will create a space where these walking wounded (mostly Hindu) souls, can face their demons and be healed on the inside.

Later, we are welcomed by familiar Sri Lankan faces – those who have journeyed with us these past six years. As we look into the faces before us, we again see the walking wounded. Their outside wounds are visible – missing arms and legs, maimed faces and bullet wounds. The blind shuffle between obstacles, their white sticks symbolic of unseeing eyes. The inner wounds, though hidden, are reflected in their visages. As each arrives we purposefully greet them, and the delight of recognition washes over both parties. Tears spill out – we are back with those who have stolen our hearts.

Then, the old man with the sad eyes greets us. Our eyes are wet, transmitting the fierce feelings we cannot verbally share. Our eyes, our "windows of the soul", reveal all as we look deep into each other's souls. He knows we love him, that for us he is the repository of all the trauma and pain of these dear Tamil people. How will we get through this day? We are already undone. But there is more. We whisper to each other that this could be one of the best days of our lives.

We stand together at the front of the large crowd with this group of friends who have come together to honour us. Our friend and interpreter, Robert, whispers that they want to perform a ceremony for us. Two gold shawls, one peacock blue, the other crimson, are placed around our shoulders and clasped at the front, an extraordinary ceremony we are told. Robert says few are honoured in this way, signifying we are now welcomed into their community as one of them. The Tamils recount how their lives have been changed because we came and continue to come. Our hearts are too full to hold all this; they split open and tears spill out unrestrained, as joy washes over us, flooding us with exquisite ecstasy.

This shared spiritual experience is one of the highlights of our lives. It strengthens the emotional bond between us. We share a common dream and vision for being signposts to a hurting world that God sees them and cares.

Worksheets on Spirituality

Connecting In Spirituality

- What is the first thing that comes to mind when you think about God?

- What are the biggest questions you have about your relationship with God?

- In what area of your life is it most difficult to trust God?

- Recently, has there been a time when you felt especially loved by God and felt especially close to Him?

- What scripture passage do you recall most often? Why?

- My communication with God is...

- I would like my communication with God to be...

- Are you able to pray together?

- What are the major hindrances in this area of our relationship?

- How might we overcome them?

My Spiritual Life's Journey

Do alone.

Draw your journey of faith in the form of a road. Symbolise people, events and experiences.

- What does the road look like?
- Who has travelled with you at different times?
- How might the road look ahead?

For example, symbolise people, events, and experiences as pot-holes, bumps, stop signs, dead end,s bridges and smooth patches

The variables of life can bring us to a sudden halt and eventually to new discoveries. These experiences of life (struggle, pain, failure, disappointment, etc.) force us to re-evaluate God, ourselves and our world.

Rest areas

Rest areas may include times of solitude, nourishment, refreshment, fun, quiet times when we listen to life and God.

Jesus said, "Come to me, all you who are weary and burdened, and I will give you rest." (Matt. 11:28).

What would help you to cultivate more rest areas in your life?

Mountaintops

Mountaintops are occasions when we get an overview of life and a joyous feeling that life is good, God is good, and it is good to be alive. They can occur through major events like a conference, or through gifts of pleasures such as sunsets, the birth of a child, a change of heart in ourselves or a loved one, repentance, etc.

Intersections, New horizons, Detours, U-turns

"Two roads diverged in a wood, and I --

I took the one less travelled by,

And that has made all the difference."

Robert Frost: *The Road Not Taken*

These include decisions and choices we make that alter the course of our spiritual journey. They greatly influence the directions of our lives. These choices are things like a move, a relationship, a job, a career, a course of study, an insight involving a mate. What extraordinary experiences in your life have revealed God's love or presence to you?

My Spiritual Life's Journey (Cont.)

Reflect on your journey in terms of major movements in your life.

- Where have you been?

- What feelings surrounded the experience?

- What feelings arise now?

- Where was God when the symbol you depicted entered your life?

- Where are you going in your spiritual journey?

- How will you get there?

Are you comfortable to share your story with your spouse? Do so if you are, or, if you are not comfortable doing this, try ito identify and name what would make it easier to share.

D. Future Hopes and Dreams

Practical ideas

> "No dream is too big, when you understand ABUNDANCE is your birthright."
> (Fearless Soul)

It is important to allow couples time to consider how they will be intentional about nurturing their emotional bond. The following are some practical ideas:

- Create an Our Marriage Journey Notebook.
  - Fill with a collection of ideas, insights, illustrations, quotes etc.
  - Identify and work together on a specific project; for example, book excerpts, articles, information on specific topics (parenting, finance, sex).
  - Write a love letter to each other.

- Put the handouts in order of priority and work through them.

- Hire an educational or inspirational video series on an agreed topic.

- Become accountable to another couple.

- Go to counselling together to get beyond a blockage.

- Study a book on marriage, complete the discussion questions and discuss.

- Study booklets on specific topics relating to marriage.

- Take a night class or correspondence course together.

- Subscribe to a magazine. Read the articles and discuss.

- Take a weekend away.

- Participate in an ME weekend each year.

- Be flexible with employment; for example, go in late one morning and make up the time later.

- Walk each day.

- Create a "Dream File".

- Create a box with surprise outings and choose one to do each month.

- Put on a massage video and give your spouse a gift of a neck and shoulder massage.

Worksheets on Future Hopes and Dreams

Future Hopes And Dreams

What I like about our marriage:

What I think could be better:

A dream that I have had for a long time and have not yet fulfilled is:

A dream that my spouse and I share and hope to fulfil is:

What immediate, measurable goal (or goals) can I set for continued growth in our marriage?

How I See My Relationships In Five Years' Time

Using these images and the whole of this sheet of paper, arrange your family as you see them. Pay particular attention to closeness and distance.

God   Husband   Wife   Children   Wife's Parents   Husband's Parents   Pets

What feelings does this picture reveal?

If you could change anything about your picture you would like to change?

Notes to Chapter 15

1. D. Allender & T. Longman III (2014). *God Loves Sex: An Honest Conversation About Sexual Desire and Holiness.* Baker Books, p. 9.
2. D. Clarke (2013). *Married...But Lonely: Stop Merely Existing. Start Living Intimately.* Siloam.
3. Ibid.
4. Ibid.

CHAPTER 16

ADDITIONAL EXERCISES

Overview
This chapter includes additional exercises for use in a ME event. The chapter is organised under the following headings.

A.   Strategies of Disconnection

B.   Sharing Our Stories

C.   The Hook-Book-Look-Took Method

D.   Intimacy Through Forgiveness

E.   Five Stages of Marriage

F.   Various ME Exercises

G.   Identifying Primary and Secondary Emotions

H.   Feelings List

I.   Three Styles of Relating

J.   Two Paths

K.   Look for the Good in Your Special Person

L.   Reflections

M.   Take Away for Reflection

N.   Couple's Covenant

O.   A Picture Tells a Thousand Words

P.   Finally...

A. Strategies of Disconnection

Karen Horney theorised a different way of viewing what she called neurosis, a term coined to label a range of psychological conditions or personality traits that do not impair physical functioning; for example, depression, anxiety, obsessive behaviour or hypochondria. These psychological conditions or personality traits are illustrated in the German poet Goethe's Faust, and due to this popular legend the name "Faust" has come to describe someone whose pride and vanity leads to his/her doom. The story is of a gloomy old philosopher who can find no meaning in life. Just as he is about to poison himself, he hears happy voices outside singing Easter hymns. As Faust considers turning to prayer, a stranger appears, Mephistopheles, an evil spirit sent by Satan. The two make a bargain: Mephistopheles will give Faust youth and worldly pleasures, if he will give his soul to him in death. This story has come to represent a person who trades their soul in exchange for the obvious benefits of youth, knowledge, wealth, power, acceptance etc. – even love.

Horney believed that the neurotic makes a pact with devil, becoming a prototype of Faust in trading dependence on God for perfection and pride - "I can make life work by my own efforts. I don't need to depend on God". She explains:

> All the drives for glory have in common the reaching out for greater knowledge, wisdom, virtue, or powers than are given to human beings; they all aim at the absolute, the unlimited, and the infinite. Nothing short of absolute fearlessness, mastery, or saintliness has any appeal for the neurotic obsessed with the drive for glory. He is therefore the antithesis of the truly religious man. For the latter, only to God are all things possible: the neurotic's version is: nothing is impossible to me. His will power should have magic proportions, his reasoning be infallible, his foresight flawless, his knowledge all encompassing. The theme of the devil's pact... begins to emerge. The neurotic is the Faust who is not satisfied with knowing a great deal, but has to know everything.[1]

Horney classified neuroses into three categories consisting of ten patterns of behaviour based on universal needs that are distorted; for example, the neurotic's need is much more intense and if the need is not met there is significant anxiety. Moreover, the nature of the need tends to be unrealistic and too central to the person's existence. These distortions occur during a child's development when legitimate universal needs are not met. They stem from a child's perceptions (not necessarily the parent's intentions) of lack of warmth and affection, lack of feeling loved and lack of feeling wanted and welcomed.

Children adopt survival responses to handle this parental indifference; Brené Brown and Linda Hartling call these "Strategies of Disconnection", utilising "Shame Shields" or self-protective armour.[2] Shame is defined as "the intensely painful feeling or experience of believing that we are flawed and therefore unworthy of love and belonging".[3] Shame Shields include the following.

1. **Moving Away** (withdrawing, hiding, silencing ourselves, and keeping secrets). The problem of parental indifference is 'solved' by withdrawing from family involvement into ourselves. We eventually become sufficient unto ourselves: "If I withdraw, nothing and no one can hurt me". As adults, needs develop into:
   - the need for self-sufficiency, independence, to never need anyone (we tend to refuse help and are often reluctant to commit); and/or,
   - the need for perfection and unassailability, never to make a mistake, and the need to be in control at all times.

2. **Moving Toward** (seeking to appease and please). Most children are overwhelmed by a fear of helplessness and/or abandonment. For the sake of survival, hostility must be suppressed and the parents won over. If this works, the compliance coping strategy becomes the preferred coping style: "If I can make you love me, you will not hurt me". As adults, needs develop into:
   - the need for affection and approval, to please others and be liked by them;
   - the need for a spouse, or someone to take over their life – "love will solve all my problems"; and/or,
   - the need to restrict life to narrow borders, be undemanding, be satisfied with little, and be inconspicuous.

3. **Moving Against** (trying to gain power over others, being aggressive, and using shame to fight shame). Horney observes that some children's reactions are not stereotypically weak or passive, but more a response like "basic hostility" that leads to an effort to

protest injustice. Over time this becomes a habitual response to life's difficulties. They develop an aggressive coping strategy: "If I have power, no one can hurt me". As adults, needs develop into:

- a desperate need for power and control over others, a façade of omnipotence (often contempt for the weak and a strong belief in one's own rational powers);
- the need to exploit others, get the better of them, use people;
- the need for social recognition and prestige; overwhelmingly concern with appearances and/or popularity (fear of being ignored, being thought of as plain, "uncool" or "out of it");
- the need for personal affirmation (fear of being nobody, unimportant, lacking meaning and substance); and/or,
- the need for personal achievement, being number one at everything, and devaluing anything one cannot achieve.

However, these Shame Shields fail to serve us as adults. as Alice Walker sums it up:

> In blocking off what hurts us, we think we are walling ourselves off from pain. But in the long run, the wall, which prevents growth, hurts us more than the pain which, if we will only bear it, soon passes over us. Washes over us and is gone. Long will we remember pain, but the pain itself, as it was at the point of intensity that made us feel as if we must die of it, eventually vanishes. Our memory of it becomes only a trace. Walls remain. They grow moss. They are difficult barriers to cross, to get to others, to get to closed - down parts of ourselves.[4]

B. Sharing our stories

These thoughts are for faith-based, Christian groups. Reflect: What are some of the ways the Christian church handles pain and suffering?

When all the parts (My Story, Our Story and His Story) come together, powerful things happen.

My Story

We are all a story of life, relationships, experiences. When our society experiences war, trauma and/or dislocation, we lose touch with our story and are left isolated and alone.

Our Story

This is the story of previous generations, but those stories are often out of touch with my personal story. Both need to be in touch with His Story.

His Story

This is about connecting with stories in the Bible. Leader couples are called to encourage each storyteller to connect with the greater stories and God's story as told by the Master Story Teller. Personal stories are linked to the greater story. Most religious traditions are linked to the larger narrative of wisdom stories.

We are relational beings and healing comes in relational change with God and each other. Larry Crabb says that people cannot be 'fixed' like a car going to a mechanic, and are not 'fixed' in isolation.[5] My story is part of our story. We are a community of broken people. As humans, we absolutely seek connection and relationships. But before we are able to deeply connect with each other, we need to connect with own souls (our own story). This teaches us to soften and suspend our judgements.

We are exhorted to love. 1 Corinthians 13 talks about being deeply connected to Our Story (a sense of community). This can be confronting. It does not allow us to live with the illusion of unity or wholeness – that we are OK, that we have no doubt, fear, loneliness, or confusion. What we are is sinful, wounded, mortal, broken. Recognition of this is the beginning of freedom. Henri Nouwen, in his book *The Wounded Healer*, suggests that unity emerges from the shared confession of our basic brokenness and consequent shared hope; our wounds call us beyond the boundaries and limitations of our humanness to encounter God.[6]

Therefore, the Christian community ought to be a healing community, not because pain and suffering are denied (or complained about or focussed on) but because pain and suffering open the path to encounter God. In this kind of community, mutual sharing becomes mutual deepening of hope. Sharing mutual suffering and weakness can lead to a renewed vision of God's promises, like the birth pangs mentioned in Romans 8:22–28. This makes our brokenness our greatest resource. God values everything and never wastes pain.

Thus, when I place my passion and search for God at the disposal of others, when I allow others to enter my life, to come close to me, to ask how my life connects with theirs, then my wounds become a channel of God's healing power, that part which speaks most deeply to others.[7] Articulation of my experiences and God's work within me can lead others out of confusion towards clarification. Sharing then becomes not superficial sharing, but a willingness to see my pain and suffering not only as part of Our Story, but a pathway to His Story (both for me and others).

Have you experienced terrible trauma? A terrible childhood? Great failures? Join the human race, as this is a vital part of Our Story. Your capacity for loving presence, compassion and endurance will be your best gift, so use it. Your authenticity will be a model that can influence others and encourage open, honest sharing.

But to do this type of caring, to be invited into the dark recesses of another soul, you have to engage hearts and souls as well as minds.[8] Our effectiveness as companions to others in times of trouble or transition will depend on:

- how well we understand ourselves;
- how aware we are of our own inconsistencies/sinful strategies;
- how well we learn from them;
- how we embrace the possibility of growth and change within ourselves; and
- how well we practice perseverance, creativity, humour, and friendliness toward our self and others.

One of the by-products of being a ME leader couple is the process of discovering oneself. Our work with others helps us discover what we need to know or make sense of in our lives. Being involved in other people's lives means being aware of our own survival strategies and how they get in the way of loving well. We need to be constantly asking questions of ourselves and others, and constantly learning how we affect those closest to us. We need to become increasingly aware of our deep thirst and how we try to fill it apart from God. Weis and Berger write:

> Ultimately [marriage enrichment] is about our humanity... less often about what we offer of our strength and understanding and more of our daily struggle with vulnerability, loss, confusion and doubt... Paradoxically it is in these... our "limitations" and our ongoing attempts to be compassionate with ourselves and our own wounds... that as [leader couples] we offer our [ME group members] the support to reconnect after traumatic wounding.[9]

C. The Hook-Book-Look-Took Method

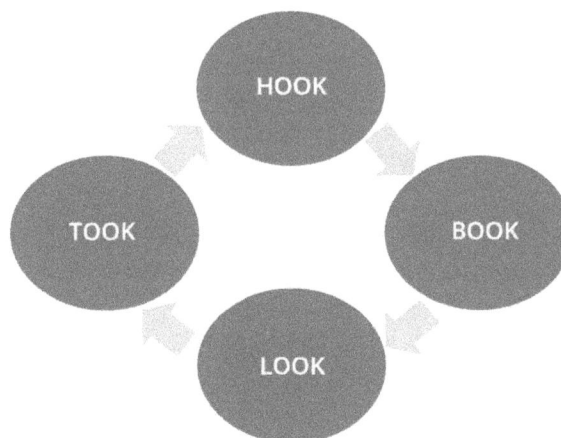

This method of presentation is for faith-based, Christian groups.

When was the last time a presentation really grabbed you? What made it meaningful? Usually, the sessions we remember were creative and helped us discover a life-transforming truth. One kind of presentation that does this is the Hook-Book-Look-Took method developed by educators Lawrence Richards and Gary Bredfeldt. This method hooks couples, communicates information and meaning, and encourages responses. Here's an overview of how this method could be used for faith-based groups.

1. **Objective:** First, consider the needs of each couple (circumstances, physical problems or emotional issues). Then consider which methods of delivery could address those needs; for instance, in one couples' retreat some of the couples were apprehensive about the future. So, a session could be planned on the best method of delivery to address this. This could be a leader couple dialogue or a handout. Richards and Bredfeldt advise making the teaching goal "short enough to be remembered, clear enough to be meaningful, and specific enough to be achieved".[10] A simple outline will help us to identify the goal of this session.

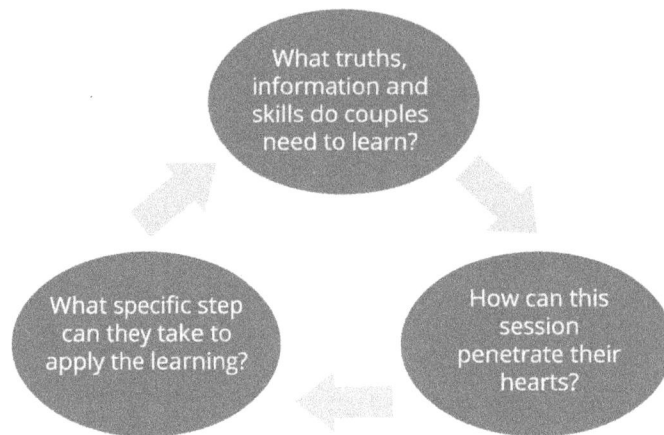

For a faith-based group, we might want the couples to focus on the fact that, no matter what our circumstances, God is in control. We want them to experience joy in the midst of difficult times; and we want them to identify one specific way to bring joy to each other that week.

2. **Hook.** Richards's method begins with the hook: grab their attention, state your goal and then transition to the information you want couples to know. Just as fishermen use hooks to get fish out of water and into the boat, an effective hook transports couples into the session. Your approach should be simple – a question, a quotation, a role-play, a dialogue or a case study about a problem they can relate to; for example, in a session on Anger and Conflict, a hook might handing out a rating scale and asking couples to rate themselves on how well they think they handle conflict in their relationship. Or you could ask, "Tell me about a couple you can relate to who handle conflict well in their relationship. What appeals to you about them?"

3. **Book.** The next step is to help couples collect and understand pertinent material. A journalist unlocks the essence of a personality or event he's writing about by doing research; you need to do the same. Read up on information about your topic. Look up definitions of key words in a Bible dictionary or regular dictionary. Ask questions (who, what, where, when, why, how) to clarify the concepts you wish to convey. The questions you use in the session should lead people to think about answers that apply to their relationship; for example, in a session on Anger and Conflict you might ask, what is anger? What does the Bible say about anger (e.g. in Ephesians 4)? Does God get angry? What angers you the most? Can you accept anger in yourself?

4. **Look.** The third step in this method is to guide the group from biblical knowledge to spiritual insight. Ask them, "What principles from this passage of Scripture can we apply to our lives?" God impresses people differently, so there's no wrong answer to this question. Here are some messages our group identified from the Acts 16 passage: God is in control, even when it may not appear that way; we can find joy in a harsh

environment; we should not be ashamed to display our faith; and non-Christians may find our joy contagious and want to know Christ.

5. **Took.** The last step is to lead couples to act on the truth they've learned. According to Richards, "Like a vaccination, the Word of God is of no effect until we can say it 'took'".[11] Help couples to choose an action step. Make sure it is realistic and something they really want to do. For example, in a session on Anger and Conflict, ask couples to dialogue about something practical they can put in place to process conflict when it happens in the future.

D. Intimacy Through Forgiveness

Intimacy through Forgiveness offers a beginning process of restoring the relationship in situations where both parties need to say sorry. As with all these exercises, the suggestion is that the person who is in the best emotional shape to start the process goes first, once you start to dialogue.

1. **Preparation:** Write a statement of what was happening to you when the situation or incident occurred which upset your spouse. Do this without defending your action; simply write down what you thought, felt, feared and hoped for at the time.

2. **Next:** Write a statement in which you describe what you understand so far about your spouse's thoughts, feelings, fears and hopes at the time. Be careful not to blame or accuse or add your own conclusions.

3. **Then:** Exchange your statements and read them. Work out who goes first. When it is your turn, use reflective listening to reach a deeper understanding of your spouse's needs and how your actions affected them. Be clear about your part in creating the problem and acknowledge this when you say sorry. If the "sorry" does not lead to forgiveness, take the time to find out just what the hurt is about and try again.

Finish with a hug, if that is what you need, and make a resolve to do better next time!

E. Five stages of marriage

1. **Romantic phase or fantasy time.** You think everything about your new mate is wonderful... and, if it isn't, his or her faults are "cute", they are not a problem. This foggy stage of young marriage is sometimes called the "honeymoon stage". It's beautiful, woolly and necessary.

2. **Disillusionment phase.** The honeymoon is over and you have your first experiences of real disappointment. During this stage you begin to wonder what you have gotten yourself into. You realise that you are indeed annoyed or hurt by some of your spouse's traits and habits. They aren't cute at all! This is a dangerous time and some marriages dissolve in divorce right here. To make the relationship work, you begin negotiations aimed at persuading your spouse to change and you promise to make changes of your own in return.

3. **Reality and power struggle.** This begins when you realise that changing isn't all that easy. It is the time when you really encounter your spouse as different. "How could you think or behave like that?" At this time we move to trying to force our spouse to change. We may argue/manipulate/threaten and try to make them what we want them to be. For some couples this stage is all about "who is going to win". Sadly, some couples stay locked in this stage for the rest of their married life. The heat dies down but the pain stays. The couple settle for resignation, which is less than they could have. Others give up the struggle and divorce.

4. **Acceptance, compromise and commitment.** This begins with the realisation that marriage isn't really about "who is going to win". Probably neither of you are going to be able to change very much and some of your expectations were pretty unrealistic. Some things can be changed but some cannot. What you are seeing is pretty much what you are going to get. You discover that your spouse's good points more than make up for their "bad" points. Clearly, in some ways, you are very different – but you are both OK.

Strangely enough, this time often involves some healthy separateness. You give up trying to live each other's lives and begin to develop your own uniqueness. In this way you invigorate your relationship. This stage ends when you realise that, despite the differences, you really do want to stay married and the commitment is not only to each other but to the concept of preserving and enhancing your growth as a couple, no matter what. Divorce is no longer an option.

5. **Creativity.** This is when you begin to understand and value the differences and to use them creatively. You work as a team, complementing each other. You support each other in your individual endeavours and delight in them. You can relax into the relationship and deal with the occasional conflicts that still arise in a way that increases your understanding of each other, your love for each other. This a rich and satisfying time, often not achieved until later in life – something to look forward to!

F. Various Marriage Enrichment Exercises

1. **Feelings.** Even when you don't say anything, I know you are feeling:
   - happy when...
   - tired when...
   - angry when...
   - sad when...
   - sexy when....
   - disappointed when...
   - contented when...
   - glad I'm your mate when...

2. **Tossing a ball or small stuffed animal.** This game is good for a second or third session of a series of ME meetings, as it is a fun, quick way to refresh memories about other people's names. It is also good to use as an energiser. Instruct participants to form a circle and toss an object to each other, calling out the name of the person they are tossing it to. The catcher is to quickly toss it to someone else. The game is more fun and interesting if the object moves quickly. Prompting is allowed!

3. **Energiser.** To energise when energy appears low. This game is musical chairs minus the chairs! While the music is playing, people are to mingle. As soon as it stops, you yell out a number and participants are to quickly form small groups containing that number of people. If they can't, they are out of the game.

4. **Museum Pieces.** Our past can be likened to a museum. Particular events are displayed and enshrined in glass cases. Ask couples to talk about a particular museum piece and revisit it in the light of their current relationship and commitment (this can be very healing).

5. **Metaphor of Our Marriage Drawings.** Distribute large sheets of paper and ask couples to draw their relationship as it is now. Instruct participants to choose one of the following.
   - Draw your marriage in terms of a landscape, city, sea or country.
   - Represent your marriage as crossing a bridge. What is on this side? What is on the other side? Where are you? Where would you like to be?
   - Draw your marriage as a gate. What lies behind the gate?

- Draw your marriage as a line, journey or road-map. Put in images and events along the way, either drawn or written. (This can be divided into sections: past, present and future).
- Use images from magazines to illustrate the story of your marriage.
- Draw significant memories from your marriage history.
- Draw a memory from your marriage associated with strong feelings.
- Select the most dominant emotion/feeling in your marriage and depict it in a drawing.
- Draw your marriage as a house. Put in the different rooms and activities. In which rooms do you spend most of your time? In which rooms do you spend the least?
- Draw or model with playdough an animal that best represents your marriage/approach to sex/way you handle anger etc. After each couple has shared the meaning of their drawing/model, pin them on the walls or create a "zoo".

6. **Swap Roles.** Draw how you imagine you would feel if you were your spouse.

7. **Control and Authority**. Each couple is to act as boss/slave. One spouse tells the other what to draw and what to use. Reverse roles. Discuss the experience.

8. **Newspaper Headline.** Distribute newspapers and magazines. Ask couples to cut out the headline from a newspaper/magazine that best represents their relationship. Variation: Instruct couples to make up their own headline from cut-outs in magazines.

9. **Crossroads.** Imagine yourselves at a crossroads or a roundabout. Draw it and your alternative decisions or directions.

10. **Where Do We Go From Here?** Ask couples to share their answers to "One day I'd like to..."

11. **Movie Metaphor.** Instruct couples to choose a movie, book or song title that best describes or represents their marriage; for example, Star Wars; Gone with the Wind; Men are From Mars, Women are From Venus; Love me Tender; Moody Monthly, etc.

12. **Husband/Wife of the Year Contest.** You are entering your spouse in a contest for Husband/Wife of the Year. Write down the qualities for which you think your spouse should be chosen.

13. **Years of Experience.** Ask couples the number of years they have been married and write on the board. Add up the totals to arrive at the cumulative total of marriage experience in the room.

14. **Photolanguage.** Supply posters for display around the room or display photo pictures on the floor or a large table, allowing plenty of room to browse. Ask couples to choose one that really speaks to them as a couple and explain why it is meaningful.

15. **Famous Couples.** Give each couple the name of a famous couple written on a small piece of paper; for example, Bill and Hilary Clinton; the Prime Minister and his wife; Queen Elizabeth and her husband; Romeo and Juliet etc. Instruct them to re-enact what happens when the husband or wife returns home at the end of the day.

16. **Three Things.** Ask couples to answer the following question to each other.
- What are three things you feel positively about?
- What are three things that need attention?
- What are three things which you can do to enhance your relationship?

17. **Desires.** Ask couples to complete the following sentence to each other: For the next twelve months,
   - I want for me...
   - I want for you...
   - I want for us...

18. **Love Letter.** Write a love letter to your spouse.

19. **Peak Event.** Draw a picture of a peak event in your marriage.

20. **Sharing Feelings.** Ask couples to talk to each other and answer the question, "I feel good when..."

21. **Write a letter.** One spouse is setting off on a space mission for an extended period of time on behalf of the human race. The certainty of their return is not established and each spouse decides to write to the other on the subject, "What you have meant to me".

22. **Feelings.** Do alone. Explore and list your current feelings and then share them with your spouse (10 min). Ask your spouse: "How many of those feelings would you have been able to identify without my telling you?" Instruct each spouse to answer: "If there is any feeling about which you are uncomfortable, then do not feel pressure to have to share it."

23. **Conflict.** Ask couples to write down a list of conflict areas and then select one of these to work on.

24. **Advertisement.** Write a short add titled "Wanted". Describe the kind of person you perceive your spouse as.

25. **Romance Group Exercise.** Distribute four large sheets of paper with a large heart drawn on each. Place them on the walls around the room. On each sheet of paper write one of the following headings:
   - What romantic name do you have for your spouse?
   - What was a romantic moment before you were married?
   - What is something romantic you have done since you have been married?
   - Draw something romantic.

   Instruct each person to contribute anonymously.

26. **Romance.** Instruct couples to complete these three sentences.
   - Something romantic I would like to do with you...
   - Something romantic I would like to do for you...
   - Something romantic I would like you to do for me...

27. **Sharing.** Instruct couples to respond to these sentences.
   - A deep conviction I'd like to share with you is...
   - A nagging doubt I want to share with you is...
   - A special experience I want you to know about is...

28. **Walk.** Line up in double file and follow the leader couple. Take couples for a walk, and ask them to share with each other a time when God made Himself special to them.

29. **Hands.** Instruct couples to hold each other's hands and express to each other: "What your hands mean to me..."

30. **Touch.** Ask couples to give each other a gentle face massage.

31. **Wedding Vows.** Write new wedding vows/promises for the future.

32. Fantasy Future. Share a fantasy about the future.

33. Homecoming. Share with each other what you expect to find when you get home at the end of the retreat.

34. Share with each other:
- Where will you be in two years' time?
- What do you think your children will be doing?

35. Share in turns. "I am saying I love you when I..."

36. Hopes and Concerns. Instruct couples to write four lists under the following headings:
- My hopes for myself are...
- My hopes for you are...
- My concerns for myself are...
- My concerns for you are...

37. Complete the following sentences.
- If you were to die tomorrow, I would regret that...
- If you were to die tomorrow, I would be grateful that...

38. In-Laws. Instruct couples to:
- list three areas where their relationship with their family strengthens their marriage.
- list three areas where their relationship with their family puts pressure on their marriage.
- write down three things they can do to enhance and/or improve their relationship with their in-laws.

39. Complete the following sentences.
- I feel appreciated when you...
- I feel romantic when you...
- I feel sexy when you...
- I feel I would like to make love in/at (a special place)...

40. Complete the following sentences.
- I find it difficult to share honestly about...
- With your help, I would like to explore honestly with you...
- I would like to do this in the following ways...

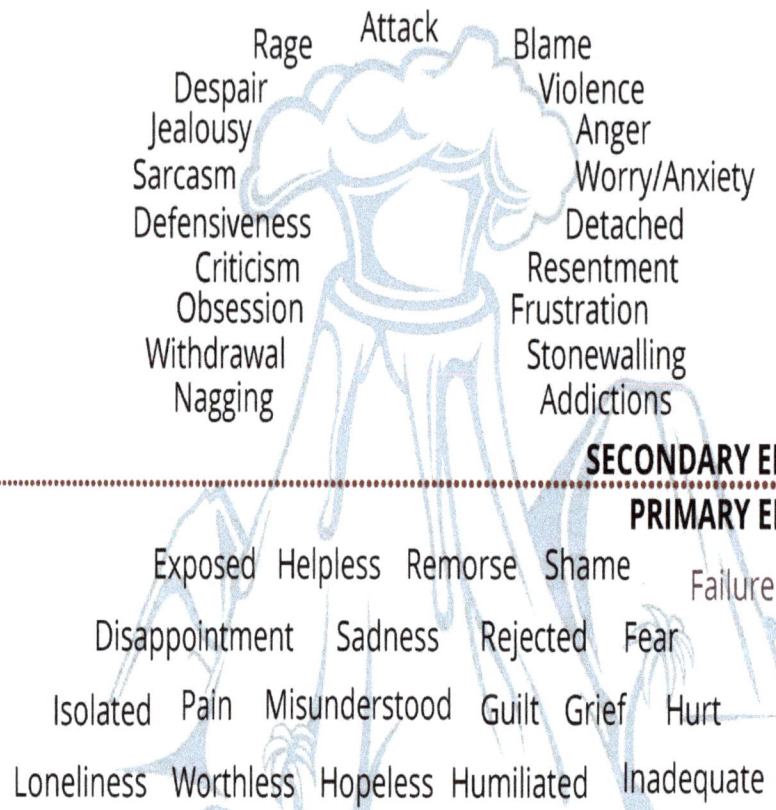

Rage   Attack   Blame
Despair   Violence
Jealousy   Anger
Sarcasm   Worry/Anxiety
Defensiveness   Detached
Criticism   Resentment
Obsession   Frustration
Withdrawal   Stonewalling
Nagging   Addictions

SECONDARY EMOTIONS
PRIMARY EMOTIONS

Exposed Helpless Remorse Shame   Failure

Disappointment Sadness Rejected Fear

Isolated Pain Misunderstood Guilt Grief Hurt

Loneliness Worthless Hopeless Humiliated Inadequate

H. Feelings List

The Gift	Feeling		Toxic
WISDOM	FEAR	Apprehension Overwhelmed Threatened	TERROR/PANIC
HEALING/GROWTH	PAIN	Sad Lonely Hurt Pity	DEPRESSION
STRENGTH	ANGER	Resentment Irritation Frustration	RAGE
REACHING OUT	LONELINESS	Isolated Forlorn Detached Desolate	DESPAIR
VALUES/AMENDS	GUILT	Regretful Contrite Remorseful	IMMOBILITY
HOPE	JOY	Hopeful Elated Excited Happy	HYSTERIA
CONNECTION	LOVE	Affection Tenderness Compassion Warmth	OBSESSION
HUMILITY/FALLI-BILITY	SHAME	Embarrassed Humbled Exposed Disgraced	WORTHLESSNESS

(Source: Adapted from: South Pacific Private, Curl Curl, NSW, Australia)

I. Three Styles of relating

Passive Avoidance/ Helpless Control	Aggressive Avoidance/ Emasculating Control	Assertive Relating
Helpless; "good little boy/ girl"; over-sensitive. Projected Image: • "I'm not important." • "I'm no good." • "Be kind to me." • "Help me." • "I'm sorry."	"Together"; capable; strong; organised; insensitive. Projected Image: • "You need me." • "Lean on me." • "I'm clever/ capable/ successful." • "I can cope." • Often "super-spiritual" and judgmental.	Realistic view of strengths and weaknesses. Appropriate humility. Sense of self comes from within, not outside of self. Projected Image: Confident, curious, open to knowing self and others, vulnerable, genuine, thankful, growing sense of courage, freedom and joy. Warm, responsive, compassionate, draws people. Personal presence and vitality.
Avoids responsibility for own feelings, behaviours and consequences. Pleases others; placates; withdraws; withholds physically, emotionally and sexually; passive-aggressive; tears; self-pity. Often never takes risks; wants to be inconspicuous; dowdy; downplays attractiveness. (This style is often the result of strong conditioning to be gentle, nurturing, caring, in order to gain approval.) Physical symptoms such as backache, headache, and gastric upsets.	Avoids responsibility for own feelings, behaviours, consequences. Dominating; aggressive; competitive; critical; controlling. (This style is often a result of strong conditioning to compete, achieve, be strong, take initiative, in order to gain approval. Or may have received strong messages that they are inferior, incompetent, stupid and have had to fight a hostile environment to get what they want.) Can expresses pent-up feelings in a hostile and violent way through physical or verbal abuse such as sarcasm, contempt. Can be charming and/ or "helpful". Often very appearance conscious. Either conforms to conventional dress or aggressively nonconformist but conforms to an admired minority.	Owns feelings, behaviours and consequences. Able to acknowledge & tolerate strong emotions. Able to express a wide range of emotions in appropriate ways, while acknowledging the other person's needs. Able to play and have fun. Able to express ideas, opinions and needs without self-depreciation or bullying others. Able to listen, communicate well, and validate others. Able to set goals and achieve them. Able to take risks; flexible; adaptable. Spirit of negotiation and reconciliation; open, honest relationships.
Unable to express genuine needs and inability to initiate action to meet own needs, therefore help has to come from someone outside self. • "If other people would respond by valuing me, I would feel valuable." • "People don't value me, therefore, I have no value." • "No one can really help me." • "God is like everyone else - He lets me down."	Others are to blame; punishes them. • "See what you made me do." • "If it were not for you..." • "If only others would... this would work."	All behaviour has purpose and choice. • "I matter"; "You matter to me."
Inferior; "poor me"; unworthy; helpless; hopeless; powerless; stupid; frightened; vulnerable; resentful (people don't care about my needs); angry.	Not much awareness. Strong need to control and frustrated when they cannot control themselves or others. Fear of failure (often denied). Alone; unloved; unlovable.	Confident. Failure is not personal but presents opportunity. Connected to others. May struggle with self-doubt and pain, but able to gain perspective. Hopeful, even in the face of confusion and despair. Passionate about life and relationships.

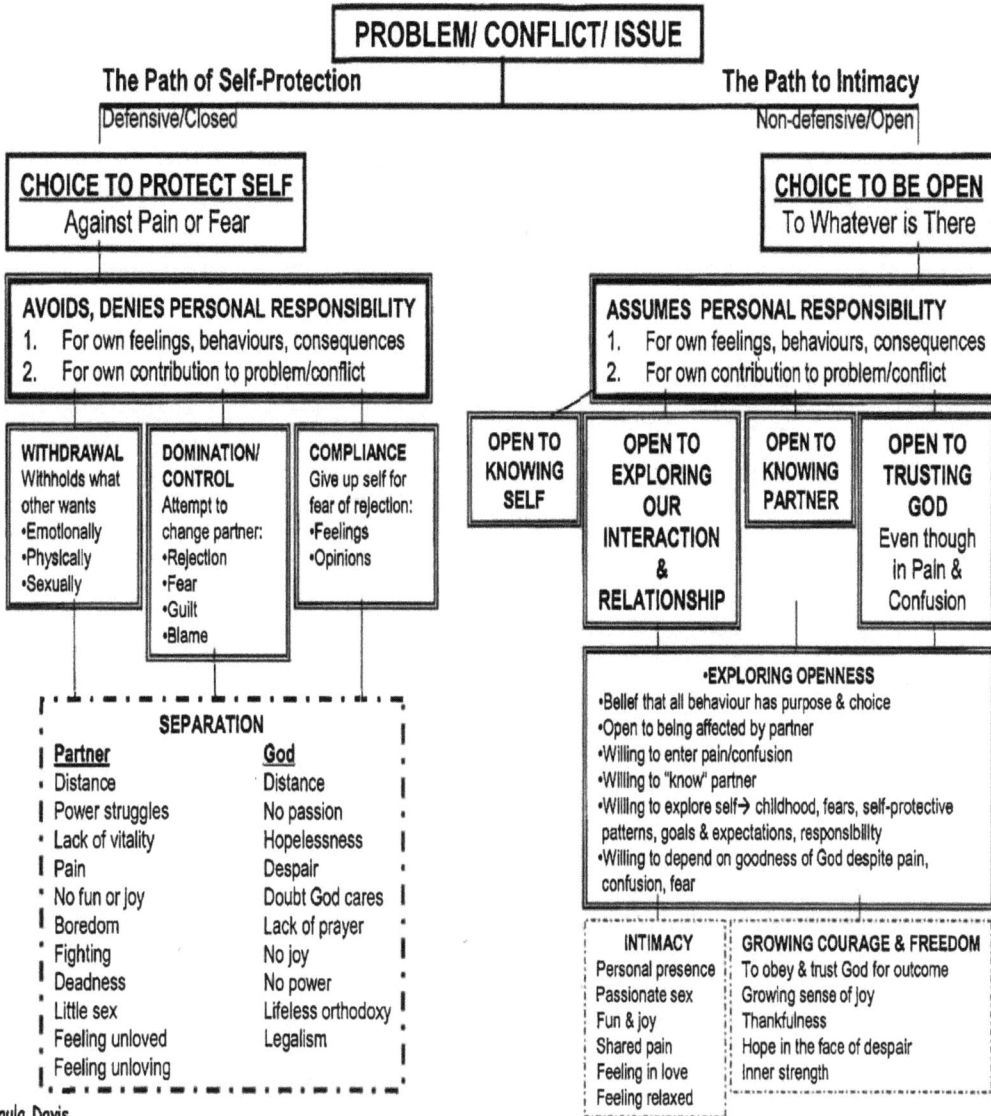

(Dr Paula Davis, adapted from J & M. Paul, From Conflict to Caring: In-depth Programme for Creating Loving Relationships, Compcare Publications 1990).

PROBLEM/ CONFLICT/ ISSUE

The Path of Self-Protection
Defensive/Closed

The Path to Intimacy
Non-defensive/Open

CHOICE TO PROTECT SELF
Against Pain or Fear

CHOICE TO BE OPEN
To Whatever is There

AVOIDS, DENIES PERSONAL RESPONSIBILITY
1. For own feelings, behaviours, consequences
2. For own contribution to problem/conflict

ASSUMES PERSONAL RESPONSIBILITY
1. For own feelings, behaviours, consequences
2. For own contribution to problem/conflict

WITHDRAWAL
Withholds what other wants
•Emotionally
•Physically
•Sexually

DOMINATION/ CONTROL
Attempt to change partner:
•Rejection
•Fear
•Guilt
•Blame

COMPLIANCE
Give up self for fear of rejection:
•Feelings
•Opinions

OPEN TO KNOWING SELF

OPEN TO EXPLORING OUR INTERACTION & RELATIONSHIP

OPEN TO KNOWING PARTNER

OPEN TO TRUSTING GOD
Even though in Pain & Confusion

SEPARATION

Partner	God
Distance	Distance
Power struggles	No passion
Lack of vitality	Hopelessness
Pain	Despair
No fun or joy	Doubt God cares
Boredom	Lack of prayer
Fighting	No joy
Deadness	No power
Little sex	Lifeless orthodoxy
Feeling unloved	Legalism
Feeling unloving	

Paula Davis

•EXPLORING OPENNESS
•Belief that all behaviour has purpose & choice
•Open to being affected by partner
•Willing to enter pain/confusion
•Willing to "know" partner
•Willing to explore self→ childhood, fears, self-protective patterns, goals & expectations, responsibility
•Willing to depend on goodness of God despite pain, confusion, fear

INTIMACY
Personal presence
Passionate sex
Fun & joy
Shared pain
Feeling in love
Feeling relaxed

GROWING COURAGE & FREEDOM
To obey & trust God for outcome
Growing sense of joy
Thankfulness
Hope in the face of despair
Inner strength

Reflections on the Two Paths

Do alone. From the list below, tick those you are presently experiencing.

In your relationship with:
Spouse

☐ Defensive/closed
☐ Power struggles
☐ Distance
☐ Lack of vitality
☐ Pain
☐ No fun or joy
☐ Fighting
☐ Boredom
☐ Deadness
☐ Lack of interest in sex
☐ Feeling unloved
☐ Feeling unloving

In your relationship with:
God

☐ Apathy
☐ Distance
☐ No passion
☐ Hopelessness
☐ Despair
☐ Doubt that God cares
☐ Lack of prayer
☐ No joy
☐ No power
☐ Lifeless orthodoxy
☐ Legalism

How do your answers connect with your style of relating?

Share with your spouse.

K. Look for the Good in Your Special Person

1. Appreciate the good things about someone important in your life. Focus on your spouse and take time to think through the following questions. In each case, try to note down specific examples.

   - What drew you to your spouse when you first met?

   - What things have you really enjoyed doing together during your relationship?

   - What things do you really appreciate about your spouse right now?

   - What are their strengths?

2. Then (and this is the important bit!), when you're with that person (now and as you move through life together) take the time to notice and acknowledge these things – their strengths, the things they do that you really appreciate, the happy times you've shared together and so on.

Complete the following sentences and take time to share them.

   - I really love it when you...

   - You're so good at...

   - Seeing you do... reminds me of that fantastic day when we...

After spending time to share your answers with your special person, think about the things you appreciated or enjoyed about your time together and share them.

(Adapted from: Happiness Action Pack, Putting the Science of Well-being into Practice. Developed by Action for Happiness with support from Headspace and Vanessa King MAPP. Retrieved from http://www.actionforhappiness.org/media/80216/action_for_happiness_-_happiness_action_pack_v3.pdf)

L. Reflections

Ask your body:

Where do you feel neglected, ineffectual, or unlovable?

What actions, activities or people help you to feel better about this?

Ask your mind:

What feeds you intellectually?

What can you do that gives you enough of that kind of stimulation?

Ask your heart:

Who and what do you love and who loves you?

What support, quiet time, or tools do you need to be able to unwind and listen to what your heart wants to tell you?

Ask your spirit:

What is your spiritual anchor?

What connects you with God?

If busyness gets in the way of your spiritual life, how could you make more time for what you value most?

M. Take Away for Reflection

- Both spouses in a relationship are the problem, and both are the solution.

- You are each 100% responsible for the system you have created through your unconscious collusion.

- Most of your complaints about each other are statements about personal unmet needs.

- "When a spouse cries out for help in extreme need, or is already massively vulnerable and is treated as insignificant by a loved one, the sense of basic trust in the spouse is shattered."[12]

- You chose your spouse because they can't naturally meet your deeper needs.

- The only legitimate powers you have in a relationship are to ask your spouse for what you need, and to change your own behaviour to meet their needs.

- You have no right to punish them for not loving you right (they are doing the best they can with who they are).

N. Couples' Covenant

I want you to know that I will demonstrate my commitment to you by:

1. Recognising the importance of your needs and helping you meet these needs as often as possible.

2. Experiencing joy and satisfaction whenever you seem to be fulfilling your needs.

3. Maintaining realistic values and expectations about you as a life partner.

4. Tolerating those attitudes, beliefs and actions of yours that are different from mine.

5. Striving to reveal myself to you honestly so that you will know who I really am.

6. Expressing my feelings to you openly and candidly in a manner which allows you to respond to me in a caring way.

7. Giving you all the freedom you need as an individual to pursue your own interests and relationships.

8. Celebrating our "we-ness" by privately creating an identity with you while publicly appreciating you.

This covenant of commitment can be renewed at regular intervals, reminding us that marriage requires trust, appreciation, and self-discipline.

O. A Picture Tells a Thousand Words

The pictures below depict a wide variety of feelings, actions and relationships. Choose the picture that most accurately reflects your current relationship, and the picture that best illustrates where you would like your relationship to be. Share your answer with your partner.

P. Finally...

Remember –

To laugh is to risk appearing the fool.

To weep is to risk appearing sentimental.

To reach out is to risk involvement.

To expose feelings is to risk exposing your true self.

To place your ideas and dreams before the crowd is to risk their love.

To love is to risk not being loved in return.

To live is to risk dying.

To hope is to risk despair.

To try is to risk failure.

But the greatest hazard in life is to risk nothing.

The one who risks nothing does nothing and has nothing – and finally is nothing.

He may avoid sufferings and sorrow,

But he simply cannot learn, feel change, grow or love.

Chained by his certitude, he is a slave; he has forfeited freedom. (Author Unknown)

If you hold to my teaching you are really my disciples.

Then you will know the truth, and the truth will set you free...

If the Son sets you free, you will be free indeed. (John 8:31–36)

Notes to Chapter 16

1. Karen Horney (1991). *Neurosis and Human Growth: The Struggle Towards Self-Realization* (2nd ed.). W. W. Norton & Company.
2. Brené Brown and Linda Hartling (2016). *Shame Shields: The Armor We Use to Protect Ourselves and Why It Doesn't Serve Us.* Retrieved from: https://catalog.psychotherapy.com.au/sq/pz_001195_brenebrown_email-32850 Catherall,
3. Brené Brown (2012). *Daring Greatly: How the Courage to Be Vulnerable Transforms the Way We Live, Love, Parent, and Lead.* Avery, p. 70.
4. Alice Walker (1990). *The Temple of My Familiar.* Pocket., p. 353.
5. Larry Crabb, (2016). Don't try to fix people [Vimeo]. Retrieved from https://vimeo.com/169299301
6. Henri Nouwen (1979). *The Wounded Healer: Ministry in Contemporary Society.* Random House.
7. Ibid
8. Ibid
9. T. Weis & R. Berger (2001). *Posttraumatic Growth and Culturally Competent Practice: Lessons Learned from Around the Globe.* John Wiley & Sons. p. 212.
10. L. Richards & G.J. Bredfeldt (1998). *Creative Bible Teaching.* Moody Publishers, p. 143.
11. Ibid.
12. S.M. Johnson (2004). *The Practice of Emotionally Focused Couple Therapy: Creating Connection* (2nd ed.). Brunner/Routledge.

APPENDIX

GROUP ACTIVITY: INSTRUCTIONS FOR PREPARING AN ME SEGMENT

Guidelines will assist you to design part of an ME session of your choice. Work on this as a couple.

Allow 1 hour to design a 30-minute segment of a ME session. The segment will consist of a 35 to 40-minute presentation to the group with the following time allocations:

- 5 minutes to explain your topic and the answers to the above questions;
- 25 minutes to present the ME segment to the group; and,
- 5-10 minutes feedback.

Questions to Ask

To help you to think through the program outline, ask yourselves the following questions:

- When will we hold this future ME event?
- Why will we hold this future ME event?
- Who is our target audience? Who will we invite? How long will the ME event be?
- Where will we hold it?
- How will we present the ME event? Will it be a weekend, a weekly event, a one-day event, etc.?

Elements to Include

A guide for the ME session segment is to include the following elements:
- Create a need;
- Convey the main concept(s);
- Use creative teaching methods;
- Include a handout, activity or exercise; and,
- Include a couple dialogue.

About Barry and Paula Davis

Barry and Paula Davis live in Sydney, Australia, have been married for over four decades and have two adult children who live with their families nearby. Barry worked as a chartered accountant in private practice. He also has a theology degree and was involved in pastoring and church planting. In recent years his vocation has centred on developing relational tools for men as they explore their inner worlds.

Paula is a clinical counsellor, supervisor and lecturer in counselling. Her doctoral thesis emerged from working with traumatised couples in post-war developing countries, exploring the transferability of Western developed psychological trauma concepts to collective societies. She has been a guest lecturer in higher education in Uganda, India and Sri Lanka.

Together, Barry and Paula have been designing relational tools for married couples since the late 1980s and have conducted marriage workshops in Australia, East Africa, Sri Lanka, India and Europe. However, they believe they are an ordinary couple living through the highs and lows of married life. They wear the label "passionate about relationships" as a badge of honour and are enthusiastic about sharing their journey because they believe their story offers hope to others.

Barry and Paula are acutely sensitive to unfairness and injustice in all societies. They possess an unshakeable desire to keep pushing the boundaries of learning to love well and to share that learning with others. Nevertheless, they enjoy lingering over a good coffee and can be found utterly absorbed in fun activities in the great outdoors. Challenge and risk attract them and they have had a go at skydiving, great white shark cage-diving, walking with African lions and zip-lining across a magnificent gorge.

Email: connectingmatters@gmail.com

Website: https://connectingmatters.com.au

www.ingramcontent.com/pod-product-compliance
Lightning Source LLC
Chambersburg PA
CBHW060958030426
42334CB00033B/3285